Aleister Crowley

THE COMPLETE ASTROLOGICAL WRITINGS

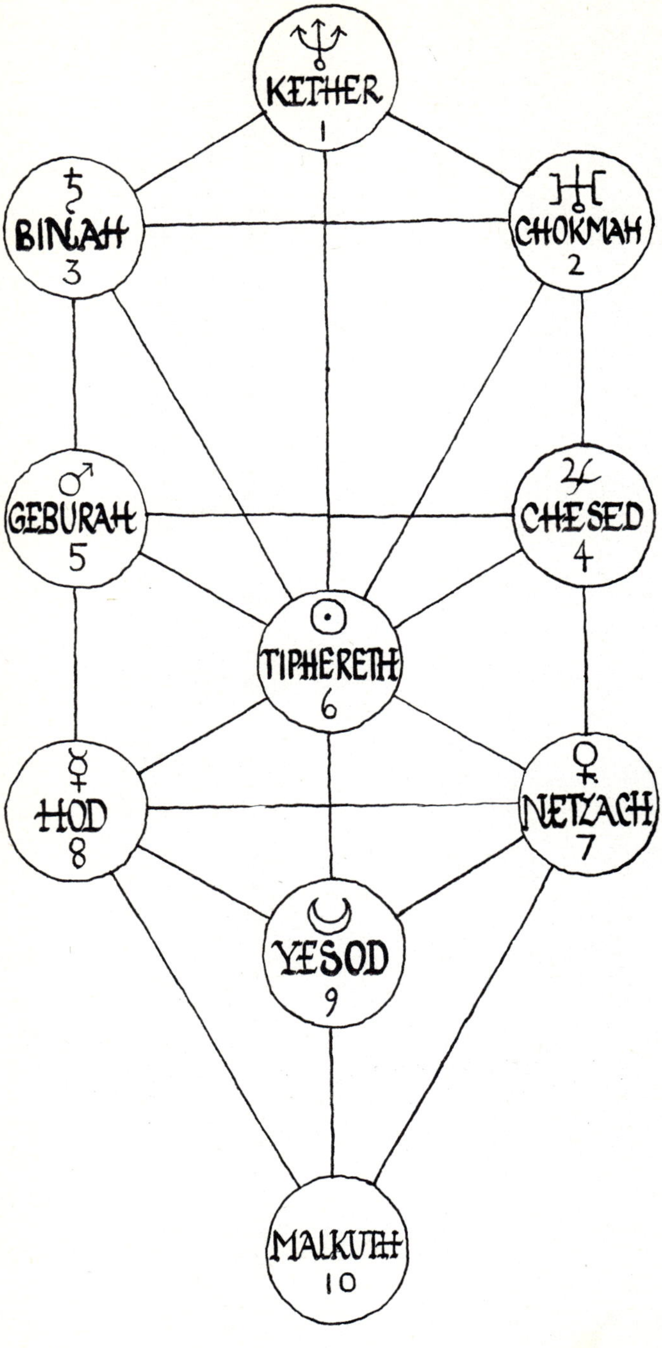

KETHER
1
BINAH
3
CHOKMAH
2
GEBURAH
5
CHESED
4
TIPHERETH
6
HOD
8
NETZACH
7
YESOD
9
MALKUTH
10

Aleister Crowley

THE COMPLETE ASTROLOGICAL WRITINGS

containing

A TREATISE ON ASTROLOGY
LIBER 536

HOW HOROSCOPES ARE FAKED
by Cor Scorpionis

BATRACHOPHRENOBOOCOSMOMACHIA

Edited with annotations by
John Symonds
and
Kenneth Grant

DUCKWORTH

First published in 1974 by
Gerald Duckworth & Co. Ltd.
The Old Piano Factory
43 Gloucester Crescent, London NW1

ISBN 0 7156 0806 1

Typsetting by Specialised Offset Services
Limited, Liverpool
Printed in Great Britain by Unwin Brothers Ltd,
The Gresham Press, Old Woking, Surrey.

CONTENTS

Editors' Introduction

The Hermetic Order of the Golden Dawn, which had lodges in London, Paris, Edinburgh, Bristol and elsewhere, instructed its members in various branches of occultism. The more advanced brethren were initiated into the secret attributions of the astrological forces to the Tree of Life – the planets were attributed to the Sephiroth, the zodiacal signs to the Paths of the Tree – and the relationship of both systems of astrology and the Qabalah to the Tarot.

Crowley began his study of astrology as soon as he entered this magical Order in 1898. He was then twenty-three years of age. His attitude to astrology was basically magical; he was not a dedicated astrologer but a magician who used astrology as one of his weapons. This meant that he was less concerned with astrology as a predictive science than as a means of assessing for magical ends his own relationships with people. Astrology therefore played a minor role in his activities, and he left only one work on the subject.

A Treatise on Astrology was written in America in 1917-18. Crowley also called the work *Liber 536*. 536 is the numerical equivalent of the Hebrew word *Masloth*, which signifies the Sphere of the Fixed Stars, i.e. the Zodiac. It is thus an appropriate number for a work on astrology. An earlier essay entitled *Batrachophrenoboocosmomachia*, which was published in Crowley's periodical *The Equinox* during 1913, is included here because it deals with the magical practice of expanding consciousness to the stars and planets. The word 'Batrachophrenoboocosmomachia' is made up of the Greek words for Frog Mind Ox World Battle, and is a play on the title of the Homeric mock epic, the *Batrachomyomachia* or 'Battle of the Frogs and Mice'. The idea behind the use of this barbarous name, *Batrachophrenoboocos-*

momachia – that is, in pronunciation or vibration – is that it is supposed to create a sense of vertigo in which the mind is freed from its ordinary bounds. Consciousness – so the theory goes – is exalted to infinity by this method.

Also included in this volume is a little-known essay of Crowley's entitled 'How Horoscopes are Faked', which appears here for the first time in book form. It was written in 1917 under the name of 'Cor Scorpionis', the heart of the scorpion, a name probably chosen because of the stinging nature of the author's remarks. The essay was published in *The International*, a monthly New York periodical which, along with its stable-companion, *The Fatherland* – Crowley was the editor of *The Fatherland* – was disseminating German propaganda in these war years.

The idea of writing *A Treatise on Astrology* – it was to be a *complete* treatment of the subject – arose out of Crowley's discussions with Evangeline Evans whom he described as 'the most famous astrologer in the States'. He said of her in his *Confessions* that she made from astrology 'fifty thousand dollars a year [but] did not know that the solar system was essentially a disk. She thought the planets were stuck at random in the sky like so many plums in a suet pudding. In thirty years of daily use of the Ephemeris, she had never observed that Neptune takes fifteen years or so to pass through a sign of the Zodiac, and told her clients that Neptune being in such and such a sign at their birth, they must possess various curious powers. When I pointed out that this applied to everyone born in three lustres, she was at first bewildered, then incredulous; and, proof being produced, angry and insulting.'

They had in fact been working together on *Liber 536*; it was to be published under both their names, and her mind and style are discernible in the text. But the collaboration broke down, and the work was never finished; Crowley was not an easy man to get on with. Evangeline Evans' views on Crowley are not extant, but here is Crowley's summary of Miss Evans: 'She wanted me to write a book on astrology for her. The plan failed through her persistent efforts to cheat me out of the profits, and her obstinate ignorance of the elementary facts of nature combined with an unconquerable antagonism to the principles of applying common sense to the science.'

As the work was not commissioned by a publisher, and was never published, it is rather difficult to see how Evangeline tried to cheat Crowley out of 'the profits'.

Crowley did not continue the work on his own. This is surprising for he had the time, the knowledge and the creative force. And when he left America for Europe in 1919, he stopped writing on astrology altogether; he had more important things to do. His first task was to found his Abbey of Do What Thou Wilt in Cefalu, where he soon set himself to write his *Autohagiography* or *Confessions*, in which, although he included his natal chart, he made no comment on the disposition of the planets.

In his old age, he published *The Book of Thoth*, his last major work, an interpretation of the Tarot, based on the symbolism of the New Aeon. The New Aeon had begun in 1904, inaugurated by Crowley's receiving from his Holy Guardian Angel (Aiwass) *The Book of the Law* or the new bible for mankind. Two pages of *The Book of Thoth* are devoted to the zodiac and the Tree of Life. They are reprinted here, immediately after Crowley's Preface.

Our thanks are due to Commander Charles Drage for his generous help with the manuscript, to Mr Raymond Mander and Mr Joe Mitchenson for the material of a footnote dealing with the theatre, and to Mr Edward Owen Marsh for several helpful suggestions.

John Symonds
Kenneth Grant

A TREATISE ON ASTROLOGY:
LIBER 536

Preface

Astrologers sometimes make mistakes. From this fact, which even they are scarcely sufficiently brazen to dispute, it follows with mathematical certainty that astrology is not a science but a sham, a quackery and a fraud.[1] Contrast its shameful uncertainty with medicine, where no doctor ever lost a patient; with law where no lawyer ever lost a case, or even with arms, where no soldier ever lost a battle!

It is true that nine times out of ten, an astrologer glancing at a stranger can tell at what hour of the day he was born. This must be guesswork, for we do not see how it is done or can be done. It is an obvious canon of all sound philosophy that unless we know exactly how things happen, we must deny that they do happen, or, if ever philosophy cannot so far close eyes on actuality, we must ascribe them to chance. Thought of this altitudinous brilliance is the guarantee of human progress; it reminds one of the sun rising over the crest of some mighty pyramid of rock and ice, crowned with the everlasting snows. True it is that in all cases, an astrologer in the front rank of his profession, gives good advice, kind, shrewd, disinterested and worldy-wise, yet inspired by a diviner wisdom such as the fact that he spends his life in the contemplation of the noblest phenomena of nature, that the Soul behind them cannot but operate to bestow; true also that any astrologer of eminence can point to hundreds of people whose life, honour, and property have been preserved

1. This is a typical example of Crowley's irony. In his introduction to *Magick* he writes: 'Frater Perdurabo [Crowley] is the most honest of all the great religious teachers. Others have said: "Believe me!" He says: "*Don't* believe me!" ' In the present work, Crowley is soon saying, 'If there be any person of the present day so ignorant as not to recognise the value of Astrology . . .'

through his advice. But what do these facts prove? What are we to think of any man who does not earn his living honestly by gambling on Wall Street, or faking antique furniture, or adulterating the food of the people, or wrecking railroads, or manufacturing the instruments of war? Why, the fellow is a cheat, a scoundrel. The idle wretch polishes off his daily 'evil' in eighteen hours to squander the remaining six in the hideous debauch of sleep.

What is to be done? Thank God, degenerate as our age may be in some respect, we have a fairly efficient police system. Well, then, send a detective to the astrologer; let her go in with her eyes red with tears; let her rock with sobbing as she tells of how her only child lies dying, and all the doctors have given up hope. Perhaps the astrologer, for all the knavery and cunning which enable him to pick the pockets of so many thousand people, may be fool enough to utter a few words of comfort. Then the matter is simple; justice can be done. The police take action, and fine and imprisonment follow. The detective is complimented on the cleverness of her plans; her salary is raised and a Free People march ever onwards, singing in the sunlight, toward that City which is God.

The age is too mealy-mouthed, too sentimental, too easy-going to deal radically with crime. Even murderers nowadays have a good chance of escaping the electric chair; and the astrologer is worse than the murderer, for he touches not the mere vile body, but the pocket. We cannot avoid death, but we can die rich. There is even an added blasphemy in the crime of the astrologer, for we know of What Awful and Beneficient Being – a name too sacred to utter lightly – the Dollar is the incarnation. Yet pause, there may be a good reason for the tenderness of the law toward the astrologer. It is so certain that any community can destroy its helpless members, especially when they are women, by hanging them or burning them, and certain communities have a splendid record and a long experience of witch-baiting: statesmanship has abandoned these methods for others less effective on the surface, it argues some wiser consideration, some subtler motive, some nobler and loftier plan for the uplifting of the human race, than the unthinking mind can grasp.

But let us put ourselves in the position of some patriotic

statesman! Here we sit, the broad and noble forehead corrugated in the agony of intense thought, the firm chin resting on the hand, the venerable beard quivering with emotions less human than divine. We brood upon the True, the Beautiful; from time to time we sigh, as we think of the Incommensurable, the Absolute, or the Greatest Good. We gaze from fearless and untroubled eyes upon the world, and the words, half-formed, die in godlike sorrow upon our lips, 'Alas, humanity!' And as we reflect, there comes to us the burning conviction that money is not an unmixed blessing. Prosperity tends to sap the morality of the Common People. Virtue flourishes in communities of simple manners and fades when luxury spreads her vampire wings, money may be a curse. We realise that many people do not use it wisely. They would be better without it. For example, the class that squanders its hard-earned dollars upon the wicked astrologer. But it is not well either that the astrologer should have it. The desire of it has already led him into crime; the obtaining of it has confirmed him in that offence against the laws of God and man. Yet to suppress the astrologer – the first, rash, noble impulse of indignation still leaves the money in the hands of those people who are no doubt better off without it. A dilemma indeed! Has political wisdom no solution? A light dawns in those eyes; the brow relaxes its tension, a beatific smile hovers dove-like on those firm calm lips. 'I will not oppress the astrologer', so the Great Idea takes shape in glory of speech: 'I will merely introduce a Bill to oppress him. Then I will advise him privately that I am his True Friend, and that for just a few thousand dollars I can prevent that Bill from passing into Law. If he cannot understand the merits of this plan – and his brain has probably been stupefied by his devotion to his foolish quackery, in which no doubt, poor creature, he has a sincere belief – then I will prosecute him once or twice under the old mild law and get him frightened. Then, surely, he will yield, and the money will be no longer where it can only do harm, in the pockets of the Common People or the wicked Astrologer, but where it can only do good, in those of the wise and Patriotic Statesman.

If this plan has sometimes failed to work as it should, it is because the Astrologer is too often obstinately impervious to all reason and good sense, as well as to manners and good taste. He may even exclaim, malicious as a dog cornered by a gang of street urchins, that on the whole he would rather go to prison. 'It is not very creditable, perhaps, to be at large in a country with such rulers.' So deplorable a temper is indicative of incorrigible vice, a perversity of the soul plainly Satanic. Such people are dangerous to a State; they may perhaps hit back. Perhaps our sterner forefathers were wiser after all; perhaps we should go after the dollars of the Common People in some other way, and deal with the Astrologer by reviving the methods of the inevitable Matthew Hopkins.[2]

Unless we can do so, and there is indeed some danger that those contemptible creatures, the Common People, might not readily acquiesce, it is to be feared that we shall see the ruin of Civilisation with its greatest glory, our unique political system, and become impotent witnesses of that catastrophe, the Triumph of Astrology.

A.C.

2. Matthew Hopkins (d.1647), lawyer of Ipswich and Manningtree, who became the notorious 'Witch-Finder' General, and an authority on the devil's mark, made by the devil's claw, which may be found on the body of the suspected person.

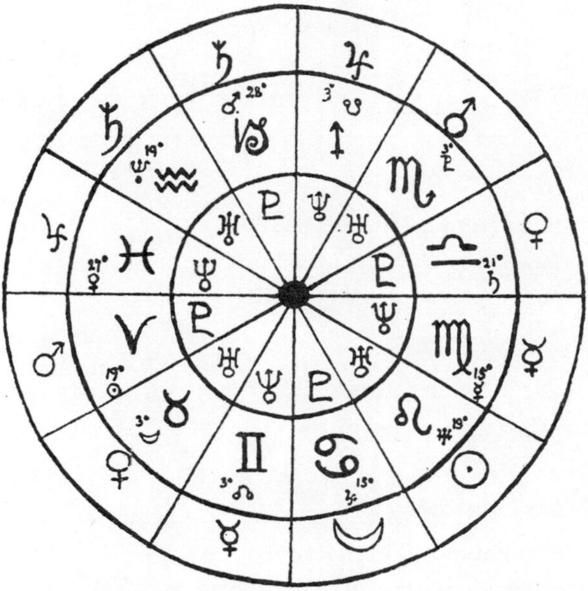

THE ESSENTIAL DIGNITIES OF THE PLANETS

The Exaltation of the Planets	Planets Ruling	Signs of the Zodiac
☉ 19°	♂	♈
☽ 3°	♀	♉
☊ 3°	☿	♊
♃ 15°	☽	♋
♄ 21°	♀	♎
☿ 15°	☿	♍
♅ 19°	☉	♌
♇ 14°	♂	♏
☋ 3°	♃	♐
♂ 28°	♄	♑
♆ 19°	♄	♒
♀ 27°	♃	♓

Herschel rules the 4 Kerubic Signs: Neptune, the 4 Common Signs, and Primum Mobile, the 4 Cardinal Signs.

A planet is in its Fall when opposite to its Exaltation; in its Detriment when opposite to its Realm.

THE TRIPLE TRINITY OF THE PLANETS

♆	The Spiritual	Self- (ego) ☿
☉	The Human (Intellectual)*	
☽	The Sensory (Bodily)	
♅	The Spiritual	Will of the 🜍 Self.
♄	The Human (Intellectual)*	
♂	The Sensory (Bodily)	
♃	The Spiritual	Relation with the ⊖ non-ego.
☿	The Human (Intellectual)*	
♀	The Sensory (Bodily)	

	Middle Pillar	
♆	The Spiritual	Consciousness.
☉	The Human	
☽	The Automatic	
	Pillar of Mercy	
♅	The Creative	Mode of action on the non-ego.
♃	The Paternal	
♀	The Passionate	
	Pillar of Severity	
♄	The Intuitive	Mode of Self- expression.
♂	The Volitional	
☿	The Intellectual	

* For "intellectual" one might say "conscious".

I
The General Principles of Astrology

The physical constitution of the Universe is the basis of the science of Astrology; and in order to explain from what principles we deduce our judgments of its movements we must endeavour to gain a clear idea of the nature of those movements.

Many people have an idea that the solar system is more or less spherical in shape. This is not the case. It is, roughly speaking, a flat disk. It whirls in one plane. The planets depart slightly from this plane, but only slightly. How this state of affairs came to be, has long been the problem of Astronomy, and it is not yet satisfactorily settled. But the general idea is that there was at one time, we do not know why or how, an enormous flaming mass revolving in space. In course of time certain heavier portions collected together by the force of gravity, and this mass being coherent, was flung off, retaining, however, its general movement with regard to space, but having also a revolutionary movement of its own in the same plane. This body constantly radiating its heat into space gradually contracted and solidified. This first body was the planet Neptune. It is by no means certain that Neptune is the most distant planet. Students of astronomy are well aware of how it was discovered. In calculating the movement of Uranus certain perturbations were discovered which could not be accounted for by any of the known planets. Astronomers were therefore led to imagine that there might be some other body yet undiscovered and probably beyond Uranus. Calculations were made to determine the probable position of such a body, which was then looked for with extreme care, and ultimately Adams and Le Verrier discovered the limits of its possible position with such accuracy that Galle of Berlin discovered it in 1846. Further observations and calculations show that there are still certain movements of Uranus not fully accounted for by Neptune; and there are also perturbations in Neptune himself which suggests that there may still be another planet outside Neptune. If so, however, the distance is probably very great indeed. Our reasons for thinking so are based on Bode's Law. Bode was a German astronomer who flourished in the last half of the eighteenth and first quarter of the nineteenth century and the law to which he has given his name is as follows.

If we take the number 4 and divide it by 10 we get the distance of Mercury from the Sun in astronomical units. The astronomical units being the main distance from the Earth to the Sun – add 4 to 3 and divide it by 4 and we obtain the distance of Venus; add twice 3 to 4 and we get the distance of the Earth; add twice twice 3 to 4 and we get the distance of Mars; add twice twice twice 3 to 4 and we get the mean distance of the asteroids. This same proportion continues, multiplying 3 four times by 2 and adding it to 4, and then dividing by 10 we get the mean distance of Jupiter. Multiplying the 3 by 2 once more we get the distance of Saturn; yet again and we get that of Uranus. With Neptune, however, the law breaks down. According to that law the mean distance should be 38.8, whereas it is only 30. No real reason is known for this law, though it is hoped that light may be thrown upon the subject by further researches in celestial mechanics and the evolution of the solar system. The law was at least of this service, that it led to the discovery of the Asteroids, which are supposed to be the fragments of an exploded planet. No satisfactory explanation of the exception of Neptune to this law has been put forth.

The same process repeated itself several times, and thus were formed Uranus, Saturn, Jupiter, the Asteroids, Mars, the Earth, Venus, Mercury. Many other bodies were formed in precisely the same way, but they lacked the principle of coherence in the same degree and, soon after separating from the Sun, themselves broke up into Asteroids and meteors, countless millions of which throng inter-planetary space. Some of these bodies, moreover, behaved at first like the sun itself, and threw off smaller bodies of the class which we call 'moons'. These were very small in comparison to the present orb, cooled quickly, and lost their internal revolutionary movement. The moon of the earth, for example, though it still revolves around the earth, no longer turns upon its own axis, and always presents to us the same face.

The important item in all this is that all these movements, complex as they are, and we have made no attempt to describe that complexity in detail, but merely to give a crude idea, take place in one plane of no great thickness and in the same main directions.

Now the fixed stars lie about the sun at distances immeasurably greater than even the farthest of the planets. It is impossible for the human mind to form any conception of the magnitude of space. These stars surround the sun completely; there is no part of the heavens in which they are not. But to resume the simile of the wheel, if we look along the spokes of that wheel, we shall perceive a narrow band of stars, and these naturally group themselves into twelve constellations disposed at approximately equal distances. We pay more attention to these stars because they lie in the same plane as the general movement of the solar system, and their influence consequently combines naturally with that of the planets. Their effects have been studied from time immemorial with the utmost care and described by ancient astrologers. To these constellations names have been given. They are as follows: Aries, Taurus, Gemini, Cancer, Leo, Virgo, Libra, Scorpio, Sagittarius, Capricornus, Aquarius, Pisces. These names are mostly those of symbolic animals. It is very fanciful to try to see any resemblance of these animals in the relative positions of the stars concerned. The names have been given because of the astrological significance thereof, and this is one of the many proofs that astrology is older than astronomy.

The materialistic school of philosophy has endeavoured to give the impression that we possess some real knowledge of the nature of the forces which we see at work around us. Such an impression is entirely false. All forces are essentially mysterious. We know from observation, comparison and measurement, how they act. We cannot even form any reasonable conception of their true character. Let us take, for example, the force of gravity. In order to explain its action, men of science have been obliged to postulate a substance called 'the ether'. They have been obliged to define this ether in mathematical terms. It is infinitely rigid, infinitely elastic, infinitely tenuous, infinitely imponderable. That is to say, it is not matter at all in any ordinary sense of the word, for it possesses qualities involving infinities and therefore is rather theoretical than actual.

In the same way nobody knows what electricity really is. There is a story of a professor who was declaiming to this effect before a class of students and wound up by thundering dramatically, 'Does anybody know what electricity is?' A student in the back of the hall, overcome by the heat or the discourse, had been half asleep. The last sentence aroused him and he sprang from his seat from habit. Then meeting the cold eye of the professor, he became embarrassed, stammered, 'I knew, Sir, but I've forgotten.' 'Just my luck,' retorted the learned man. 'There was only one man in the whole world who knew and he has forgotten.'

If we take even so simple a phenomenon as the expansion of bodies through the action of heat, we are equally involved in mystery. There is a sort of theory that for some reason the molecules of a body move more violently when what is called heat is applied to them, because heat is conceived of as a mode of manifestation or accompanying attribute of motion. But these molecules are themselves quite theoretical. Their existence has been invented in order to explain certain phenomena of chemical action. These imaginary molecules are composed of yet more imaginary atoms, which were defined, as the name implies, as ultimate indivisible particles of homogenous matter, but that was just a century ago, and since then, all sorts of other phenomena have been observed which make it impossible any longer to imagine the atom as indivisible – hence has arisen a new hypothesis, that of electrons, and when you inquire of the physicist as to whether these electrons are matter, he may tell you that, on the whole, the least unreasonable theory is that which supposes them to be merely strains in the ether. In other words, the things which are, have been resolved by science into combinations of things which are not. If you ask a modern chemist or physicist for his definition of matter, he will reply to you in terms identical with those which were used by the philosophers of the Middle Ages to define Spirit.

The astrologer is more frank than the professor of other sciences. He does not endeavour to conceal his ignorance beneath an elaborately embroidered cloak of metaphysical phrases. He is content to accept the dictum of the Schoolmen, *omnia exeunt in mysterium*, [everything ends in mystery], by which they meant that if you follow any idea far enough – if you keep on asking how and why and what, instead of resting contented with a superficial, half-way explanation, the result is always the same. You reach the blank wall of the inconceivable. If there be any person of the present day so ignorant as not to recognize the value of astrology and base his judgment on materialistic groups, let him read Herbert Spencer's *First Principles*. In that book which ranks with David Hume's as one of the most masterly treatises on nature, as seen by scientific scepticism, he will find it prove with admirable lucidity that no possible theory of God or of nature is satisfactory to the mind. Nay more, he shows that no such theory is even intelligible to the mind.

As practical people, we shall therefore do well not to worry ourselves too much about metaphysics. We had better acquiesce in the statement that everything is relative and confine ourselves to observing and measuring the forces which we perceive in action. It is not an argument against Astrology to inquire why does the movement of a certain planet produce certain effects. We do not know any more than the physicist knows why a nerve contracts on the application of an electric current. We do not wish to make so philosophical an inquiry. We are only concerned to inform ourselves as to whether it acts. Theoretical *a priori* considerations must not be advanced in astrology any more than any other science. Such considerations have been the curse of every science. They have done more to retard the progress of science than any other form of human folly. The reader should study the works of T.H. Huxley[3] on this point. In

3. Thomas Henry Huxley (1825-1895), English biologist who invented the word 'agnostic'. He defended Darwin's *Origin of Species*, 1895, against the attacks of Bishop Samuel Wilberforce.

former days people would begin their deductions from what they supposed to be an indisputable proof of the attributes of the Divinity. Whenever they came across a fact which appeared out of harmony with this preconceived idea of His nature they tried to explan away the fact, but as facts are 'chiels that winna ding' they saw that their castle in the air must tumble and consequently resorted to the expedient of burning any person alive who appeared interested in the discovery of awkward facts. Such a policy was naturally suicidal.

Now, astrology has nothing whatever to do with any theories of nature. Like every sane science, it contents itself with the true scientific method. Suppose we are on a shooting range – we see a puff of smoke and hear a report. In another part of the ground almost immediately afterwards, we hear a bell ring or see a flag wave. There is no reason whatever to suppose any connection between these events. They may be pure coincidences. Suppose, however, we see the same thing happen a hundred times running or even suppose that we see the flash, hear the shot a hundred times and that on seventy or eighty occasions the waving of the flag followed, the situation becomes entirely different. We have, then, a right to say that there is, in all probability, some causal connection. It would however still remain incomprehensible to us, why a flash in one part of the earth should cause the waving of a flag in another part. There would be nothing to tell us that there was a preconcerted arrangement between the shooter, the marker, and even if we were subsequently informed that such was the case, we should still be at a loss for the motives of such an arrangement, and in order to discover these we should have to dive into a dozen sciences, ballistics, history, ethnology, and I know not how many more. At the end of all that we should find ourselves up against the great metaphysical problem which we have already dismissed as improbable.

But it would be quite fair for the observer to draw certain practical deductions. If he noticed that the flag was waved immediately after the shot was fired on a thousand consecutive occasions, he would be perfectly justified in predicting that the next time the flash came the flag would follow. This prediction, like any other, would not be a certainty. It would only be a very strong probability, but humanity habitually acts on probabilities of this kind. If I walk down Fifth Avenue, a motorcar may smash a wheel or skid or in some other way go wrong and interfere with my peaceful promenade upon the sidewalk, but I shall be a great fool if I avoid the sidewalk for any such reason. In other words I habitually predict that no such accident will occur. So far things have fallen out according to my expectations.

Now when an astrologer predicts that a person with Mars in the seventh house afflicted will make an unhappy marriage, if he marry at all, he is employing precisely the same qualities of sound reason and judgment based on scientific observation and comparison of innumerable facts. He has observed and noted and tabulated; filed among his papers are hundreds of horoscopes in which this position occurs and in every case, the person born with this position has been unfortunate in wedlock. He is, therefore, absolutely justified when he sees another such figure in predicting unhappy marriage.

It must not be expected that any responsible astrologer claims to be absolutely right. There are extreme complexities in the study of astrology. It appears that there are certain unknown forces which may interfere with even the most probable judgment. There are times, for example, when a person may pass through very bad aspects without feeling any ill effects. For some reason or other, those aspects have not been excited to action. There are a dozen theories to account for this apparent irregularity. It is not possible in this brief introduction to go into them fully but there are so many and so subtle forces to take into consideration that it is occasionally impossible to divine astrologically why any given event should take place even when the matter is considered after it has happened.

There is another and exceedingly important point – 'forewarned is forearmed'. If a person appears to be in danger of drowning, one can avert the threat by keeping him away from water. This is one of the most useful functions of astrology. It may be, let us grant, that the astrologer is mistaken, that there is not really any danger as supposed, but it cannot do his client any harm to act sensibly and every good astrologer is full of worldly wisdom and commonsense. These considerations apply specially in horary consultations when the astrologer is sought on account of some pressing anxiety or trouble; such natural good judgment as the consultant may possess is at such times interfered with by the disturbance of his mind and the counsel of the astrologer cannot be otherwise than beneficial.

However, it would be absurd to rate so low the claim of the astrologer to help mankind. On certain main points, such as the connection of the personal appearance with the sign rising at the time of birth or the position of the Sun in the Zodiac, as the influence of Saturn in the tenth house or Mars in the Ascendant, and a thousand others, the probability of cause and connection is so enormous that no sane person who studies the facts with intelligence and without prejudice, can fail to be convinced that astrology is a positive, constructive and all but infallible science.

Just as in fractional distillation, the first vapours which come over are very different in character from those which arise from the application of greater heat, so the successive formation of the planets has given them very varied natures. The subtle influence which is disengaged from them and shed upon Earth by their rays has been carefully studied and will be described in the pages of this book. There is nothing particularly repugnant to reason in this theory. One has the obvious analogy in better-known department of physics.

We have daily experience of the difference in the effect produced by the rays of the Sun and those of the Moon, and we have only to extend this conception in order to include the other planets. But there is an *a priori* difficulty in accepting the postulate that the aspects of the planets have any effect. Let us consider this matter carefully. What in the first place do we mean by the aspects of the planets? The aspect of one planet to another is the angle subtended at the eye of the observer by any two of them. Thus, when the Moon is full, we say that the Sun is in opposition to the Moon, and this means that if a straight line were drawn from the Sun to the Earth and produced it would pass through the Moon. Now, we do know that this particular aspect has an influence upon Earth, an influence due to that force called gravity. When the Sun and Moon are in opposition they pull in opposite directions, they counterbalance each other. The earth is consequently not pulled out of shape so much as when they are in conjunction and pulling together. The effect is measured by the tides. But this is not at all the doctrine of aspects. As the Moon passes away from the pull, these forces act at a gradually diminishing angle, and the effect upon the tides also diminishes in a gradual and proportional manner. The astrological effects do not work in this way at all. It is at the exact moment of opposition that the effect is produced. As soon as it is 15 or 20 degrees away, it no longer exists, and it is very puzzling, from the philosophical standpoint, why this should be so. Mars approaches the square of Uranus, let us say, and there is a tremendous earthquake. A week later the aspect has passed and we get, not as one might suppose, lesser earthquakes, but no earthquakes at all. One is tempted to say hastily that this is unreasonable, and it has been brought forward as an argument against astrology. Fortunately, however, we have a very good analogy in the science of optics. Take a pair of field glasses, put them to your eyes and look out upon the landscape – it is all blurred. Move the screw backwards and forwards, the blurring increases or diminishes somewhat, but there is one particular position of those glasses which is peculiar to their relation with your own optic lenses in which the image suddenly stands up, clearcut and luminous. A glass is either in focus or out of focus, and although a slight deviation produces less blurring than a larger one, yet there is a perfectly sharp line of demarcation. There are other analogies such as the phenomenon of the boiling of water; at 99 centigrade, water is still not boiling, at 100 centigrade it is boiling, and from a physical standpoint, there is more difference between the water at 99 and the water at 100, than between the water at 99 and the water at 1. However, we do not know why the rays of the planet only influence each other, only blend their action when they strike the earth at particular angles. The science of astrology is at present largely empirical. We know that certain events on Earth follow certain configurations of the heavens. We have observed these events so frequently that we feel sure that there is a cause and connection between them, but no astrologer pretends that he understands the nature of their connection. The reader will remember that David Hume, who has never been refuted, regarded causality itself not merely as unproved and unprovable but as inconceivable.

There is a school of philosophers called the Casualists who maintained that every event was a direct volition of the Deity. When the apple becomes detached from the tree and falls to the ground the reason is this: first, God wishes the apple to become detached; second, God happens to wish the apple to reach the ground. It is not only unphilosophical, they say, but blasphemous, as limiting the power of the Creator, to assert that one effect necessarily follows another. It is impossible to controvert this position by logic, however repugnant it may be to our commonsense to accept it. The importance of indicating the possibility of such a position is this: to show that from a standpoint of pure reason, the statement that high tides are connected with the new moon is exactly as absurd as, not more absurd nor less absurd than, the statement that the conjunction of Saturn and Mars bodes ill for empires. If there is any distinction to be made between the logical quality of these two propositions, the logician has yet to be born who finds it. If we accept one more readily than the other, it is because it rests upon more universal observation, but it is perfectly empirical and the fact of our having a beautiful theory to account for it does not in any way strengthen the original credit it deserves. The reader may perhaps remember that Charles II asked the Fellows of the Royal Society why it was that if you filled a bowl of water to the brim, you could put a live goldfish into that water without spilling it, whereas if the goldfish were dead it would immediately overflow. They consulted upon the matter and quarrelled violently over it in the manner of metascience, returning ultimately to the 'merrie monarch' with no less than nine learned and satisfactory explanations. It had never occurred to one of them to try experimentally whether the king's statement was correct. The making of theories has been, from time to time, a great curse to science. The tendency is to generalise from insufficient evidence, and having formulated on hypothesis, to deny or neglect any facts which do not immediately fit into it. The demonstration of Immanuel Kant that the so-called laws of Nature are in reality only the laws of the mind, is one of the most valuable contributions that was ever made to thought. It is not true that two and two make four – it is only true that we are obliged to think so.

The bearings of this are very important to astrology. What astrology needs is more human observation. The astrologer is obliged to reason from data which are often inaccurate, and sometimes deliberately falsified. He is asked, in short, to make bricks without straw. That he has produced so marvellous a pyramid of truth is therefore enormously to his credit. The method employed in this book will be strictly scientific. Facts have been collected, selected, co-ordinated, and deductions have been drawn from them with the most rigid adherence to the canons of truth, the method of science, and the rules of logic. Every statement is based upon the accumulated experience of centuries, as handed down by tradition and in treatise, and the fundamental knowledge thus acquired has been sifted again and again by applying to it the tests of evidence which accrues daily in private research. It is not pretended that such knowledge is final. It is possible that new facts may be discovered at any moment, which will modify the opinions hitherto entertained. As a case in point, the discoveries of Uranus and Neptune have gone far to revolutionise astrology. Many problems which baffled the ancient astrologers have been solved by those events. There are still many unsolved problems in astrology. To give a simple example: Jupiter passing over his own place in the fourth house might bring inheritance. This might happen with the utmost regularity, four out of five times in a man's life; the fifth time, no. Why? A dozen suggestions might be made. None of them might satisfy the intelligence. It is thinkable, however, that the discovery of yet another planet might offer a clear and obvious solution. Astrology is in the position of every other science. A great deal is known, but there is a great deal more which is not known. It at least ranks with all other sciences in the devotion and skill of its votaries, in their acuteness and intelligence, and in their desire to bring practical benefits to their own knowledge within the reach of every member of the human race.

The Master Key to Astrology

It has often been a source of bewilderment to the student that with such small variations in heaven, they should be so large on earth. Everybody has just as many signs and planets as everybody else; yet one man is a nobody – in fact most men are little more – and another is more than half divine. No study of aspects as such can explain the fact. They work more or less when they are far from being exact; and on the theory of probabilities it would seem as if at least a third of the human race should be of noble calibre. As a fact, hardly one man in ten thousand leaves even a transient mark on his generation. How is this? The problem has always baffled astrologers and encouraged their critics. In fact, till now no astrologer has fairly faced it. If we do so now, it is because we have solved the problem and place the key in the hands of humanity.

What is the difference between an amoeba and an elephant? The cells of which an elephant is composed are one and all not very dissimilar to the amoeba. The difference is that one is varied and organised, an harmonious republic; the other remains single.

What is the difference, to go higher in the scale of evolution, between a monkey and a man? The answer is similar. It is not so much the size and weight of the brains that differ; some men with small brains have been the intellectual superiors of men with large brains. But if we take the brain of an ape and that of a man from their envelopes, a radical difference becomes immediately patent. The convolutions in the ape are few and simple; in the man they are many and complex.

There lies the great secret: the men who mould the destinies of humanity are the most evolved and therefore the most highly complex types. They are not men who have small interests here, and small functions there; they have built up every factor in their being into a single composite pattern. Often the manifestation of the complex will be widely divergent, on the surface; but this is only another symptom of the complexity. All this is explained by astrology.

A glance at the horoscopes of the greatest men of whom we have record shows that generally speaking the planets form exact or very close aspects and also – this is the important point – that all or very nearly all, the planets are interwoven. Sometimes we see two or three complexes in a nativity; perhaps even four; and these have no close relation with each other. Such horoscopes are those of commonplace people. It is as if they had several strands in their nature which had not been properly interwoven. As a result there are times when one is at work in its own feeble way; then it is forgotten, and another comes into operation. This lack of continuity is fatal to the performance of any constructive work. If such a person should acquire fame, it is the result of some action suddenly conceived and executed, or of an accident.

A few examples of great horoscopes will make these points certain:

Shakespeare, to begin with, has all nine planets in a single complex. Five of them are in aspect with 3 degrees, only one is more than 10 degrees from the very furthest.

Dante maybe said to have two complexes, one of five planets, all within 6 degrees; another of four all 9 degrees; and one complex is only 9 degrees from the other.

Michael Angelo has six planets within 6 degrees, with a seventh only 4 degrees, and an eighth only 3 degees away.

Petrarch has six planets within 6½ degrees, and the other three within 10 degrees.

Sir Richard Burton has five planets within 5 degrees, and the other four within 7 degrees.

Bismarck has seven planets within 10 degrees, the other two within 4 degrees.

Edison has six within 11 degrees, the others within 8 degrees.

Shelley has five within 8 degrees, three within 2½ degrees, and the other only 6 degrees from a conjunction with one of the larger complex.

Zola has all nine with 11 degrees; Copernicus eight within the same limit.

Goethe has two distinct complexes, one of six planets within 13 degrees, the other three within 7 degrees.

Napoleon has six within 10 degrees, three within 5½ degrees and three within 7 degrees.

Balzac has four within 9 degrees, five within 10 degrees, and the two complexes are related within 7 degrees.

Wagner has five within 5 degrees, three within 6 degrees and the last only 5 degrees away.

Baudelaire has five within 10 degrees and the other four within 10 degrees also; the one complex is but 7 degrees from the other.

Pasteur has six planets within 6½ degrees, two within 3 degrees and the Moon which stands aloof is by far the least important of the host of heaven.

Swinburne has six planets within 5 degrees, the rest within 1¼ degrees.

If we had chosen to include minor aspects, such as 45 degrees and 135 degrees, or the quincunx and quintile, an even stronger case could have been made out, but it is undesirable to introduce too much subtlety into an argument of this sort; we prefer to base it only upon obvious and patent facts.

In the investigation of any nativity, it is quite useless to content oneself, as is too frequently done, with the consideration of planets in pairs. These will give details of the native, it is true; but it is the complex which decides on what scale these details are to be interpreted. Zola had Saturn trine to Mercury, which made him great in construction. But had not this aspect been merely part of a mighty complex, it would have made him a good merchant, a lawyer, or something comparatively common.

Shelley's conjunction of Mars and Jupiter is very differently effective to that aspect in J. Pierpoint Morgan![4] Why? Because they form parts of complexes of quite opposite

4. John Pierpoint Morgan (1837-1913), American financier of vast wealth, and celebrated art collector.

natures. The mere fact that one is in Leo and the other in Libra would not account for the difference. And here it is that we must emphasise the necessity of looking not only for the complex, but for the key to it. Two men might have identical aspects, and yet be utterly different just because in one case the Lord of the Ascendant was Mars and in the other Venus. It is not always easy to divine the secret pivot on which a complex swings. The Lord of the Ascendant is usually the cardinal point but if there be several planets or even one very strong planet rising, he may be overwhelmed by them or it and his place in heaven, as it were, usurped. And it is of the utmost importance that his fundamental planet be detected with accuracy; for it makes all the difference in the world whether we regard the other planets as modifying Saturn or modifying Jupiter. If the native be a Saturnian at heart the trine of Jupiter will favor his selfish plans; if a Jupiterian, the trine of Saturn will restrict and balance his enthusiasms. The conjunction of Sol and Venus which made Shelley so glorious an incarnation of Light and Beauty would hardly have acted in that way had Scorpio, not Sagittarius, been in his Ascendant. It is the Lord, Jupiter, culminating in conjunction with Mars and Neptune, that determine the disposition and the superiority of Sol in Leo to Venus that made effective the manifestation of that disposition in the heart through art; had those planets been influenced by Pisces, for example, it would have shown itself in some soft shadowy way.

Enough has been said for a preliminary account of this matter. In the course of these papers we shall pile Pelion upon Ossa, and Ossa upon Olympus,[5] in demonstration of this secret of the Astrological Complex.

The Technical Elements of Astrology

Matter as we know it, consists always of three dimensions, no more, and no less; length, breadth and thickness. Anything

5. 'Pelion, a wooded mountain near the coast of Thessaly. Otus and Ephialtes, according to Greek mythology, heaped it on Ossa, and Ossa on Olympus, in their attempt to overthrow the gods' (*Oxford Companion to Classical Literature*).

which has not these qualities is subjective.

The subject of pure mathematics deals with subjective conception.

It is based upon a series of arbitrary conventions.

Mathematics is a device for simplifying our thoughts with regard to the numerical relation of objects.

A point has position, but neither parts nor magnitude.

A line, length without breadth.

A circle is a continuous line, such that there is a point from which all straight lines drawn to it are of equal length.

The solar system is not a circle, because for one thing, it is real, objective, three-dimensional, while a circle is imaginary, subjective and two-dimensional, but it somewhat resembles a circle in its general mathematical properties, although the path of Neptune which bounds it is by no means circular, but we speak of it loosely as a circle for convenience.

The Zodiac, too, is not by any means a circle, for the stars which comprise its constellations lie at very varied distances from the Sun; but we speak of it as a circle for convenience.

Mathematicians have divided the circle into four quadrants for convenience.

Mathematicians have divided the circle into three hundred and sixty degrees, arbitrarily for convenience, although there is some connection between this division and the length of the year which was at the time of the division not accurately known.

There are also, the following arbitrary and conventional divisions.

First, there is the division into twelve signs of thirty degrees each, these signs corresponding roughly with the principal constellations.

Each sign is divided into three parts called decanates, each containing ten degrees.

Each sign is divided into six parts called quinaries, each containing five degrees.

The degrees themselves are divided into sixty equal parts called minutes, and each minute is divided into sixty parts called seconds.

When a planet is observed to be in that part of the heavens where is any particular constellation, it is said to be in that constellation, although of course the planet is very near, and the constellation very far away.

However, the rays of the constellation and those of the planet are parallel and their influences are in consequence combined. Thus, if we say that Mars is in Aries, we mean that a person standing upon the earth and looking at the sky would perceive the planet Mars apparently situated among those stars which form the constellation known as Aries; and as the influence of Aries is sympathetic with that of the better side of the nature of Mars, we should call Mars strong.

The Twelve Houses of Heaven

If an observer, standing upon the earth, perceived the Sun rising at the moment of the Vernal Equinox, he will call the position of the Sun the cusp of the Ascendant, dividing the apparent path of the Sun into twelve houses, each of thirty degrees. The first house will consist of the thirty degrees immediately below the Sun; the second house of the next thirty degrees, etc., the thirty degrees immediately above the Sun constituting the twelfth house.

At the moment of the Vernal Equinox, the Sun is entering Aries, and therefore at his rising, we say that Aries occupies the first house. By the time that he has reached his setting, he is still in Aries, but the opposite sign Libra is now in the east, and so we say that Libra occupies the Ascendant. As the divisions of the Zodiac are not quite equal, the signs do not exactly correspond with the houses. For example, at London, Aquarius rises in about one hour and eight minutes; that is it takes an hour and eight minutes for the first degree of Aquarius to be replaced on the Ascendant by the first degree of Pisces; while in the case of replacing Leo by Virgo, the time required is two hours and forty-eight minutes.

The astrological import of the twelve houses will be described in detail in dealing with the action of the planets in passing through them.

The Aspects of the Planets

If an observer standing upon the earth fixes the position of any two planets in the sky, he will find that he must shift the position of his telescope through a certain angle. At certain angles, as has been previously explained, the influence of the two planets react upon each other, and those angles are called the aspects. These aspects are as follows:

1. Conjunction.
   Planets are said to be in conjunction when the angle between them is zero. That is to say that the telescope does not have to be shifted at all in the plane of the Zodiac.

2. Parallel.
   Planets are said to be parallel when the angle between them is zero. That is, the telescope does not have to be shifted at all in the plane at right angles to that of the Zodiac.

3. Semi-sextile.
   The semi-sextile aspect is 30 degrees.

4. Semi-square.
   The angle is of 45 degrees.

5. Sextile.
   The angle is of 60 degrees.

6. Square or quartile.
   The angle is of 90 degrees.

7. Trine.
   The angle is of 120 degrees.

8. Sesqui-quadrate.
   The angle is of 135 degrees.

9. Opposition.
   The angle is of 180 degrees.

These are also certain lesser aspects: 72 degrees, 144 degrees, and 150 degrees. These are of very little if any importance and can, generally speaking, be neglected. The semi-sextile and semi-square aspects are also weak, especially the semi-square. The same is true of the sesqui-quadrate.

In the old-fashioned traditional astrology, there was a convention to consider the trine, sextile, and semi-sextile aspects as good; the quartile and opposition as bad and the conjunction as doubtful. Modern research, however, has led us to modify this very crude conception. In this book will be found numerous examples of exceptions to this rule, which is merely a rough generalisation.

The parallel aspect is of great, but little understood, importance. Its principal function appears to be to confirm and strengthen other aspects. It is most effective when the parallel is near zero; that is to say when the forces of the two planets in parallel lie as nearly as possible in the great plane which contains the total force of the solar system.

How to Set up a Figure of the Heavens

In the present state of the science of astrology, it is not necessary, or even desirable, to strive after great mathematical accuracy, such as is needed by astronomers. Reasons for this are numerous.

1. It is very rare that the time of a nativity is known with accuracy. Nor is it certain even exactly what moment should be taken, even suppose that the birth took place at the Lick Observatory, with all the astronomers in the world in consultation at the bedside of the mother.
2. It is not quite certain what exact moment to take as the time of the formation of an aspect. Sometimes the effects appear to advance slightly and sometimes to delay.
3. Even were all these points satisfactorily settled, the judgement of the expert astrologer depends on the human factor, on the personal equation. The most successful astrologers are not those who pay the most attention to the mathematics of the subject, but those whose natural gift in this direction is trained and developed by experience.

It is a very easy matter to set up a figure of the heavens

suitable for an astrological judgment. Any person with even moderate training in mathematics can learn to do it in an hour. The instructions now to be given will enable him to do this in comfort.

The first thing to be done is to provide yourself with an Ephemeris, which may be obtained through any bookseller. The present generation of astrologers, as a rule, employ that issued by 'Raphael' and we shall suppose the student to possess it. At the left hand of the left hand page will be found the date and the day of the week. Pick out the day which you require.

In the next column is given the Sidereal Time. We need not here enter into what that means. We merely give the rule. If the hour and minute for which you set up the figure is for afternoon, add that hour and minute to the Sidereal Time for the day. If it be before noon, find out how much before noon, by subtracting the hour and minutes from twelve hours (thus eight o'clock in the morning is four hours before noon) and subtract the result from the Sidereal Time. If, in the first case, the time obtained is more than twenty-four hours, subtract twenty-four hours from it. In the second case, if the time before noon is greater than the Sidereal Time, add twenty-four hours to the Sidereal Time. You then turn to the end of the book and look at the Tables of Houses for the place for which you wish to set up the figure.

Now take the blank form with which you have provided yourself, a circle divided into twelve parts. At the top of the Tables of the Houses you will see the Sidereal Time marked on the left-hand side. Run your eye down the column until you find the nearest approximation to the new Sidereal Time which you have made by adding or subtracting the hours as stated above. Now, against the house in your blank figure which is marked ten, put the sign and degree which is given in the column next to the Sidereal Time in the Table of Houses, and fill in the others as far as the third house accordingly. From the fourth house to the ninth no figures are given, and it is not necessary that they should be given, for the fourth house is equal and opposite to the tenth, the fifth to the eleventh and so on. Thus if 16 Cancer be on the cusp of the tenth, 16 Capricornus will be on the cusp of the fourth.

Having filled up all the twelve houses in the manner indicated, you can now turn back to the other part of the Ephemeris.

You then proceed to insert in this figure the planets in their proper places. For example, suppose 24 Virgo is on the cusp of the eleventh house and you find the Sun marked as in 22 Virgo, you put him slightly in front of the cusp; if in 26 Virgo slightly behind it. The daily motion of the Sun is always within about 3 minutes of a degree and it is, therefore, quite unnecessary to make any calculations depending upon the hour of the horoscope. It is quite sufficient to take the noon position, accurate to the nearest degree. Thus, suppose he were marked 16-5-52 Libra, he can be put in the figure as 16, even if the actual time is near midnight. A little common sense is all that is necessary. We then consider the position of the Moon; the Moon's daily motion is very large; it is sometimes as much as 15 degrees or even a little more. It is sometimes as low as 12 or even a little less, but this works out approximately as a degree every two hours. In the Ephemeris, the positions for both noon and midnight are given. You should take noon or midnight according to whether the hour of the horoscope is nearer the one or the other. By allowing half a degree an hour you will get the Moon's position correct with quite an inappreciable and negligible error. Thus suppose the time you want is 9 o'clock in the evening and the Moon at midnight on that day is in 8 degrees, 37 minutes of Taurus, all you have to do is to subtract a degree and a half, which will give you 7 degrees of Taurus. You then go on to the right hand page of the Ephemeris, which gives you the positions of the other planets.

Neptune never moves more than a minute or two in the twenty-four hours; Herschel rarely more than two minutes; Saturn rarely more than seven; Jupiter rarely more than twelve; Mars rarely more than fifty; and it is therefore quite unnecessary to mark down more than the nearest degree. Venus, however, occasionally moves over a degree, and you should consider the hour of the horoscope in deciding where to place her. Thus, suppose she is in 19-39 Aries, you would mark her as 19, if the time were long before noon, 20 if it were afternoon. Mercury moves still faster, sometimes covering over 2 degrees in the 24 hours, and you will be proportionately a little more careful in deciding his position.

The Nodes of the Moon are given in the Ephemeris in the upper right-hand corner of the page; they move very slowly, and no trouble need be taken to correct their position for the hour of the day. (Note: It will be observed that the Ephemeris purports to give the aspects, especially those of the Moon on the right-hand part of the page. The young astrologer will be wise to neglect these and work them out for himself, as only the exact aspects are given, and there may be many astrologically applicable which are not noted on the particular day for which he is setting up the figure.)

It will be noted that sometimes planets are marked as retrograde. This never applies to the Sun or Moon, and it is only important in the case of Mercury and Venus from the point of view of setting up the figure. If in casting your eye down the columns, you see the number diminish rather than increase, you know that the planet is retrograde, and in such a case, the later the time of your horoscope, the further back instead of forward, will be the position of the planet.

A little confusion is caused by the fact that the movement of the Zodiac is in an opposite direction apparently to that of the planets. This is, of course, not really the case. Even the so-called retrograde movements are due to the fact that the earth in moving so much faster than the other planets makes them appear as if they were going backwards. It is a similar illusion to that by which the lower half of a cartwheel appears to be moving backward; or as a local train appears to an express when the latter passes it. However, the point to be observed is this; owing to the rapid revolution of the earth, the observer at any given spot sees a new sign of the Zodiac rise every hour or two, whereas the Sun remains in the sign of the Zodiac for a whole month. If, therefore, you set up a figure of the heavens for sunrise, and another for noon, it will appear as if the planets had all gone backwards, whereas of course, in reality, they are moving forward. It is hoped that this simple explanation will clear up any difficulty which there may be experienced by the young astrologer in setting up his figure.

There is a very useful and simple check on his calculation. If the time for which he is erecting the figure be near sunrise, he will find the Sun near the cusp of the Ascendant; if near noon about the cusp of the tenth house; near sunset, the seventh; near midnight, the fourth and for intermediate times, in intermediate positions. Until he has set up a few dozen figures, he had better always use this to check his calculations.

We have tried to make these instructions as simple and practical as possible, omitting any refinements or complexities, but if they are not found perfectly easy to follow, the student after repeated trials, but not before, should get a practising astrologer to show him once or twice how the thing is done.

The General Principles of Judging a Figure

Having set up a figure of the heavens, the first thing to observe is the rising sign, and the student should turn to that part of the book in which its effects are described.. He should then notice whether the sign is in any way complicated by the presence of planets in it, and again he should turn to a corresponding portion of the book, if this is so. He should then look at the ruler of that sign, notice its position in the zodiac and also in what house it is situated, and he should see whether this ruler is in any way complicated by aspects. In every case he will find a part of the book in which these conditions are described. He must then repeat this operation with every sign in turn.

Having gone through all this preliminary work, he will be well on the way to form a judgment. He will be wise to regard all these as so many details, like a box of bricks from which he can build a house. Some factors will strike him as extremely important; others as less so. The more he considers the figure, the more salient points will leap into the focus of his imagination, and by setting his intuition at work and employing his creative faculties to eke out his judicial, he will obtain a mental picture of the horoscope as a whole, which, though reposing securely upon the foundation of the facts of the planetary positions, is something more than the sum of those facts. To draw an analogy from painting itself, a masterpiece by Velasquez is, if you analyse it, a set of patches of color, arranged in a peculiar manner, but to say this is not in any way to describe the picture. An astrologer who says that because certain positions and aspects exist, such and such a result must follow, is not a good astrologer, but a bad astrologer.

The more he concentrates upon the bare material of his calculations, the worse his judgment is likely to be. Indefatigability is a good servant but a bad master.

The expert astrologer takes infinite pains with his figure; he endeavors to fulfill Carlyle's absurd definition of a genius,[6] but having assimilated the whole horoscope, he forgets it or only refers to it casually to confirm the general impression which it makes upon his mind. The real judgment is obtained by rising to the height of the situation, having absorbed everything that the figure has to teach. The astrologer places it in the alembic of his imagination. The full current of his genius overleaps the dam of his data and sweeps it away. What he attains is not merely reasonable – it is reason informed and illuminated by his lofty intelligence.

It is for this reason that the plodding, painstaking astrologer is as useless as the same kind of college professor. There is no branch of human activity in which rules are of any real importance. It is the privilege of every great creative artist to break the rules. If Wagner had followed out the academic laws of harmony, music would still be in the morrass where the dancing-master musicians of Mendelssohn's era would have left it. If Whistler had attended to the platitudes of Ruskin,[7] Queen Victoria would still be on the throne of England. One cannot judge poetry by counting the syllables on one's fingers, and the wooden melodies of Dryden and

6. 'An infinite capacity for taking pains.'

7. James Abbott McNeill Whistler (1834-1903), American painter of outstanding ability and wit, author of *The Gentle Art of Making Enemies*, 1890. In 1859, he settled in London. Twenty years later he sued the great critic John Ruskin (1819-1900) for libel. Ruskin had called his 'Nocturne in Black and Gold' a pot of paint flung into the face of the public. Whistler won the case but was awarded only a farthing damages. The costs of the case bankrupted him.

Longfellow are not more, but less musical than the unregulated outburst of Whitman.

The astrologer claims to be a creative artist as much as the poet, painter, or musician; and he will never attain to real greatness in his profession if he allows himself to be bound down too tightly by tradition, or even by the calculations of his own experience.

We are all human, but we are only worthy of the name of human, insofar as we are divine. Inspiration, and nothing else, distinguishes humanity from the beasts that perish.

The General Signification of the Planets, Signs and Houses

The planets

In the sections of this book in which each planet is described, will be found an essay upon its nature, but in order that the reader may gain some preliminary acquaintance with the subject, we shall here give a summary.

Those who are familiar with Greek and Roman mythology, will be able to gain a very considerable knowledge of this subject by merely contemplating the attributes of the Gods whose names are given to the respective planets, and there is, on the whole, no better method of studying the subject, for it is not by accident that those names were given, but after a careful consideration of the astrological influences.

In early times the sea was not navigable in the sense which we now use the word. The voyage of Odysseus from one end of the Mediterranean to the other was considered worthy of celebration in the greatest poem which antiquity has transmitted to us. To the Ancients the sea was an unknown and terrible monster. It was filled with every kind of fabulous and appalling being, and there was something peculiarly frightful about it. It was the personification of the unknown, and the great river Oceanus which girdled the whole earth was bounded only by the gloomy shores of Hades. On the other hand, the dwellers upon the coast of Greece and Italy, many of them living in islands, were perfectly familiar with the sea in its playful moods, and a number of gracious legends are equally associated with the name of Neptune. Then again, they were well aware how a sudden storm will transform the 'measureless laughter of the loud resounding sea'[8] into the shriek of an insatiable fury, pitiless and murderous. These qualities are resumed and embodied in the astrological conception of the planet Neptune.

Uranus or Heaven was the Father of the Gods. To the Ancients, the Gods represented a terrible and incalculable force. The Gods were incommensurables. It was impossible to foretell what they would do at any given moment. They could raise up or throw down careless of tears or prayers. The whole of pagan literature is saturated with this conception. They were too exalted for men to understand – they were passionless and immutable, and yet they could descend upon the earth and mix in the affairs of men. The 'blameless Ethiop' entertained Jupiter and called him friend, exactly as did Abraham in the Biblical story. But it was imprudent to look upon their faces – at any moment they might be setting traps for the unwary. They might seduce him through pride, or fill him with ungovernable desires which would lead to his destruction. It is true that all benefits of humanity came from the Gods. It was the Gods who instructed mankind in every art and science, but they would also act in the most unexpected and diabolical ways. If these ideas be rightly apprehended, the reader will know a great deal about the nature of the planet Herschel or Uranus.

The eldest born son of Uranus was Saturn. Saturn is, in the first place, the patron of agriculture, and also the God of generation. The age of Saturn was the 'golden age'. At that time virtue thrived – men were industrious, simple, austere and yet happy, but Saturn also represented time, and it was said of him that he devoured his own children. For this reason, he was associated with the phenomenon commonly known as death. In the collapse of ancient civilisation, when life was no longer understood in its right relation to existence, when the worship of Attis, Adonis, Osiris and other mutilated or murdered Gods became general, Saturn became confused with the Jewish Shaitan. Time, life, and all the

8. A quotation from the *Agamemnon* of Aeschylus.

conditions of existence were regarded as evil, as the result of malevolence. 'Other-worldliness' had destroyed the simple acceptation of the facts of life which characterised paganism. The later conception of Saturn is, therefore, principally that of heaviness, weariness and age, of ill-will to men, and of peace upon earth, only the peace of the grave. Meditation upon these remarks should give a fairly good general idea of what the astrologer means by the influence of the planet Saturn.

It has been said above that Saturn devours his own children, but on the occasion when the child Jupiter was born, its mother deceived Saturn by giving him a black stone instead of the infant, and thus the life of the child was saved. He grew up, dethroned his father and made himself king of the Gods. The ancient conception of Saturn having already deteriorated into that of the oldster, the man past his prime, whose powers are failing, yet who ruled his household with severe discipline, often amounting to tyranny, Jupiter took his place in the respect and affection of mankind, as the type of mankind at its prime, the prosperous, portly, kindly, fatherly man. His power was indeed terrible, but he exercised it, on the whole, with wisdom and beneficence. The Hebrew conception of Jehovah is not very different from the Roman conception of Jupiter, but the latter God has not those qualities of vengeance which scripture attributes to the former. Jupiter occasionally punished some particularly outrageous case of blasphemy or some attempts to usurp his power, but he was pre-eminently the father of his people. His authority and dignity were enormous. One could not easily approach him, but on the other hand, he was rarely angry and even when not invoked, was looking down from heaven to see whether he could not do anything for the good of his children. This slight sketch will give a fairly accurate general idea of the influence which astrologers attribute to the planet Jupiter.

Mars was the God of war among the Romans, and it is surely unnecessary to discuss the nature of war in this year of our Lord, 1915. Mars is the soldier, brave, energetic, stern, violent, fierce, brutal, resourceful, though not perhaps particularly intelligent. He is quick to anger – with him it is a word and a blow. He seeks 'the bubble reputation even in the cannon's mouth'.[9] It is these qualities which are summarised in the astrologer's idea of the influence of the planet Mars.

We must now leave, to some extent, the classic mythology, for the Sun in the mind of the astrologer has a wider, deeper, truer conception than that which the Romans gave to Apollo. It was one of the secret doctrines of paganism that the Sun was the source, not only of light, but of life, and if we are to understand the force which the astrologer attributes to the Sun, we must endeavor to follow out this arcane mystery. The Sun is by far the most important of the planets, for he represents the life of the man himself. He is the axle of the wheel; the other qualities are secondary. It is true that, like Apollo, he gives swift life and swifter death, and also that such essential ornaments of life as art and love are intimately connected with him, but in the Roman system, Apollo was not the greatest of the Gods. One could not say that without him nothing could subsist, and this is, of course, true of the Sun. The religions of Syria and Egypt, which were principally solar, permeated classical beliefs and gradually affected the conception of Apollo. There is a certain later identification of him with the suffering God of Christianity, Free-masonry and similar cults.

It must not be understood that we wish to diminish the importance of the other planets. The point which we wish to emphasise is this, that if the Sun be afflicted, no amount of benefit from the other planets will make up for that deprivation. The whole subject of the Sun, is however, so vast and so important, that it is really impossible to summarise in a few words, what the astrologer implies by the force of the father of our system.

The astrological conception of Venus leads us back to classical ground once more. Venus was born of the ocean in its smiling mood. She was born in an oyster shell, which connects her with the symbolism of the worship of the reproductive powers of nature. She is, therefore, connected with Neptune in his most smiling mood and with her father Jupiter. Venus is an idealised conception of woman, without

9. *As You Like It*, Act II, Scene 8.

any base admixture. She is love, grace, beauty, tenderness and enthusiasm. She inspires art, and wherever she goes it is with dancing and music. Moreover, and this is very important from our present point of view, she yields, moreover, she tempts strength. The consideration of these points will enable the student to gain a clear conception of the astrological idea of the influence exercised by the planet Venus.

The God Mercury has several forms. In the first instance, he is a playful, mischievous, prankish boy. He is the *enfant terrible* of the Gods. It was the custom of patriarchal peoples to use the boys of the tribe to take messages, as the men could not be spared from the more important works of the household. It is, therefore, natural that Mercury should be the messenger of the Gods. In later developments and amplifications of these ideas, we see Mercury bringing forth the fruit of which they are the seed. He is the master of science and knowledge and the inventor of music, though not so much the executant as Apollo. But the childish knavery persists, in that subtlety, acuteness and wisdom, so that Mercury became also the patron of all kinds of thieves and rogues. Furthermore, especially in his Egyptian form, Tahuti or Thoth, he invented the art of writing and became a patron of letters which again connects him with the idea of a messenger. The astrologer, therefore, considers the planet Mercury as pre-eminently influencing the intellect, with all its splendour, trickeries and basenesses.

One of the favorite epithets of the Moon-Goddess among the Romans was Trivia, she of the three ways, because she had three forms. She is woman, both as mother and as child; this dual capacity completing that conception of womanhood of which Venus is described above as only one part. There is, however, a certain sinister aspect of the life of a woman to understand which we must go back once more to a consideration of the life of primitive people. In the early communities, a woman who was past child-bearing was past her usefulness; whatever might have been her service to the community, they were forgotten. She sank into contempt and hatred, which she naturally reciprocated by using the sublimation of the arts which she had learned in dealing with men in order to annoy them. Even today in India, as well as in some other communities which it is unnecessary to particularise, the old women are looked upon with fear and detestation.[10] It is supposed that she spends the whole of her time in making mischief. Among superstitious peoples, she would, therefore, obviously acquire the reputation of being a witch. The waning moon was, therefore, taken as the symbol of every kind of devilry. She is Hecate, the Queen of the Stryges. A good modern picture of this idea is given in *Macbeth.*

The third aspect of the Moon is that suggested by the facts of nature, her swift motion through the heavens and her changeful appearance endow her with the qualities of fickleness and instability. This is connected with the waywardness and inattention which we notice in young children. There are, therefore, these main points to be considered. First, she represents the life of woman herself in exactly the same way as the Sun represents the life of Man. Secondly, she represents woman in her aspect as mother as opposed to that of wife, and she also represents the child in the earliest ages, before the mind, which is Mercury, is fully developed and the little creature is not much more than a bundle of appetite, moods and emotions. Thirdly, she represents in woman very much what Saturn does in man, but this only when she is waning and afflicted. Consideration of these points will enable the student to understand fairly well what the astrologer means by the influence of our satellite.

There are two other points to mark in a horoscope to which we have not previously referred. Some astrologers nowadays neglect them, saying that the influence attributed to them by the older searchers of the stars has now been explained by the discovery of Uranus and Neptune, but we have seen horoscopes in which their influence is extremely marked and we think that it will not complicate the subject unduly if we briefly indicate their functions and nature.

They are the Nodes of the Moon, which are the points at which she crosses the ecliptic. They are called in astrology Caput-Draconis and Cauda-Draconis, the head and tail of the dragon. The influence of the head of the dragon combines in

10. This is no doubt an exaggeration.

a peculiarly sudden and violent manner the effects of the Sun, and Jupiter, and it is therefore favorable for beginning any great operations. It is particularly helpful to the study of the loftiest, purest kind of occult science and it lends great force to the student of such matters.

The tail of the dragon, which is always exactly opposite to it in the heavens, has a precisely opposite influence. It is very good for ending a matter, but implies sudden losses just as the head of the dragon indicates sudden gains. It is invaluable to the student of the more physical and practical types of occultism.

Neither the head nor tail of the dragon forms aspects with the planets. Their only importance in their position in the horoscope.

The signs

The Universe is one, omnipotent, omniscient, omnipresent. Its substance is homogenous but this substance cannot be said to possess the qualities of Being, Consciousness and Bliss, for these are rather the shadows of it, are apprehended by the highly illuminated mind when it comes near thereto. Time and space themselves are but illusions. This substance [of the Universe] has received many names. The Hindoos call it Parabrahm, Atman and so on. The Gnostics call it the Pleroma. The Qabalists call it the White Head, the Smooth Point, the Ancient One, the Concealed of the Concealed. In later times, it was called God, or the Absolute, or Spirit, and even Matter. All, however, agree about its attributes and these are mostly of a negative character. Because of its essential one-ness, the Greeks called it the One, and we here so consider it, for One is the first positive manifestation in computation. Since, therefore, this substance is one, homogenous and self-conscious, it cannot be manifest in any way while it is in that state. It is sufficient to know that it did divide itself into two equal and opposite courses, which have been variously described by different schools of philosophy as male and female, or active and passive, or fire and water, or being and form, or matter and motion, or the Yin and the

Yang,[11] or again personification such as Shiva and Shakti,[12] and in fact any other pair of deities of the first order. This dual principle, exalted as it is, comes a little nearer to the limits of the human mind, for that mind is itself dualistic, our consciousness being composed of subjective and objective, the ego and the non-ego.

It is possible to dissolve this duality back again into the unity by a mystic process, but the natural course taken by its own combination is to form a third entity, partaking of the qualities of both, yet possessing an independent existence. Thus is formed the descending triangle of father, mother, son, the Yod, Hé, Vau of the Qabalistic Trigrammaton and the pre-Christian trinity of such Gods as Isis, Horus, Osiris, or many others whose names will readily occur to the reader. In the ancient Greek philosophy, of Parmenides, Empedocles, Heracleitus, the Eleatic Zeno and even in the philosophy of Pythagoras and the Stagirite,[13] these three principles are recognised under the names of fire, air and water. They are connected with the three possible states in which one can conceive the Universe – Being, Not-Being, and Becoming. The more carefully Plato and Aristotle are studied, the clearer these points become. It must, however, be understood that these principles are all active and causative – they still pertain to the divine hierarchy. In a word, to the Yetziratic World[14] of Rabbi Ben Simeon.[15] However, from this trinity of actives [i.e. fire, air, water] is consolidated a passive which, to continue the termination of the physicist school of philosophy, is called earth. The whole of this doctrine is admirably resumed, although amplified in the Sephirotic[16]

11. The feminine (Yin) and masculine (Yang) elements or the negative and positive forces in Chinese philosophy.

12. Shiva (the Hindu deity typical of Pure Consciousness) and Shakti (Shiva's Consort) are the negative and positive aspects of the one substance Crowley is discussing.

13. i.e. Aristotle.

14. The World of Formation as opposed to the Material World, Assiah, in the Qabalistic system. It is equivalent to the Astral Plane as distinct from the mundane sphere.

15. Rabbi Schimeon Ben Yochai, from whose writings the mystical Jewish treatise entitled *The Zohar* was compiled.

16. The Qabalah is composed of ten emanations known as the Sephiroth.

system. This division forms an extremely satisfactory base for any scheme of classification, and it has been necessary to enter thus briefly into pure philosophy because without some comprehension of first principles, it is impossible to obtain any idea, not so much of what astrologers mean by the signs of the Zodiac, but why they mean them. For the twelve signs are divided into four triplicities in this order, fire, earth, air, water, beginning with Aries; and each triplicity classes its members under the regimen of the three actives. Thus, Aries represents the fiery part of fire, the most active and violent manifestation of that element; Sagittarius is the watery part of fire, the passive and tractable form; while Leo represents the airy part, the balanced, perfected and stable part of it. In nature, Aries might be compared to the lightning, Sagittarius to the rainbow, and Leo to the Sun. Similarly with the element water. Cancer is its active form. This must not be misunderstood; water is in its nature passive and receptive, yet in this are certain active qualities, for example the power of solution. Pisces is the reflective, passive, quiet form of the elements; and Scorpio harmonises and fixes these two. Thus, Cancer would be symbolised by clouds, rain, streams and rivers; Pisces by wells and pools, and Scorpio by the sea. With air, again, Libra is air in its most active form, the interpenetrating garment of the globe. Gemini represents it in absorption and modification as the breath and mind of man. Aquarius harmonises these two ideas. In Aquarius the air is stable and fixed to such an extent that it partakes of the nature of water; it is the bearer of water, like the clouds themselves.

Turning to earth, we perceive the same subdivision. Capricornus is the earth, considered as a formative force; mountains in particular are analogous to it, because they are salient and rugged, offering obstacles. Virgo is the earth in its passive form – fields and pastures, which as it were yield themselves naturally to other influences. Taurus combines these ideas – the stable and fixed course of earth, which we can only interpret as the essence of labour.

It is hoped that these few simple preliminary remarks will aid the student in the beginning of his investigation into the meaning of the signs of the Zodiac from the standpoint of natural philosophy.

We must now consider an entirely different element, but a most important one, which enters essentially into the fundamentals of the astrological conception of the Zodiac. It is first necessary to call the attention of the student to the fact that all ancient religions were symbolic celebrations, either of the forces of nature in the macrocosm, and so primarily of the Sun, or of the forces of nature in the microcosm and so primarily of generation.[17] In other words, all religious ideas are related either to the life of the earth, or to the life of man. Owing to the numerous accidents which occurred in the gradual development of civilisation, and in particular we would refer to the growth of the Roman Empire, these ideas became, to some extent, confused. Political considerations entered into theology; adaptations and compromises were made by priests who had become ignorant or careless of the true traditions, and we accordingly find that these two lines of thought are interlocked to such an extent that not all the acumen of scholars, even of initiated scholars, can satisfactorily dissociate them. To take one striking example, it is very strange that the spring festival which we now call Easter should be connected with suffering and death, as in the case of Attis, Dionysus and some others. The solution is given by considering what death is – we will not say a euphemism or a blind truth, but a mystic truth, which only initiates of the highest class are likely in any way to understand. But the obvious meaning is given by the fact that the birth of the Sun and of the year occurs nine months later at the winter solstice when Sol enters Capricornus. The crucifixion symbolism of the Sun, which is connected with his crossing the equator should really be referred to his entering into Libra rather than into Aries, and nearly all the confusion which has arisen is due to this original mistake. The entry of the Sun into Aries properly signifies his resurrection, but it is not at all the time to symbolise his suffering, and descent beneath the equator from which he rises, symbolically speaking, after three days and nights, that is to say six months.

17. What Crowley is getting at in this passage is the contrast between the Sun in the Macrocosm and the Phallus in the Microcosm, the Phallus being in his words 'the sole vicegerent of the Sun upon earth'.

We have, fortunately, a very remarkable document, the book of the Atu of Tahuti, more commonly known as the Tarot.[18] Scholars are at issue with regard to the origin and antiquity of these extraordinary designs and it is no part of our present purpose to discuss so vexed a question. Indeed we will acquiesce readily in the contention that even in the Middle Ages the designs had been debased and corrupted by ignorant copyists, and that they stand in urgent need of restoration, but at least a very remarkable degree of truth has been retained and it is by careful consideration and study of these cards that we are able to draw a clear conception of the necessary sequence and significance of the signs of the Zodiac. There are, in all, seventy-eight of these cards; sixteen of them are court cards, king, queen, prince and princess in each of the four elements. There are also the four aces, representing the divine root of the force of each of the four elements; there are thirty-six cards numbered from 2 to 10 representing the 36 decanates of the Zodiac; twenty-two cards remain and these refer to the twenty-two letters of the Hebrew alphabet, of which three are attributed to the three active elements, seven to the planets (for it must be remembered that the discovery of Uranus and Neptune is quite recent) and twelve for the signs of the Zodiac. To this last series we now turn our particular attention. The following is the list:

Aries, the Emperor or Pharaoh
Taurus, the Pope or High Priest
Gemini, the Lovers
Cancer, the Charioteer
Leo, Strength
Virgo, Prudence or the Hermit
Libra, Justice
Scorpio, Death
Sagittarius, Temperance
Capricornus, the Devil
Aquarius, the Star
Pisces, the Moon

18. The 22 keys or trumps of the Tarot. These are attributed to the 22 paths of the Tree of Life.

These titles are not in all cases of any great significance. They were no doubt given in later times merely on account of some salient feature in the designs. It is therefore necessary to give some account of the designs upon the cards.

1. The Emperor shows a crowned king seated with orb and sceptre upon a cubical stone, on which is marked a red eagle. His arms are so placed as to form a triangle with the apex upwards, and his legs are crossed. This triangle above a cross is the alchemical sign of sulphur, which represents the element of fire in a very sublimated and sacramental form. It is easy to see the analogy between this drawing and the sign of Aries, which is ruled by the fiery planet Mars and in which the Sun is exalted and triumphant. It is the return of the year, when earth is renewed and all life awakens again to its fullest activity.

2. The Pope is figured in his pontifical vestments, crowned with the triple tiara, which, of course, in more ancient times was but the yellow crown of Osiris, and represents the creative force which linked man with divinity. His hands are upraised in blessing and at his feet kneel four persons in such a position that their five heads are at the point of a pentagram, the star of the microcosm, the symbol of God made man. This card, therefore, represents incarnation. In the ancient mythologies, particularly in India among the worshippers of Shiva, in Syria among the worshippers of Mithras, and in Egypt among the worshippers of Apis, we find the Bull is the symbol of the Redeemer. We also find Isis and Hathor, represented by the cow, it being from them that the Redeemer springs by incarnation. The Sun in Taurus then is a fixation on Earth through woman of the fire of the Sun in his exaltation. Taurus means bull, is ruled by Venus, and in it the Moon is exalted. It is also a passive feminine earthy sign.

3. The card called the Lovers is a very peculiar symbol. It represents the expansion and dispersion in air of that fiery force which has been fixed on earth. Its conventional form represents a youth standing between two women, one fair

and one dark. These represent the waxing and waning Moon. Above the heads of this group is flying a winged god, a child, bearing a bow and a quiver full of arrows, one of which he directs against the head of the youth. It is a symbol of inspiration, of the growth of the mind of the youth. Modern designers have mistaken this winged God for Cupid, but he is really a form of the Sun in which that luminary is considered as a vehicle of a divine force beyond him, the Creator of all. This is an identification of Mercury with the Sun. (It is not generally known how intimately the myths of Hermes and of Dionysus are connected, and there is no space to prove the identification in this place.) In the life of the year, this card represents the shooting of buds, the blossoming of flowers, which occur when the Sun is in Gemini in the month of May.

4. The card called the Charioteer represents a crowned king standing in a chariot, drawn by two sphinxes, one black and one white. At the corners of the chariot are four pillars, which support a canopy of azure, covered with stars. The meaning of this card and its connection with the sign Cancer are quite obvious. The Sun enters Cancer at the summer solstice, that is at the period of his greatest triumph, his extreme northern declination, the height of summer. The sphinxes are, of course, day and night. The canopy of stars is the abyss of heaven and the four pillars are the seasons. In his hands the King bears a cup and this is connected with the symbolism of the Holy Grail. In connection with the life of Mars it represents the quickening of the child in the womb of its mother, which takes place three months after conception, as symbolised by the Sun in Aries. Cancer being a watery sign, this period is the receptacle of the force of the previous quadrant. It is governed by the Moon and here we see its connection with the symbol of the mother, while the exaltation of Jupiter in the sign refers to the divine influence presiding over the incarnation.

5. The card called Strength represents a woman closing the mouth of a lion. This in the life of the year symbolises that the fruits of the earth are now safe from the devouring elements which endanger them during the spring. It is the

fixation of the fire of Aries, and a similar sense of security and triumph reigns also with regard to the life of man. It is a period of security, of fine weather. The arduous work of ploughing is over. The harvest is gathered in; there is no further fear of starvation during the winter, which is already foreseen. It should be remembered in case this explanation seems trivial to us moderns, who by the advance of science have made ourselves permanently secure against famine,[19] that in the times when these cards were designed, the case was entirely different. Dwellers in modern cities never think about the harvest unless they are gambling in cereals; but to a family in ancient Egypt or Chaldea, it was the constant preoccupation and anxiety. This card is a hieroglyph of the old aphorism that salvation comes to the woman whose courage and fortitude assure the preservation of the race, and again in the life of the year, it shows the benefit obtained from her housewifery. Remember that among all primitive people the women do all the hard work of the field.

6. When the Sun enters Virgo, the harvest is already secure, and the fruits of the earth ripen. The symbol upon the card called the Hermit is therefore very easy to understand. It represents an aged man, hooded and cloaked, bearing a long staff and a lamp. At his feet before him goes a serpent. This man is Hermes, the messenger of the Gods, he who taught science and letters to men. It is only in the modern design that this man is old, and this is owing to confusion in etymology. The word Hermit has nothing to do with Hermes; it comes from the Greek *Eremitos*, one who lives in a desert, and it is because hermits, as known to the people of the Middle Ages were usually old men, that this card Hermes was replaced by a figure of a hermit. The lamp, staff, cloak, and serpent are clear indications that the original design represented the messenger of the Gods. He symbolises the developed mind of man, the prudence and foresight which causes him to gather up the fruits of his ploughing and sowing and reaping into granaries, for Virgo is the last sign of

19. Crowley was writing in the good old days of 1915 when the threat of over-population was not sufficiently appreciated.

summer. The Sun is already prepared for his crucifixion upon the equator. Virgo is an earthy and mercurial sign and so represents the fixation of the intellect in practical ways.

7. The card called Justice represents a grave woman with austere and solemn countenance. In her right hand she holds an uplifted sword, in her left a pair of balances and she is seated on a throne. At the entrance of the Sun into Libra, the days and nights are again equal, and this card is a fitting complement to the Emperor who presides over Aries. This is the moment of the crucifixion of the Sun who now descends below the Equator for the remaining six months of the year. Libra is ruled by Venus, but Saturn is exalted in the sign, and this indicates, with reference to the life of man, the sorrow and burden of the woman. It will be noticed that the sceptre in the hand of the Emperor, the symbol of creation and destruction is replaced by the sword which destroys. It is this woman who executes the fiat of the Almighty, who has appointed that every rise shall be equilibriated by a fall.

8. The card called Death is just as simple a representation as Justice was. The card shows the figure of a skeleton in whose hands in a scythe, cross-hilted, with which he is reaping a field, on which are to be seen the heads and hands alike of crowned kings and beggars. When the Sun enters Scorpio it is the death of the year. The leaves fall, nature putrifies. Scorpio, the balanced form of water, is under the rule of Mars, and its meaning in alchemy is always corruption and putrefaction. This process is necessary to rebirth, and that such is the office of death is shown by the fact that the handle of the scythe is in the shape of a cross, the sacred emblem of salvation in which the true light exists, but in a concealed form. For the letters of the Latin word Lux are formed by the arms of a cross.

9. The card which rules over Sagittarius is called Temperance, and it represents the final operation in the Great Work. The card shows a woman in whose girdle shines the Sun. Upon her head is the crown of the twelve stars of the Zodiac. Beneath her feet is the Moon; in her right hand, she bears a

cup; the water from which falls upon a lion in the midst of a fire and in her left is a torch whose fire illuminates an eagle that crouches upon the sea. Between these symbolic animals is a caldron boiling over a fire and the lion and the eagle emit from their mouths into the caldron two streams. The picture is so full of signification, that one cannot enter into it in this place as fully as one might wish, but the main point to be observed in this is that in the life of man, this represents the triumph of the woman over the destructive forces of nature: by tempering and equilibrating the opposing forces, she has succeeded in preserving that which was entrusted her by the Emperor, the active and creative force which she develops. The sign Sagittarius is ruled by Jupiter, and this is again an indication of the triumph of the father.

10. We now come to an exceedingly sinister card, the Devil. In this symbol, the makers of these hieroglyphs have been exceedingly cautious. It has seemed to them very necessary to hoodwink the eyes of the uninitiate. Apparently, the card represents the figure of a satyr or demon. He is standing upon an altar, and four other demons are worshipping him. It is simple to deduce from this that he refers to Capricornus, the goat, ruled by Saturn and having Mars exalted therein. In this exoteric reading, we see denoted earth at the end of December, an element one might say actively malevolent. The student will remember that the festival of Saturn was held at the entrance of the Sun into Capricorn. The Sun has reached his greatest Southern declination. It is the culmination and finality of death, but a deeper philosophy finds a deeper meaning in this card. It is noticeable that this Devil bears the torch and cup as did his predecessor. It is also remarkable that he and his four worshippers are placed at the points of the pentagram, which, as we said before, is the symbol of God made man, the peculiar hieroglyph of Christ. It may also be observed that the devil is standing upon the cubic stone, and this fact is not unrelated to that upon which we have animadverted in our discussion of the Emperor.

The torch and cup are the same symbols as the sceptre and orb, in a slightly different form, and the pentagram or pentacle has previously occurred in the card of that other earthy sign Taurus, which we call the Pope. We must then regard this Devil as the Emperor in disguise, beneath a veil, and the symbolism of the whole will become clear, when we recall what festival has replaced the Saturnalia,[20] what was the principal event in the world's history which occurred at the entry of the Sun into Capricornus. This card consequently represents esoterically the complete triumph of the creative force initiated by the Emperor. It is the birth of the Sun. In the life of the year, too, this is not only the period of the Sun's greatest declination, but it marks the moment of the beginning of his return. It is the supreme optimism, not of the short-sighted folk whom William James called the 'once-born',[21] but that of the thrice-born who regard life and death equally as parts of a sacrament. This card was redrawn by Eliphas Lévi,[22] who harmonised it with the ancient representations of Baphomet.[23] In it he shows the complete equilibration and triumph of all forces and in particular the perfect wedlock of spirit and matter. The older form is, however, deeper and subtler. Particular attention should be paid to the planet Mars who represents the energy of the Sun. In Aries we saw him at work, in Scorpio in apparent defeat; here he is exalted in the house of Saturn himself. It is the force of life triumphant in the palace of the King of Death.

11. The card called the Star or Hope is of a very gracious and beautiful character. It represents a woman kneeling by the bank of a stream. In her hands are vials of water; with one she fills the stream, the other she pours over her own head. Above her shines the star of Mercury and at her side is a rose-tree about which a butterfly is flitting. As Sagittarius

20. The Saturnalia, the greatest pagan festival, which took place in December, answered roughly to our Christmas.

21. See William James, *The Varieties of Religious Experience.*

22. See Eliphas Lévi, *Transcendental Magic.* Lévi's design of 'the Sabbatic Goat', which hardly captures a baleful atmosphere, appears at the beginning of the section entitled 'The Ritual of Transcendental Magic'.

23. The bestial deity adored by the Knights Templars. Crowley took the name of Baphomet when he assumed control of the magical Order of the Oriental Templars (O.T.O.).

represented the triumph of the woman, so this card represents the recognition of that triumph; the festival of the purification of the virgin occurs in this part of the year. The sign Aquarius means water-bearer. The old astrologers gave Saturn as its ruler, but modern thinkers on this subject have inclined to suppose that this position may more properly be given to Uranus. However, there are some considerations that make Saturn very suitable and one of these is that in regard to the life of the year, February is the month of the greatest inactivity; it is also the month in which the heaviest rains fall and soften the earth for the plough. There is a very strange signification which must further be noticed. There is a reference to the story of the flood. The earth is the ark in which the precious grain is carried and kept safe from the destroying elements during the period of their greatest rage. This ark in connection with the life of man is also symbolical of woman, and the flood itself is the amniotic fluid.

12. Now we come to the last, and in some respects the most curious of these designs. The card shows the Moon waning. She shines upon a landscape which shows low hills crowned by two towers: directly beneath her winds a narrow path between them, and on each side of the path is a jackal, the sacred animal of Anubis, the watcher of the Gods and the guardian of the threshold. In the foreground is a pool of water, from which emerges a beetle, the symbol of Kephra, the Sun at midnight. The entire picture is very characteristic of the moment before dawn, both of the day, and of the year, and it also represents in regard to the life of man, that preliminary period of trouble, darkness and illusion which characterises woman before she has discovered the purpose of her existence. This is further indicated by the fact that Pisces is the right house of Jupiter, so-called, and in it Venus is exalted. This sign is however given by modern astrologers to Neptune, for this reason, that if we interpret this hieroglyph on the plane of the mind of man, it represents this present state of doubt; the dawn in him of the capacity for full spiritual illumination.

The houses of heaven

The first house describes the individuality and temperament of the native; also his physical condition and appearance. It also describes all those things which pertain to him as an individual, irrespective of heredity, circumstance and environment.

The second house gives information with regard to the possessions of the native, and his capacity for increasing them. This does not include gain by inheritance or legacy, nor does it refer to his aptitude for business.

The third house deals, in the first instance, with the mentality of the native, and in general with every kind of medium through which he interprets his personality to his fellows. It also describes short journeys, by which is meant those in which his main interests are not involved, and which are undertaken casually. It also describes his brothers and sisters, near relations, and neighbors, in which terms are included those acquaintances or friends whose connection with him are intellectual rather than emotional.

The fourth house describes the birthplace and the home of the native. It further designates his prospects in regard to inheritance, especially from the father; it describes the father himself. A further signification is that of houses, lands and any property connected with the earth, especially mines. From it indications are drawn with regard to the latter years of life, the place of death and the end of the matter in general.

The fifth house describes the affections of the native, his pleasures including gambling, and the desires of his heart. It has an especial signification with regard to his *vita sexualis*. It also describes his children.

The sixth house describes the health of the native, and other things intimately connected with his body, such as his food and clothing. It has also a very secret and peculiar reference to the occult development of his ego. It further describes his relations with any persons whom he may employ to serve him in any function, not merely domestic servants and it indicates his relations with small animals, particularly domestic pets. It is further related, in a very special way, to agriculture, and also to any speculations he may undertake, exclusively for the purpose of gain without any idea of amusement.

The seventh house describes the partners of the native, primarily in marriage, but also in business and in other affairs of life which demand the co-operation of another person. It also deals with litigation, and describes any person openly opposed to the native.

The eighth house indicates the probable length of life and the manner of its termination. It indicates any gain which the native may have through legacies or bequests.

The ninth house is the house of science and religion. It deals also with long voyages, that is to say, voyages to which great importance is attached, and which are closely interwoven into the life of the native. It describes his capacity, but even more his aspirations in the matter of spiritual advancement and will indicate the nature of his religious teacher.

The tenth house describes the occupation of the native and indicates also his career. Upon this house his fame depends, as also his rank and honour among his fellows. It describes the employer, master, or superior of the native and his relations with the government of his country. Finally it denotes the mother.

The eleventh house is the house of friends. It describes those persons to whom the native is naturally attracted, and the character of his relations with them. It also describes his ambition, but this must be carefully distinguished from his aspiration on the one hand, and from his desire, on the other.

The twelfth house is the house of restraint and describes any influence which may, in any way, restrict his free-will. It also describes his secret enemies and the characters of any intrigue in which he may take part or which may be aimed at him. It refers also to any secret associations with which he may be connected. It also signifies large animals, such as horses and the fortune of the native in respect to them. Finally, it indicates any places in which he may be in which discipline is the first consideration.

There is a rough and ready method of ascertaining the fortunes of any person indicated as pertaining to the life of the native by shifting round the horoscope so that the house which describes that person is in the Ascendant. For example, the wife's mother is indicated by the fourth house; the mother's brothers by the twelfth, and so on. But this is a very rude, crude, amateur, inaccurate, and unscientific way of judging, and should not be resorted to if the horoscope of the person in question is available.

Man and the Universe

A proper understanding of the planets, and indeed of the Universe itself, is only to be obtained by a knowledge of the doctrine of correspondences between the microcosm and the macrocosm.

God made the Universe from nothing, and therefore, as the Pantheists say, He is in all. But this is only part of the truth; for also He made all, and remains immune from His creation. Into these high mystical truths it is no part of our purpose here to enter. Suffice it to say that the Universe is to be regarded as a copy of God, a shadow of God, or even an incarnation or materialisation of God. Man likewise is made in His image. To recover the substance from the shadow is the task of the Adept; to compare the lesser image with the greater is the task of the astrologer.

Even at the outset of this study, certain salient analogies leap to the eye. In particular, we see in the planets the seven ages of man.

First, the Moon, changeable, passive, easily moulded, gentle, pure, dreamy – the child.

Next, Mercury, the youth at puberty, no longer changeable, but swiftly flashing, keen to know, self-conscious, often full of tricks and conceits.

Then, Venus, full of grace, tender, the new consciousness again become passive to absorb impressions from the world about it, eager to find a mate, devoted to art or religion.

Now comes the Sun, the adult, still agile, but steadier, active, brilliant and creative, the young man rejoicing in his strength.

Mars follows. The man becomes less occupied with self, plunges vigorously into the turmoil of life.

Jupiter symbolises his development from his strife into

victory and rule. He is the head of his business, the father of a family.

Lastly comes Saturn, austere, grave, heavy, the hand of age upon his shoulder, and so, the end.

What then of Uranus and Neptune? These planets represent parts of man which are beyond time, or at least beyond the petty cycles which we usually mean by time. It is not often enough that we consider the disproportion of human and astronomical time. The distances of the fixed stars, are so great that we seem to see a different order of being. In point of fact, the stary universe is just about 10,000,000,000,000,000,000,000 times as big as ours; and, curiously enough, our universe is just that much bigger than the universe of bacteria. Here are then three scales of creation, and only three, appreciable by us at present; this thought should serve to simplify our understanding.

Now, Uranus and Neptune represent those parts of ourselves which apprehend these vaster mirrors of the All-One. Fix this in the mind, and almost all their peculiarities will be explained.

Uranus is an exceedingly occult planet. Dark and dreadful, he is the Klingsor[24] of Parsifal. He moves mysteriously in strange paths; he wears a mask of terror. He is infinitely slow, and yet infinitely sudden, like a snake. He represents the true magical power in man, capable of nameless evil, yet vital and necessary to his being; moreover capable of redemption and, when redeemed, the greatest power possible for good.

Of course, in beings of small development, these great powers do not exist. Uranus is for them merely the cause of eccentricity, or folly; if well-placed and aspected, the cause of scientific ardour, philanthropy, and the like.

Neptune is altogether the complement of Uranus. He is the outpost of the Solar system, and receives the influences of the stars. Here, he is the vice-regent of Nuit, the Star Goddess. For this reason he represents the eternal, just as the Sun does; but he is the circumference, while the sun is the centre; the Mother, and the Sun the Father.

24. The evil magician in the Grail Legend. His *Chateau Merveil* was a diabolical travesty of the Castle of the Holy Grail.

He is thus remote, lonely, lost in dreams and aspirations of holiness; brooding upon cosmic things, wooing the stars like Pierrot singing to the Moon. And so, in lesser natures, he brings masquerade, comedy, a trickiness and sprightliness which have a core of sorrow. And often, too, when aspiration goes astray, drugs and drinks are invoked to cure the melancholy, the void, the ache for the infinite – for all men do not understand that only He who struck off the soul, scattering it as a spark of His own fire, can satisfy its cravings.

This is a very significant point; Uranus also causes drug habits and alcoholism, but in this case it is a vice, a bestiality; with Neptune it is virtue strayed, a spirituality thwarted.

These remarks have been diffuse and incoherent beyond excuse. But they will have served their turn if they have exhibited a point of view, a method of study. Without that attitude and that gesture no man may come to a comprehension of the cosmos.

II

Neptune

The Mind of the Father said 'Unto Three!' and immediately all things were so divided.

This oracle, attributed to Zoroaster, refers secondarily to the division of Nature into the three active elements of fire, air and water. [The fourth element] Earth is but a mixture of these three in divers proportions. In this division, according to Greek theology, the kingdom of Fire fell to Hades or Pluto, that of air to Zeus or Jupiter, and that of water to Poseidon or Neptune.

Neptune is, therefore, the Lord of Ocean, and especially of that Oceanus the great river that girdles the whole earth.

It is not wise to laugh, as the shallow laugh, at the supposed absurdities of old geography. The earth is not a flat plate, but the solar system is; and on the rim of this plate is that lonely sphere, Neptune, the outpost of the fortress of the Sun. So that it was a most happy accident that this planet was called by the name of the Lord of Oceanus.

Such is the far-off base, in the wise and true dreamland of the philosophers, of the palace of our knowledge. Let us see how their strange symbols have been hints of truth, how from the root of poetry has grown the tree of prose.

First, consider Neptune as a lonely sentinel patrolling the confines of our camp. Think of the solitude and darkness of that mysterious and eternal journey, what thoughts must bloom. Mystic, austere, romantic, will they not be? What messenger comet may approach from utmost space? The spirit of adventure thrills the blood, frosted as it is by that contact with a space of icy-nothingness, save (it may be) meteors and dark stars. Neptune is always starlit; at its distance from the Sun, our Father, is hardly bigger than any other star. So Neptune gallops through sempiternal night with his source of heat and motion too remote to cheer him, but with hope, faith and love.

How spiritual, how star-pure, must then be the secret thoughts of such an one, the hermit of the solar system? How indomitable, how lonely, how refined must be his moods.

Yet there is something in solitude which set men dreaming. Not always is that dream the starry aspiration of the Knight vowed to some inaccessible lady, often there steals through the faery window a glint of some fantastic mirth. In lighter moments, there is something of the troubadour, and even of the Pierrot, in his melancholy craving for the inaccessible. For it is not in the Neptunian nature to reach harbour. He longs for love and friendship; did he gain them he would retire. For nothing can satisfy that thirst of things infinite; there is no goal attainable. Neptune is man's boundless spirit; heaven itself is too narrow for his desires. So into his nature comes the gay coquettishness; he becomes conscious of his own anguish; and this is externalised as a love of masquerade. He knows that love is unattainable; and so he plays at love. He knows that happiness is beyond his reach; and so he seeks it by a violation of the limits of existence. His true nature, thrilled through by the wisdom of the stars with whom he holds such raptured communing in the centuries of that timeless vigil, leads him to mystic trances, to visions of deity, to mysterious marriages with elements beyond our system. For he, the Ishmael of the planets, never turns his face towards the Sun.

But if he be not steeled to endure exile, to attain the snowy summits of omniscience and bliss by means of the wise eremite, then the false nature mocks the true. In revels, fantastic and fond, in comedies bitter at the core, in the use of strange drugs or of perverse delights, in soulless and neurotic waking dreams, he seeks to satisfy his soul.

Ah, Neptune is the soul!

And does not this fit the sea? Is not the sea at once infinitely calm, and infinitely angered? Does not the sea take strange shapes, break up the light into a myriad fantastically coloured flaws? Illusion and art, chameleon and dragon, that is the sea! Is not the sea now tender, now adorable, sunkissed, now terrible in its torment, a whirl of insatiable desires? Did not Sappho fling herself into the sea, and did not Undine draw thence the bitter joy of her veins.

Are not the sea's moods unstirred, unplumbed, and do they not harbor monsters more terrible than the fancy of antiquity ever invented? Ay! Take the ocean of Odysseus and of Jason, of Mandeville[25] and of Swinburne; let the romance and the terror, the mystery and the unearthly joy of all the artists of the world direct your glance; look upon the sea through their eyes, and draw into your soul the wonder and the wantonness of it. Then understand how proper is the Ocean as an image of the soul, how proper is Neptune to be the ruler of the Ocean. The soul!

Yes, there is the word! Neptune is the soul, with all its naked nerves played upon by rays of alien systems, malicious, capricious, fairy, or else like harp-strings swept by some player from beyond, too subtle and divine for His melodies to reach the ears of mortals.

Only that sympathy, that yearning, that other-worldiness in ourselves, that influence of Neptune in our own horoscopes, enables us to catch a far-away echo of that lyre, faint, silvery music of the Psyche of our inmost being.

It was of Neptune at his noblest that the poet[26] wrote:

The Hermit's Hymn

Mightiest Self! Supreme in self-contentment!
Sole Spirit gyring in its own ellipse:
Palpable, formless, infinite presentment
Of thine own light in thine own soul's eclipse!
Let thy chaste lips
Sweep through the empty aethers guarding thee
(As in a fortress girded by the sea
The raging winds and wings of air
Lift the wild waves and bear
Innavigable foam to seaward), bend these down,

25. Bernard Mandeville (1670-1733), physician and satirical writer, author of *The Fable of the Bees.* His leading idea was that 'private vices are public benefits'.

26. Crowley is referring to himself. See *The Collected Works*, 1905, vol. 1, page 25.

Touch, draw me with thy kiss
Into thine own deep bliss,
Into thy sleep, thy life, thy imperishable crown!
Let that young godhead in thine eyes
Pierce mine, fulfil me of their secrecies,
Thy peace, thy purity, thy soul impenetrably wise.

All things which are complete are solitary;
The circling moon, the inconscient drift of stars,
The central systems. Burn they, change they, vary?
Theirs is no motion beyond the eternal bars.
Seasons and scars
Stain not the planets, the unfathomed home,
The spaceless, unformed faces in the dome
Brighter and blacker than all things,
Borne under the eternal wings
No whither; Solitary are the winter woods
And caves not habited,
And that supreme grey head
Watching the groves; single the foaming amber floods,
And O! most lone
The melancholy mountain shrine and throne,
While far above all things God sits, the ultimate alone!

I sate upon the mossy promontory
Where the cascade cleft not his mother rock,
But swept in whirlwind lightning foam and glory,
Vast circling with unwearying luminous shock
To lure and lock
Marvellous eddies in its wild caress;
And there the solemn echoes caught the stress,
The strain of that impassive tide,
Shook it and flung it high and wide.
Till all the air took fire from that melodious roar;
All the mute mountains heard,
Bowed, laughed aloud, concurred,
And passed the word along, the signal of wide war,
All earth took up the sound,
And, being in one tune securely bound,
Even as a star became the soul of silence most profound.

Thus there, the centre of that death that darkened,
I sat and listened, if God's voice should break
And pierce the hollow of my ear that hearkened,
Lest God should speak and find me not awake,
For his own sake.
No voice, no song might pierce or penetrate
That enviable universal state.
The Sun and Moon beheld, stood still.
Only the spirit's axis, will,
Considered its own soul and sought a deadlier deep,
And in the monotone mood
Of supreme solitude
Was neither glad nor sad because it did not sleep
But with calm eyes abode
Patient, its leisure the galactic load,
Abode alone, nor even rejoiced to know that it was God.

All change, all motion, and all sound are weakness!
Man cannot bear the darkness which is death,
Even that calm Christ, manifest in meekness,
Cried on the cross and gave his ghostly breath,
On the prick of death,
Voice, for his passion could not bear nor dare
The inter-lunar, the abundant air
Darkened, and silence on the shuddering
Hill, and the unbeating wing
Of the legions of His Father, and so died.
But I, should I be still
Poised between fear and will?
Should I be silent, I, and be unsatisfied?
For solitude shall bend
Self to all self-fulness, and have one friend,
Self, and behold one God, and be, and look beyond the
end.

O Solitude! how many have mistaken
Thy name for Sorrow's or for Death's or Fear's!
Only thy children lie at night and waken –
How shouldst thou speak and say that no man hears?
O Soul of Tears!

For never hath fallen as dew thy word.
Nor is thy shape showed, nor as Wisdom's heard
Thy crying about the city
In the house where is no pity,
But in the desolate halls and lonely vales of sand;
Not in the laughter loud,
Nor crying of the crowd,
But in the farthest sea, the yet untravelled land.
Where thou hast trodden, I have trod;
Thy fold have been my folk, and thine abode
Mine, and thy life my life, and thou, who art thy God, my
God.

Draw me with cords that are not; witch me chanted
Spells never heard nor open to the ear,
Woven of silence, moulded in the haunted
Houses where dead men linger year by year,
I have no fear
To tread thy far irremeable way
Beyond the paths and palaces of day,
Beyond the night, beyond the skies,
Beyond eternity's
Tremendous gate; beyond the immanent miracle.
O secret self of things!
I have nor feet nor wings
Except to follow far beyond Heaven and Earth and Hell,
Until I fix my mood
And being in thee, as in my hermit's hood
I grow the thing I contemplate – that selfless solitude!

Neptune in the Zodiacal Signs

The influence of the zodiacal sign upon Neptune operates only in a limited manner. As Neptune takes fifteen years or so to pass through a sign, generalisations must be observed. Were we to say 'Neptune in Aries indicates the martial temperament', it could be translated 'All/persons born between 1861 and 1875 have the martial temperament'; but where we are considering the modification of some other planets by an aspect of Neptune, it is clear that there will be a difference between the action of Neptune when he is in Aries and when he is in Taurus. His characteristic as the Zeitgeist will act and that most efficiently upon the other planets.

We shall now proceed to a study of the action of the signs upon Neptune, asking the reader to bear this limitation carefully in mind.

Neptune in Aries

There is very little sympathy between the hard, practical, fire and energy of Aries and the cold sensitive Neptune. The combination makes for disruption; its aspect to another planet, other things being equal, is likely to be somewhat upsetting. Those aspects which we describe as good will be not so good when Neptune is in the sign, as if he is in one more harmonious with his nature. In all cases of war and other businesses requiring initiative and energy, the influence is likely to be particularly unfortunate. Neptune may be regarded as taking away all the good points of Aries, and replacing them by the very opposite qualities – the passive for the active, the soft for the hard, the sensitive for the forceful. In the particular technical case of the sailor, the indications are not so objectionable, though it seems unwise to entrust the welfare of a fleet to an Admiral with Neptune rising in Aries. Such an appointment could only be excused by some extraordinarily good aspects from such planets as Mars and Jupiter.

When Neptune is a determining force in questions of health, he will perhaps cause the affliction to take place in the head rather than in another part of the body. Rather than repeat this remark in every sign, one may briefly indicate here that it should be modified in each case by altering the word head to the part of the body indicated by the sign.

Neptune and the other planets

In that baser and narrower astrology which concerns itself solely with the material plane, Neptune appears as a malefic. One may go so far as to say that he seems more sinister and obscure a malefic than even Saturn. The reason for this is that he represents the influx of a spiritual element which cares nothing at all for the affairs of this earth. The other planets deal with the relative; they are commensurables; Neptune intrudes upon them as the absolute and incommensurable. He represents in life the effect of the squared circle and the double cube in mathematics. For those who are devoted to the spiritual he is, therefore, wholly good; for others wholly bad. He wrests them from serenity.

Conjunction generally means confusion, unless the natures of the conjoined planets be very harmonious. The conjunctions of Neptune are therefore ominous to the conjoined planet unless there be other support.

Opposition generally means conflict and exhaustion; both planets lose in force. The quartile aspect means attack; both planets become more brutal. (This is not always necessarily bad: for example, Sun quartile Mars in a question of Health might seem a rude robustness.) The sextile aspect is friendly, bringing out the softer qualities of both planets.

The trine aspect resembles the alliance of two great kings. They mutually support and defend one another; the strength of both is brought out in its best form. This aspect is more important when the planets are large and slow-moving.

These remarks should be taken into consideration in the study of the following. For convenience and brevity the aspects have been classed simply as friendly and unfriendly; and they must be modified according to the map whose interpretation is demanded. The exact plane, on which the *effect operates*, depends of course upon the houses in which they are situated, or which they rule.

Neptune and Uranus

These two planets are of supreme importance in the affairs of the spirit. (For example, they were conjoined at the birth of the poet Baudelaire, and when in *exact* opposition announce the birth of a Master of the Temple. Events such as these are cosmically more important than the fall of empires.) Their natures being so potent and opposite, they refuse to harmonise; every aspect that they make is the signal for battle in the wars of the world-soul. And, the Universe being in motion toward Absolute Truth and Beauty, every such battle is a victory for love.

In otherwise unimportant nativities, the friendship of these planets implies a struggle of the soul, a self-analysis probably long and bitter, but almost certainly ending in victory for the higher. This may manifest itself in the outer in strange ways, not indicative to the thoughtless of what is really taking place. We may find a recluse, an amiable crank, a fanatic, a self-torturing saint.

In those horoscopes which are otherwise important, and give more or less immediate fame to the native, we expect a friendship of Neptune and Uranus to make him principally a reconciler of certain deep antimonies. They were within 3° at the birth of Herbert Spencer,[27] who reconciled the warring tendencies of religion and science with his doctrine of the Unknowable; and exactly conjoined in the horoscope of Baudelaire, who united good and evil in his moral infinite. The same is true of Pasteur, who revolutionised medical science; and of Copernicus, who founded modern astronomy by his extraordinary and world-upheaving discoveries. Also of General Grant,[28] who reunited America, and of Paul Kruger[29] who broke the British Empire. Neptune and Uranus were sextile for Cecil Rhodes[30] and near trine for Napoleon.

Of those who attempted similar or lesser problems, we may quote Sir Edwin Durning-Lawrence,[31] the Shakespeare-Bacon crank, who had these planets semi-sextile; Dr Orville Owen,[32] nearly sextile; 'George Eliot' had them within 4° of

27. Herbert Spencer (1820-1903), English philosopher who, under the influence of Charles Darwin, attempted to reconstruct the whole range of human thought as a 'social evolutionist'.

28. Ulysses Simpson Grant (1822-1885), Republican, became 18th President of the U.S.A. He had been commander-in-chief of the Union Army in the Civil War.

29. Paul Kruger (1825-1904), Boer leader and President of the South African Republic, discouraged the Boers from supporting the Zulus against Britain in 1878-9 on the grounds that 'one must never join with savages in war against a civilised nation'.

30. Cecil John Rhodes (1853-1902), British statesman, financier and pioneer imperalist who helped to open up Africa and established the British colony of Rhodesia.

31. Sir Edwin Durning-Lawrence Bart (1837-1914), Member of Parliament for Truro, 1895-1906.

32. Orville W. Owen, author of verse plays, flourished at end of the nineteenth century.

conjunction. They are also close to semi-sextile in the nativity of Joseph Smith![33]

As previously observed, there is not so great a difference between the friendly and unfriendly aspects of these planets. The conflict is perhaps more terrible in the latter case and may rage unabated throughout the life. But in such contests, the battle is more important than its results. Luther, who split Christianity in half, had these planets in a fiery sign within 10° excited by the violence of passion implied in a close conjunction of Mars and Venus. They are united in the horoscope of Ruskin, whose radical criticism of art and life made so famous a fiasco, and semi-sextile in that of Swinburne, whose Muse petered out before he had written six years, as also in that of Tennyson, who strove to make merchandise of poetry. Tennyson had also Mars conjoined with Uranus, making him a toady and selfish scoundrel.[34] Savonarola had them sextile and perished in the flames which he himself kindled. Dante, who had them quartile, made of his own heart, hell, purgatory and heaven. Sir Richard Burton, England's greatest linguist and explorer, a magnificent poet, a most original thinker, had them in exact conjunction in the third house.[35]

On the whole, then, one may consider aspects of these planets as 'on the dangerous edge of things' where, as Browning says, our interest lies. The bigger and more threatening the aspect, the better for the world at large, if not for the peace and comfort of the native. The minor key of strife, the lesser phases of the soul, often mean mere eccentricity.

Beware of people born on 4 November 1880, or thereabouts and on or near 3 December 1900.

Neptune and Saturn

The aspects of these two planets are extremely powerful, as the one fills the defects of the other, while maintaining the plane of high mentality. Their combination is not so spiritual

33. Joseph Smith (1805-1844), the founder of the Mormon sect.
34. Tennyson was one of Crowley's bugbears; hence these insults.
35. Sir Richard Francis Burton (1821-1890) was one of six people to whom Crowley dedicated his six-volumed autobiography, *The Confessions of Aleister Crowley*, 1969 (in one volume).

as that just considered, but for this very reason it is more obvious and more puissant in everyday life.

The first point that strikes the observer is that both planets are solitary, and, therefore, in a mundane sense, sad. When unfriendly (and in this case the conjunction is definitely evil, unless both planets are very powerful or well supported by more genial orbs) they bring misfortune and melancholy. The native is lonely, a recluse, occupied with forebodings or, in the best case, with ascetic and austere thoughts. He probably lacks sympathy and may be a cynic or misanthrope. He is difficult to approach; he repels. Yet though slow and unpractical, he is liable to be the slave of whims. Often old age brings definite melancholia. George III, the 'old, mad, blind, despised and dying King' of Shelley's sonnet had these planets in conjunction.

Fortunately, however, the influence is frequently transmuted into art, the art of the *Weltschmerz*. Coleridge, Chopin and Alfred de Musset[36] all had this conjunction. All three are representatives of the minor key. In the case of Coleridge, the conjunction of Venus is added and the softening influence of this planet increased his sentimentality on the one hand and drove him to opium on the other.

Oscar Wilde had these planets in quartile and although both were well aspected, Saturn by Uranus and Neptune by Mercury; the influence proved fatal. (Neptune was in the house of public enemies and Saturn in the tenth, the latter always brings fame and downfall.)

The aspect 150° ordinarily unimportant seems most malefic in the case of these planets. For example, Charles I and Dreyfus[37] both suffered from this. In political life the

36. Alfred de Musset (1810-1857), French poet, playwright and novelist whom Sainte-Beuve described as 'a child of genius'. Excessive indulgence in sex and alcohol brought him to an early grave.

37. In 1894, Alfred Dreyfus, an officer of the French General Staff, was convicted of spying for Germany, and sentenced to lifelong imprisonment on the dreaded Devil's Island. Dreyfus happened to be a Jew, and his trial behind closed doors and conviction plunged France into anti-semitic fervour. The letter convicting Dreyfus was a forgery. In 1897, the statesman Georges Clemenceau, 'The Tiger', who was to lead France to victory in the First World War, started his fight for a re-examination of the case. Four weeks later, the novelist Emile Zola

influence is very strong, but very treacherous. Gladstone had these planets in conjunction in the 11th and although he had always hosts of friends, he was always being ruined by cabals.

Rossetti, another case in point, was melancholy, and suffered terribly from sensitiveness. Neptune was in conjunction also with Mars and he ended in madness. A trine of Sol made him a great artist in spite of this misfortune.

There is a very extraordinary case of the conjunction of these planets on the cusp of the tenth house, where, helped by Jupiter, the native had what may also be called a double mind. Not only could he do two things at once, but he could never do less!

The friendly aspects are extremely fortunate, giving extraordinary competence in one's profession, a complete mastery of technique, superadded to tremendous energy and creative force, great vitality and capacity of comprehension. The effect of the trine aspect is shown in such superb careers as those of Michael Angelo, Pasteur and Lord Roberts.[38] Even the sextile and semi-sextile aspects are of great value in the race for fame. George Sand, almost the only feminine artist since Sappho, had them sextile; and Petrarch and Adelina Patti semi-sextile. Every one of these cases shows the artistic temperament at its best and most triumphal; each shows vast capacity for detail, as well as for magnitude of aim; each

---

joined the ranks of the Dreyfusards, and published his celebrated manifesto, *J'Accuse*. France divided into two hostile factions, those for the Army and France and those who were for Dreyfus or simply against the people on the other side. Among the Dreyfusards were not a few anti-semites. In 1898, Major Walsin-Esterhazy, another officer of the French General Staff, was dishonourably discharged because of embezzlement. He hurried to a British journalist and confessed that under orders from his superior, Colonel Sandherr, he had forged Dreyfus's handwriting on the incriminating document. The following year the Court of Appeal annulled the original sentence against Dreyfus, and gave him ten years instead of life. A week later, the President of the Republic pardoned Dreyfus, but it was not until 1906, when Clemenceau became Prime Minister, that Dreyfus was acquitted. French emotions over the *Affaire Dreyfus* have not yet entirely subsided. Dreyfus died in 1935.

38. Frederick Sleigh Roberts, 1st Earl Roberts of Kandahar, Pretoria and Waterford (1832-1914), British field marshal. He commanded the British forces in the Boer War (1899-1900).

assures a fame based on the respect due to singleness of purpose and purity of heart.

Neptune and Jupiter

The religious and genial effect of Jupiter turns Neptune to a warmer shade of blue. Thus we find a kindly, easy-going humanitarian style of mysticism in such men as Colonel Olcott,[39] Petrarch and Lord Lytton[40] who had these two planets sextile. (In the case of Petrarch a square aspect of Sol and Luna tinged his work with the insight of realism, the quartile is admirable to strip off illusion, and the semi-sextile of Saturn added the austerity and purity which we praise.) In the horoscope of Shelley, Mars and Jupiter are both conjoined with Neptune in the ninth house. It is not saying too much to affirm that Shelley created the 'religion of humanity'. Mars and Jupiter conjoined give more force than any other combination, and we must contrast Shelley with J.P. Morgan,[41] (1837-1913), in whose nativity they are in opposition to Neptune. One shows the power of ideals, the other the power to work against them. Similarly, without Mars we find Maeterlinck, a flabby pseudo-mystic, a humbug, an amateur, the internal soul of Neptune at issue with its vestment Jupiter; religion robbed of its essence and become a vampire. Yet had only Mercury lent aid, he might have been at once the greatest of poets and the greatest of religious teachers.

The square aspect is not so exhausting. It gives tremendous realism in religion and statesmanship or in ethical teaching whether through art or directly. Thus we find Zola (expressing himself in art owing to the semi-sextile of Venus) as a builder of social theories based on ruthless realism. Yet that realism, unknown to itself, is founded on a thoroughly romantic idea. The railway engine in *La Bête Humaine* and the still in the *L'Assommoir* are much more symbolic than

39. See note 201.

40. Edward Robert Bulwer, second Baron and first Earl Lytton (1831-1891), novelist and Viceroy of India. His occult novel *Zanoni* impressed Madame Blavatsky. He entertained Eliphas Lévi at his fantastically romantic stately home, Knebworth House in Hertfordshire.

41. See note 4.

anything in Ibsen or Wagner. They live and move and have their being and the characters of the story are puppets in their hands.

The same criticism applies to the work of Pico de Mirandola,[42] who had the same aspect, as had Cecil Rhodes[43] and Brigham Young,[44] who both strove to fashion empires, each in his own way, one with a new religion, the other with money. Each had the romantic aim; each had the realistic, even brutal method (Rhodes' trine of Sol gave him added glory, wealth and success).

Turning to friendlier aspects, we note Lewis Carroll, whose semi-sextile of Venus (in the Ascendant) added to the semi-sextile of Jupiter, made him not only a religious artist, but a lover of children. (The pettiness of the aspects is, however, a limitation. It is almost safe to say that no horoscope is really first rate without good aspects or strong positions of the male planets Sol, Mars or Saturn. Jupiter is too comfortable to move the world alone; he likes things as they are.)

Of the trine aspect we have one shocking example. The rising Moon of Alfred Dreyfus[45] was squared by Mars, and Saturn in the seventh house afflicted Neptune in the Ascendant, a mundane opposition and a close aspect of 150°. But the frightful calamities brought about by these positions were counteracted in the end by the trine of Jupiter to Neptune.

To return to our opening remark on the warmth and colour of the soul on whom these planets throw harmonious rays, we have two supreme examples of the trine aspect, Johann Wolfgang Goethe and J.M.W. Turner. Compare these with the nativities already cited in regard to the trine of Saturn and note the larger humanity and less strictness. Each

42. The Christian Qabalist, born 1463, died 1494. According to Eliphas Lévi, Pico de Mirandola was of the opinion that 'in Black Magic the most barbarous and unintelligible words are the most efficacious and the best'. Crowley was of the same opinion. See *Magick*, ch.9.

43. See note 30.

44. Brigham Young (1801-1877), Mormon leader and head of the Latter Day Saints of Salt Lake City. At his death he had seventeen wives.

45. See note 37.

master of his art in an equal degree to Michael Angelo and Pasteur, yet both more vivid, more all-embracing, less single-minded. It will depend largely on one's own horoscope as to which pair one chooses as more useful to humanity; but to any intelligent mind the nature of the difference is obvious, and consideration of the point is extremely instructive as illustrating the disparity between Jupiter and Saturn in their influence on Neptune.

Neptune and Mars

The influences of these planets are so opposite in nature that not even their strongest and most favourable combination seems productive of much good. Neptune tends to render Mars unpractical, to make him hold his hand at the very moment when his only chance is to strike with all his strength. In Charles I and George V, we find the trine aspect; Edward VII had the sextile. In each case we find a certain weak amiability of character combined with a certain talent for intrigue. This is no such great defect in one not a crowned head. Chopin had the trine, but this was made rude by a square of the sun, and strengthened still further by Saturn and the Moon. He could then succeed in art; but who will doubt that he would have made a disastrous ruler? The feeble, dreamy, almost imbecile W.B. Yeats[46] has Mars and Neptune trine; but the combination gives him power in a shadow-world of his own. Again, we find the semi-sextile aspect in the sentimental twaddling Ruskin, though Mercury conjoined with Mars lent him eloquence.

Theodore Roosevelt[47] has the sextile of Mars; and this means political adroitness – as Edward VII also enjoyed. But the ex-President has also squares of Jupiter and Venus, lending a certain rugged and impetuous strength to what is, in its essence, a somewhat puerile idealism.

The square of Mars is sometimes better than those aspects

46. Crowley never lost an opportunity to deride W.B. Yeats. They met as members of the Hermetic Order of the Golden Dawn in 1898. See John Symonds, *The Great Beast*, 1971, and Ellic Howe, *The Magicians of the Golden Dawn*, 1972.

47. Theodore Roosevelt (1858-1919), a Republican, became the 26th President of the United States.

usually called favourable. It takes away the impracticality of Neptune and the obstinate blindness of Mars is cured by imagination. Hence we find this aspect in such horoscopes as those of Jay Gould[48] and William III of England. Tchaikovsky, too, has this; and in addition Mars is in close conjunction with the Sun. William Jennings Bryan[49] has Mars in the tenth house, square to a conjunction of Neptune and the Sun. Despite other bad aspects, Mercury square Jupiter and Saturn opposition Luna, this has given him his moment of success.

The conjunction is usually disastrous in the long run, though it may spell temporary success. It is the strength of fanaticism and we find it in Wilhelm II[50] (fortunately for him the trine of Luna and the square of Venus add weight and dignity to the combination, besides turning its angry energy to peacefulness; hence he is able to say that he had kept Europe at peace for 43 years) and also in King Ludwig of Bavaria, the patron of Wagner, a monarch whose tragic history is well known, and in that more terrible apostle of an idea – Robespierre.

No doubt this conjunction has in it the threat of furious madness. Napoleon I has this aspect, but Mars is in close sextile with Jupiter and Uranus in trine. The composer Richard Strauss also has this but with sextile of Venus; so that his epilepsy is turned to artistic ends and his ravings are musical. Another fanatic, Shelley, has this conjunction; in his case the benefit of Jupiter made his mania humanitarian. Rossetti again became mad, having this conjunction but a trine of Sol made him the great and versatile artist that we

48. Jay Gould (1836-1892), the American railway magnate and speculator.

49. William Jennings Bryan (1860-1925), American politician and orator who campaigned for the Presidency on the ticket that the United States should adopt a silver currency. 'America is being crucified on a cross of gold,' was his cry. He was not elected.

50. The Kaiser, Wilhelm II (1859-1941), whose megalomaniac behaviour played a great part in causing the disastrous First World War. Of him, Churchill wrote: 'Nevertheless history should incline to the more charitable view, and acquit William II of having planned and plotted the World War. But the defence which can be made will not be flattering to his self-esteem.'

admire. A curious case is that of Dumas *père,*[51] who had these planets in opposition; but their influence is masked by the overwhelming conjunction of Venus, Jupiter and Saturn.

On the whole it is to be asserted that no aspect of Mars and Neptune is very desirable, unless assistance is found from some third sphere. Mars is blunt, brutal, blind, material, obvious, frank, angry; Neptune is the opposite of all these. Neptune is the eighteenth-century planet, the star of Versailles, the spirit in Watteau,[52] Verlaine,[53] Ernest Dowson;[54] all this is utterly abhorrent to Mars. Louis XV made even war itself an affair of uniforms and ballrooms; the Revolution turned even the theatre to shambles. It is remarkable how Mars comes to put an end to Neptune; 1914 is to the decadents (cubists, futurists and the rest in whom art has turned to disease and dementia) just as the Terror came to rip up the frilled fooleries of the Oeil-de-Boeuf.[55]

Such help as aspects of these two planets afford lies chiefly in the paths of intrigue. Machiavellianism is the result of their combination. Where a talent for intrigue, assisted by the will and the power to cut a knot occasionally by the dagger, means success, then a strong aspect of Mars and Neptune may avail not a little. Many of the mediaeval Popes are thus

51. Alexandre Dumas (1802-1870), French novelist and dramatist, author of *The Count of Monte Cristo, The Three Musketeers* and other popular works, was the founder of French Romanticism. His son, Dumas *fils*, author of *La Dame aux Camélias*, continued the tradition.

52. Antoine Watteau (1684-1721), great French pâinter of poetic sensibility and remarkable technical facility.

53. Paul Marie Verlaine (1844-1896), French poet, companion of the youthful and extraordinary Arthur Rimbaud, whom he shot and wounded in a quarrel in Brussels. For a while he taught French and drawing in an English school. His great lyrical gift, combined with his life of debauchery made him a culture hero among the young. In a fit of pique and sibling rivalry he smashed the bottles which contained the pickled foetuses of his mother's miscarriages. Havelock Ellis and Arthur Symons visited him towards the end of his life, which he spent as a devout Catholic.

54. Ernest Christopher Dowson (1867-1900), English decadent poet of some merit who lived his short life in misery and poverty exacerbated by drugs. He was a contributor to *The Yellow Book* and *The Savoy*, the leading literary periodicals of the time.

55. Ante-chamber of the Great Hall of the palace of Versailles.

favoured by the stars. (Mars and Uranus have a not dissimilar influence, and are found with equal frequency in such cases.) In modern times these methods are slightly and superficially altered; but their essence remains the same. For social and court intrigue we substitute the chicaneries of law, use political pull, buy judges, bribe legislatures; while for the use of the dagger and the poison bowl, we have meaner, deadlier more cowardly and more treacherous – the newspapers.

Neptune and Sol

The exact contrary of our remarks on Neptune and Mars is true of Neptune and the Sun. He enlightens all that is dim, strengthens all that is weak, in the most distant of the planets. As Neptune is the circumference, Sol is the centre, of the system. She is the image of the soul of the Great Mother, as he is of the Father. Hence, they are complementary to, one may almost say necessary to, each other and their interaction is wholly harmonious. In people with such aspects, we may look for a completeness of nature which is bound to spell success. There will be a radiance diffused from the personality; a joyousness tempered by divine sadness, a melancholy transformed into abundant joy. The least assistance from a third planet will give the key in which the melody is to be played, for Sol, and Neptune are so self-sufficing when together that they have no particular tinge; therefore the rest of the horoscope will depend much on the other planets. One can only say of this particular combination that it forms a steady, grand, harmonious harp which the Artist can thrill with the 'music of the spheres'. Of concrete examples of the operation of this law, we have too many and must content the reader with a selection.

Probably the greatest singer in the world, Adelina Patti,[56] has Neptune in conjunction with the sun. (Her career was determined by Mars in his own house in the fifth, trined by Uranus.) Other conjunctions are those of Savonarola,[57] to

56. A coloratura soprano of unrivalled fame (1843-1919).

57. Girolamo Savonarola (1452-1498), the great Florentine preacher and reformer who denounced the follies and luxuries of the time, attacking the notorious Pope Alexander VI. He was excommunicated, imprisoned and burnt.

which Mercury was added, determining him as scholar and mystic. A conjunction of Venus and Saturn only ten degrees away made him fanatic and ascetic. Erasmus, again, the one great light of scholarship in the Middle Ages, had this conjunction aided by the moon. Mercury and Venus conjoined in the Ascendant, Libra, were the factors that decided his life. Edison, like Savonarola, has Neptune with the Sun and Mercury. Here Scorpio rising, with its lord well-aspected in the third house, makes practical science the basis of the life. Gladstone has these same two planets semi-sextile to Neptune; they are on the cusp of the Ascendant, and gave him his ambition, eloquence and force. William Shakespeare had Sol and Luna in conjunction semi-sextile to Neptune, the latter being in the tenth, the house of fame. Jupiter and Saturn were also in exact conjunction in that same tenth house.

Petrarch has Mercury and the Sun conjoined and square to Neptune, but helped by Jupiter and Saturn. Neptune is in the fifth, the house of art, love and beauty. Emile Zola had a conjunction of Sol and Luna semi-sextile to Neptune; the latter is semi-sextile to Venus; showing the artistic outlet of his energy, while the square of Jupiter indicates his anti-religious standpoint, and the opposition experienced by him from the clerical party.

Chopin has Neptune with Saturn square to the setting Sun, and Neptune is in the worst place for him, the nadir. This gave the wistfulness and melancholy to his work. Fortunately, the energy of Mars and the purity of the Moon united to save him. Tchaikovsky has the square, but Mars is with the Sun.

Queen Elizabeth of England had the opposition of Sol and Neptune, in the tenth and fourth, both ill places – the reverse gives the best places and this accounts for her dynastic failure as well as for her actual success as a ruler and defender of her country. (Sol is in close trine to Saturn, giving her the resolute stability of moral character which we associate with her name; and Jupiter is rising.)

George V of England has a sextile of the Sun and a trine of Mars, but Jupiter imprisoned in the twelfth squared by Uranus may lose him his throne.

We now turn to the trine aspect, and find indeed a galaxy. T.H. Huxley[58] had this, and his work not only as a man of science but as a philosopher, must endure for ages, while the harmony of his personal character was the admiration even of his bitterest enemies. Rossetti had this and it made him divine, despite the evil influence of Mars. General Grant,[59] one of the three political lights of America, also had this trine. So had Cecil Rhodes,[60] though a square of Jupiter baulked him and he died leaving his work unfinished. Copernicus, too, had this aspect; and despite a square of Venus, (a comparatively unimportant pawn in so great a game) he accomplished the revolution of astronomy. In this case a conjunction of Uranus and a trine of Saturn assisted. Hence the cosmic scope of his world-shaking achievement.

Michael Angelo has this trine, with a conjunction of Mercury and Venus rising, sextile to Jupiter. The Moon and Uranus conjoined in Scorpio trine to Saturn in the fifth house, gave him his majestic comprehension of art, and his creative energy and power of execution.

In conclusion, one can but reiterate that a favourable aspect of these two planets in strong position and well-dignified, especially if they are helped by good angles of other planets, is one of the most fortunate circumstances possible, an asset in life to be preferred to almost any other.

Neptune and Venus

The combination of Neptune with Venus is as generally evil as that with Mars, but for precisely opposite reasons. Venus, it is true, means love, beauty and grace, tenderness and the rest: but unless these qualities are stiffened by some male element, they mean in practice, mere weakness, sloppiness, sentimentality. The old alchemists described Venus as having 'external splendour and internal corruption' and astrology bears this out. Venus is the false gold, the corrosive and poisonous copper. We shall find this dictum amply confirmed in our exemplifications. Venus is too like Neptune to be a

58. See note 3.
59. See note 28.
60. See note 30.

good mate for him; she is the 'visible soul of Nature' of which he is the invisible; and (as we learn in *The Chymical Marriage* of Christian Rosencreutz[61] it was forbidden to the seeker to look on Venus. Hence even the best aspects of these two planets declare a soul so passive and impressionable that the rest of the horoscope has too much power; and even if this power be 'good', it is not well in the end. Only actual strength from some steadier planet joining in the combination itself, can assure a real success. In other words there must be something so to dominate that the Venus aspect becomes but a junior partner in the firm. Hence in the horoscopes of such brilliant men as Zola, Goethe, Brigham Young, and Theodore Roosevelt we find the aid of Jupiter; in that of Coleridge we find Mercury and Saturn coming to the rescue. Copernicus was saved by a trine of Sol. Where Venus alone with Neptune means success, it implies Hypocrisy or Sentimentality. For example, Queen Victoria had these planets trine and her age is still a byword among men. Swedenborg had them sextile and his religion is back-boneless, a cult of cranks without virility. Backhaus has them conjoined and we find a pianist whom one can only call 'accomplished'. Kruger had the trine aspect and no viler old humbug ever ruled though the conjunction of Mars and Jupiter not far off made him also vigorous, astute and brave. Wilhelm II,[62] with the quartile, risked the very existence of his country again and again by his culpable determination to keep the peace of Europe; Louis XVI with the sextile lost his throne and his head by refusing to sweep away the mob with a 'whiff of grapeshot'. Tolstoy had the conjunction, and was a sentimentalist to the point of lunacy; Dickens with the square, ruined his magnificent genius for satire (Saturn on the cusp of the third, in his own Capricorn square Mars in his own house Aries) by the worst kind of Victorian squeamishness and imbecility. Theodore Roosevelt once more, in spite of the brutal force of realism given by the square of Jupiter,

61. The pseudonym of Johann Valentin Andreae, author of *Chymische Hochzeit*, Strasbourg, 1616, translated as *The Chymical Wedding* by E. Foxcroft and published in London in 1690.
62. See note 50.

and the violent energy supplied by the sextile of Mars, has the square of Venus, and his catchwords, his appeals to the cruder and baser idealism have ultimately choked him. Sir Alfred Harmsworth (Lord Northcliffe)[63] has the sextile aspect, and he is but the statesman of the street corner, the purveyor of mental sewer-slush to the gutter-mind. Undoubtedly these aspects give persuasive power; but it is only the foul power of hypocrisy. It rests upon illusion. All that is dim and faery in Neptune, instead of being confined is made horrible by the essential falsity and worthlessness of the unredeemed and vampire Venus, who is not Venus-Urania, but that Lilith[64] that haunts the dreams of evil men, that feeds on sleeping children, the first and most fatal of all the demons of the pit.

Neptune and Mercury

The aspects of these two planets are very favourable. Mecury lends intellectuality to the mystic planet and Neptune redeems the cold brilliancy of the star of reason. At the same time, Mercury is the trickster, and Neptune the master of masquerade, and these, in combination often produce a whimsicality or perversity whose benefit depends chiefly on the rest of the horoscope. In good ways it may mean wit, in bad crankiness and faddism. It sometimes gives logic divorced from common sense.

In W.E. Gladstone, the semi-sextile (aided by the Sun) gave eloquence and political adroitness; thus he was the greatest orator and parliamentarian of his period. Edison, with a stronger form of this double aspect, is the master-mind of his age in practical applications of science. Petrarch, too, has the Sun and Mercury square to Neptune, and we find his eloquence and passion unequalled. Dante who harnessed intellect and mysticism to the chariot of satire and invective, had Mercury and Neptune sextile. Coleridge has the semi-

63. Alfred Charles William Harmsworth (1865-1922), 1st Viscount Northcliffe, British newspaper proprietor, founder of the *Daily Mail* and *Daily Mirror* and father of the yellow press.

64. According to Rabbinical tradition the demonic Lilith, the 'mistress of spirits', was Adam's wife during the 130 years he spent apart from Eve. With the appearance of Eve she vanished.

sextile and his table-talk was the delight of his contemporaries. So had Luther, whose intellect and eloquence shook the world. Both these had additional helps from other planets. A third case is Ruskin, whose prose remains an enduring monument of his era. Napoleon, whose intellect, not only as a commander, but a lawgiver, has few parallels, also enjoyed this aspect. Alexandre Dumas[65] has Mercury trine, and despite the evil aspect of Mars, wrote the most brilliant novels of adventure that exist in the French language. Savonarola has this conjunction with Mercury and Sol; he was the most eloquent and learned doctor that even Florence can blazon on her shield. Balzac has these planets in opposition but helped by a semi-sextile of the moon; from this we can divine his sword-sharp intellect, his infinite comprehension of mankind, and his summary of it all as a comedy or masque. The square excites a bitter cynicism, as in the case of Byron. Philip Bourke Marston,[66] the blind pre-Raphaelite poet, has them in opposition; he is the most clear-sighted and realistic of the artificial school.

Of the fine power of the trine we have two brilliant and perfect examples; Oscar Wilde and Bernard Shaw. The wit of these two is absolutely typical of the aspect. The lesser sextile is exemplified by George du Maurier, the author of *Trilby*, for many years an illustrator of *Punch*, and his delicate humour and timid satire are still admired. Harmsworth, a clever unscrupulous journalist, has Mercury trine Neptune, but there is a sextile of Venus which has turned all to ill (also he has the Sun in opposition to Saturn and squared by the Moon; Saturn is in the tenth; he will end with a crash). The conjunction sometimes produces a great religious teacher, such as Rudolf Steiner.[67] The opposition is more likely to cause a certain inhibition in true religious thought, and to turn the impulse to the vagaries of faddism, to intellectual acuteness without any sense of proportion.

65. See note 51.

66. Philip Bourke Marston (1850-1887) a mournful poet, friend of Rosseti and Swinburne, who went blind, lost his betrothed and died young.

67. The founder of the mystical doctrine of Anthroposophy, the science of man in relation to the cosmic forces.

Such is the case with Eustace Miles, who proposed to reform the world by a diet of health foods, and who loads his after-dinner speeches with puns on the names of the persons present. Hereward Carrington[68] goes even further and proposes complete starvation as a cure for all the woes of man. Logically, he is right of course! Fortunately, a trine and sextile of Uranus came to his rescue and maturity has brought him some degree of wisdom, or at least of common sense.

Enough has been said; it must now be clear to all in what way these planets act and react; how their operation is chiefly to determine the qualities of the mind, and particularly speech which is the issue of the mind. It is not a great combination for the artist, who asks more of the planets of fatherhood and of creative energy. Most of the examples that we have given impress us rather as brilliant than as profound. Gladstone was too clever to be a real statesman; Edison never made a discovery in abstract science; Petrarch is not in the first flight of poets; the star of Coleridge has but three narrow rays; Luther was not a deep theologian; Ruskin was but an artist manqué; Napoleon never cut at the roots of his political oaks; Dumas is but a narrator; Savonarola never did more than scourge the symptoms of the evil he attacked; Byron never wrote first-rate poetry; Marston is but a sorry rhymster; Wilde and Shaw have done nothing immortal; Harmsworth is a byword for shallowness, stupidity and sensationalism; du Maurier was a hack, Steiner a quack. Balzac, it is true, was the greatest novelist that trine has yet brought forth; but the Mercury and Neptune aspect is of secondary importance in a horoscope which has Venus and Mars in conjunction semi-sextile to Jupiter in the tenth, Sol being also in the tenth only seven degrees away. It indicates his point of view, and even to some extent the method of his work; but the greater gods must be made to speak in order to explain his capacity and energy and his ever-crescent and immortal fame.

68. The author (with S. Muldoon) of *The Projection of the Astral Body*. He was the model of the character Morningside in Crowley's novel *Moonchild*.

Neptune and Luna

The remarks to which duty forced us when on the subject of Venus and Neptune must be made even more severe if we are to deal adequately with his relations with the Moon. For Venus has a certain ease and jollity; the Moon is cold, dim, mother of illusions. She is utterly dark, unless the Sun himself lend her of his light. Alone she is but the planet of witches; strange beasts prowl in the darkness; poisoners gather their deadly herbs beneath her as she wanes. Neptune, too, is an 'octave' of Luna; so that in combination they bring the maximum deviation from balance; and all unbalanced force is evil. We accordingly find an excessive weakness and effeminacy, expressing itself in peevish melancholy, often associated with ill-health, and with addiction to drugs and drink. The strong characters, the great men, who have these planets in aspect have them either unimportant as in the case of Wagner, who has them sextile, but has the Sun rising (on the exact cusp of the Ascendant) trine Mars sextile Jupiter, semi-sextile Mercury, an array which utterly outshines them – or assisted by some masculine benefic. Thus Shakespeare's semi-sextile is also a semi-sextile with Sol; Erasmus has Sol as well as Luna in conjunction; Zola has Sol and Luna conjoined sextile, as well as aspects of Venus and Jupiter; Chopin's sextile is fortified by Mars and the Sun; Philip Bourke Marston's[69] opposition is also an opposition to Mercury, and besides he had the conjunction of Mars and Jupiter as the dominant factor in his horoscope. Wilhelm II has a trine of the Moon, whence his physical misfortune,[70] and his weak love of peace; fortunately Mars conjoined with Neptune in the tenth kept that weakness from becoming criminal.

George Eliot has the two planets semi-sextile; hence the ultra-femininity of her nature and her wish to masquerade as masculine. The Emperor Franz Joseph[71] has them square; his life has been a tragedy too great for tears. Robert Louis Stevenson has them in conjunction; there is a typical case –

69. See note 66.

70. Kaiser Wilhelm had a deformed left arm.

71. Franz Joseph (1830-1916), emperor of Austria and after 1867 emperor-king of Austria-Hungary.

the frail, anaemic, delicate, refined, wistful, gentle creature utterly unfitted by his personality to fight in the world and only saved by Venus on the cusp of the eleventh, implying help of friends (she is trined by Uranus) from constant disaster. There is also a conjunction of Sol and Mars in the eighth (culminating) implying sudden and unexpected strength in hours of despair, but of course it killed him in the end. Saturn rising (second house) is more melancholy still, especially as he is within 2° of the opposition of Jupiter.

Dreyfus has the same aspect, a conjunction, and it made him the sport of a most evil fortune, despite the trine of Jupiter which could do no more than secure his ultimate rehabilitation. The trine aspect is again found with Guy de Maupassant and to this, no doubt, we may attribute his nervous subtlety. But he has Venus rising in conjunction with Jupiter and Mars, an overwhelming force of character to counteract the otherwise weakening effect.

As a final example, we have the notorious Mabel Collins,[72] whose Neptune is not only in conjunction with the Moon, but trine Mars, square Venus and sextile to a conjunction of Saturn and Uranus. Such a hotch-potch of aspects is too confusing ever to be good. Hence her Neptune in the fifth, the house of pleasures and of art, ruined that part of her life. Her books were but medleys of mania, ill-written, pretentious and ignorant and her pleasures were unsavoury to the last degree.

To sum all, we may say that while the combinations of Neptune and Luna may be most fortunate in stimulating the imagination, in conferring subtlety and depth of thought, and in making the character pure, aspiring and gentle, this will rarely be the case unless in other respects the horoscope is unusually strong. So recondite and obscure a mode of thought as is implied will most assuredly suffer shipwreck from the storms of life unless the ship of the Soul be armoured with the triple brass and iron of some other planets better calculated to resist the buffeting of the waves of circumstance.

72. The theosophist, author of *Light on the Path* and *The Blossom and the Fruit.* She was another of Crowley's bugbears.

Neptune in the Twelve Houses of Heaven

It is to be understood that the indications given below refer only to simple cases – they are modified according to the sign in which the planet is situated and according to the aspects which it makes with other planets. As it is, of course, impracticable to give a separate account of all the possible combinations, it has been necessary to put down the single, separate, simple effects of every element of which the configuration of the heavens at any moment is composed, leaving the student to combine them for any particular case, in accordance with his judgment, experience and ability.

Neptune in the First House

It is usually easy to recognise persons who have Neptune rising. Even at the first glance it is apparent that they are not as others. The sensation given is difficult to define, but it is unmistakable. They seem, in some way, peculiar, strongly individual, yet not with any common kind of strength. The general racial characteristics will be determined more by the sign rising, the planet which rules that sign and the aspects to that planet, but it is practically always possible to determine whether Neptune is in or close to the Ascendant, for his influence is concentrated in the eyes. These are often grey or blue of a rather cold shade, but whether this be so or not, they have a peculiar magnetic quality. The effect is often weird and startling. There may be some hint in it of perversity or madness. They are coldly penetrating yet sometimes shiftly and secretive; so characteristic is this appearance that only a few observations of people who possess it are necessary to familiarise the student with it. This indication is often especially valuable when the hour of birth is not accurately known, for if Neptune happened to be rising, there can be no possible doubt, and the figure may then be cast for the appropriate hour with perfect confidence.

The moral and mental characteristics of people with Neptune on the Ascendant are singular and subtle. The action of Neptune, taking place as it does, in the remotest fastnesses of the soul causes deep-seated upheavals of the personality.

Nothing so upsets the normal indications drawn from the sign and ruler as the presence of Neptune. It does not modify them it introduces an entirely new influence from a finer and more powerful plane. The first result of this circumstance which attracts our notice is that the character often betrays a contradictoriness, a whimsicality, a perversion, or introduces some fantastic element of mockery or masquerade. In some natures, this will be very profound and far-reaching; in others shallow, even superficial. This question must be determined by consideration of the relative strength of Neptune, essential or accidental, with the rising sign and its ruler. We may, however, mention a few of the principal observations which have been made, especially characteristic of its effect. In younger souls, such as have not freed themselves, even partially, from the gross influences of the physical, a yearning of the spirit which Neptune represents, is likely to manifest itself in seeking after strange gods. The use or abuse of those drugs which break down the limitations of time and space and seem to develop the individual, though only temporarily, at the expense of his environment, is frequently to be seen. For exactly the same reason, abnormal vices are resorted to by the Neptunian. The common satisfactions of life appear to him banal – he has not yet developed that mastery of his own soul and of the soul of the Universe which brings the seeker after the hidden mysteries of life back to sanity. The advanced soul knows that life is a dream, but he knows also that it is a divine dream. He no longer mixes up the planes. In the beginning of his search, inspired by a sense of dissatisfaction he imagines quite naturally, that by reversing the natural order of things, which he has decided to be bad he will attain to good. Indeed this state of thought is probably necessary for everybody at some time or other. However, by following out his path, he comes to the conclusion that, after all, things are no better upside down than they were the right way up. He will then, sensibly enough, take the easiest way – he will become content with life, no longer in the unthinking way which is characteristic of the lower animals, but through his having gained a divine wisdom. No doubt he and everyone else in the world, are but players on a stage, shadows in a dream, but he sees also that in this play he should make the best of his part. In this dream, he should not invoke the powers of the nightmare.

For these reasons, as well as because of our own understanding of the divine tolerance which pours the smile of the Sun and the tears of the rain alike upon the just and the unjust, we must not blame Neptunians for those peculiarities which seem to our elder judgment to be destroying his soul. In extreme cases, it may be necessary that the soul should be allowed to destroy itself, for only through destruction lies redemption. Our attitude, therefore, should be sympathetic. We should endeavour to understand these wonderful impulses. It will be useless for us to endeavour to suppress them. They are divinely ordered, but we may advise the control of these passions where they seem to us to be doing more harm than good. It will be well to remember that the source from which they spring is irrepressible. It comes from the depths which are the very seat of character, and any attempts to deal harshly with them are fore-ordained futile. Our attempts would only excite opposition and that opposition would be justified, for to our worldly wisdom, it would array in battle the army of the all-wise Providence of God.

There is one characteristic of a rising Neptune, which is excessively annoying to the person possessing it. This has been described by Edgar Allan Poe in his story 'The Imp of the Perverse'. The mind of the individual may be perfectly made up, his judgment may be sound and his desire unhampered, but at the moment of putting his will into execution he balks and jibs. Ibsen has pictured the same quality in his description of 'The Troll in Us', but perhaps the clearest and most succint of all the accounts of this curious quality is given by St. Paul in his *Epistle to the Romans*, Chapter 7, verse 15-24.

This is not to be confused with the war of the flesh against the spirit, which takes place constantly in all of us, or with doubt, hesitation, vacillation, and the conflict of impulses, or the difficulty in striking a balance of judgment. It is pure perversity.

The quality of aspiration to things beyond the limits of life is common to all Neptunians and in elder souls which have passed through the purifying fires, in those same minds which possess knowledge and understanding of the cosmos and have learned how to deal with passion and emotion, it assumes a less devastating form. There is still the determination to attain to the Bourneless Beyond, but the method which appeals is carefully reasoned instead of being instinctive, and common sense takes care that neither health, reason, fortune, or social relations, is put in danger. A person thus gifted may study strange sciences, but he will not go astray in them, will devote himself during every moment of his spare time to prayer and meditation, but will not become a fanatic; will adopt mystical practices which might appear entirely foolish to the average man, but he will probably keep his own counsel in the matter.

The gamut of Neptune's influence is thus seen to extend far from the darkest abyss of hell to the crown of the heaven's evershining mountains, but the underlying impulse is always the same. It is the hunger for the infinite. The drug-fiend, the psychopath, the lunatic and the saint are all members of the same family and that which divides them is not the result of any differentiation in the soul, but rather in the degree of knowledge and experience. It is his mentality which separates St. Francis of Assisi from the Marquis de Sade, and in judging any particular horoscope, the characterisations of the native must be determined by those houses and planets which govern the mind.

To recount a few of the less important Neptunian qualities, the same impulse which causes an Ignatius Loyala,[73] a Gilles de Rais,[74] an Indian Yogi or a Napoleon to determine to be something extraordinary makes impractical persons with less sense of actuality, determine to pretend to be something extraordinary; hence we find people who assume

73. St Ignatius Loyola (*c.* 1491-1556), founder of the Society of Jesus. His *Spiritual Exercises* is a system of rules, prayers and self-examination designed to train the whole man for the Christian life.

74. Rais or Retz, Gilles de (1404-1440), marshal of France, munificent patron of music and the arts, satanist, murderer of innumerable children. The original 'Bluebeard', he died on the end of the hangman's rope. J.K. Huysmans described his horrible activities in his novel *Là Bas*, 1891. Crowley was banned from delivering a lecture on Gilles de Rais to the Oxford Poetry Society in February 1930. It was later published.

titles to which they have no right, who love to wear extraordinary clothes, who smother themselves in exotic perfumes, or who make up their faces. This idea may again express itself in a different kind of action; such, for example, as love of intrigue, of playing practical jokes, of hoaxing their friends or the public, or of playing some part upon the stage of life, which is not altogether natural. Better balanced persons will probably manifest this tendency by actually going on the stage, where the impulse finds a legitimatised and accepted expression.

In all these matters, it is rare to find a true creative tendency. Mimicry and imitation are the rule, but there is usually a certain spice of originality involved. As an example of a whole period under Neptunian influence, we may cite the time of Molière, the seventeenth century, when everybody masqueraded. It was not merely the valets and maids who pretended to be their masters and mistresses, but the nobles themselves could not conduct the most ordinary flirtation without pretending to be shepherds and shepherdesses of the time of Virgil. It has been necessary, this, lest the student confound this quality with the coarseness, quite inexcusable, of snobbery.

The Neptunian is usually a somewhat irresponsible person, he is very inconstant and his moral character appears weak, because it is based on what seems mere impulse or whim, rather than on judgment, inspired by self-interest. He usually knows that he is making himself ridiculous by his antics, but the elfishness of his spirit leads him to continue with them, and a hint of opposition will often cause him to exaggerate the errors of which his friends complain.

Neptune also gives a disposition to wander, a discontent with the place where one happens to be; we make no apology for quoting Baudelaire's prose poem 'Anywhere, anywhere out of the world', which gives a most eloquent picture of the spirit of which we are speaking:

> This life is a hospital where every sick man is possessed with the desire to change his bed. One is anxious to bear his sufferings in front of the stove, and another thinks that he will get better beside the window.

It seems to me that I should always be well wherever I am not; and this question of removal is one which I ceaselessly discuss with my soul.

Say, my soul – poor, deluded soul, what do you think of going and living in Lisbon? It must be warm there, and you would become as lively as a lizard. It is on the waterside; they say that it is built of marble, and that the people have such a hatred of vegetation that they pluck up all the trees. – Ah! there is a landscape to your liking; a landscape made with light and mineral, and a liquid mirror to reflect them!

My soul replies nothing.

Since you love rest so much while contemplating movement, would you like to come and live in Holland, the land that brings happiness? Perhaps you would find amusement in that country, whose picture you have so often admired in museums. What do you say to Rotterdam, you who love forests of masts, and the ships moored alongside the houses?

My soul remains dumb.

Would Batavia smile on you perhaps more sweetly? There we should find the spirit of Europe wedded to the beauty of the tropics.

Not a word. Can my soul be dead?

Are you then come to such a point of enervation that you take pleasure only in your own happiness? If so, let us away to those countries that are the emblem of death. I have it, poor soul, we will pack for Torneo. Let us go farther still, to the far end of the Baltic, still farther from life, if it is possible. Let us set up our camp at the Pole! There the Sun strikes the earth obliquely, and the slow alternation of light and night suppresses variety and increases monotony – that better half of nothing. There we may take prolonged baths of shadows, while, to amuse us the Aurora Borealis will send us from time to time its rosy sheaves, like the reflection of the fireworks of Hell.

Then at last my soul broke forth, and wisely did she cry, 'No matter where, no matter where, so long as it is out of the World!'

It follows from all that has been said that the purely Neptunian type lives almost entirely in and through the nervous system. Very often his body is frail, delicate and flower-like, but the soul in him burns strong and may easily wear out the scabbard. At any time when the physical functions are depressed, and the nerves cannot obtain that supernormal energy which they so insistently demand, the result is likely to be hysteria and nervous breakdown. Persons, who suffer in this way are, perhaps, fortunate, for the warnings of nature in such cases are insistent, and medical treatment, by insisting upon absolute rest and quiet, can restore them to health. Where the body is stronger and responds with more alacrity to the extravagance of the nervous system, the result is likely to be worse. For then, insidious and often incurable disease obtains a hold, before the patient is aware of it. Such troubles as locomotor ataxia, general paralysis of the insane, softening of the brain, and other obscure lesions may perhaps be caused in part by this influence. Worry and all its attendant ills are very often Neptunian in origin. One may conclude by mentioning certain other wasting dieases whose nervous origin is not yet understood by the less advanced schools of orthodox medicine.

Neptune in the Second House

It should first be remarked that unless Neptune is well into the second house or has some planet rising before it, it may act upon the character very much as if it were actually in the Ascendant. If this however be not the case, its full influence may be expected upon affairs connected with money and possessions. By this, one should not understand so much vested interest, inherited property, or even the whole fortune, however this may be derived, but rather those things which are immediately available at any one time, and more particularly the earnings of labour, if the native is engaged in such.

The effect of Neptune in these matters is very singular; money is itself a somewhat mystic and elusive commodity. It has the unusual property that a large sum is in many ways much less than a small sum. Any schemer will tell you that it is much easier to get five thousand dollars than five. This is one of the reasons why there must always be extremes of wealth and poverty. The whimsicality of Neptune harmonises very well, therefore, with the nature of the second house, and taking one thing with another, the native is not likely to find himself in any great poverty. If his bank account in terms of actual cash, appears small, this need not imply distress. He may have a sort of Bohemian easiness about the matter. He is likely to regard money as a very fluid article, coming and going without apparent reason. It is likely to come when he least expects it, and to fly away from him when his grip is most tightly clasped upon it. There will always, too, be something abnormal about the nature of the means by which money is procured. Straightforward, honest effort is not usually on the programme. If you offer to such a person a simple, honest, certain means of making money in large quantities, he will throw down your proposition. He will want to improve upon it by the introduction of some fantastic comedy of duplicity, which will sound very well and completely ruin the scheme. The idea of a square deal is somehow offensive, and such people are therefore usually in financial low water. It has been said of one of them that he would spend a thousand dollars in the hope of cheating someone out of thirty cents.

People with this characteristic are, of course, extremely suspicious that someone may be trying upon them the game they would try on others, and they will deprive themselves of a thousand dearly longed-for pleasures to avoid the suspicion that someone has got a box of cigarettes out of them.

It must be thoroughly understood that these characteristics are not at all dishonest in the proper sense of the word. By dishonest one means a person who, knowing clearly what is right, does deliberately what is wrong, and there is no trace of crime in the Neptunian temperament. It is pure wanton perversity.

The general instability of the financial position will probably work out in many curious ways. Money will often come in through perfectly legitimate channels, but in every case, there is a probability of loss. In some way, quite beyond the control of the native, who may use all sorts of precautions, perhaps thrift, pushed to a perfectly absurd extreme, then suddenly a fantastic impulse will arise, and cause the whole amount to be lost in a manner which a grain of common sense, not so large as the proverbial mustard-seed, would have prevented.

There is, of course, also a strong tendency to gamble. Unless the fifth house be very strong and fortunate, disaster is to be expected.

In some case where the rest of the horoscope is well balanced, particularly with regard to the moral character, the influence of Neptune may be more controlled and legitimatised. This will especially be the case, if he have some favourable aspect. The income may then be derived from operations of a Neptunian character. The native may profit through the stage or through such business as the sale of pictures, especially 'old masters' painted in Philadelphia, the dealing in antiquities, the establishment of 'bucket shops' and in general all those affairs in which values are dependent principally upon the caprice, and those which make their profit from human vanity and love of Sham. Beauty parlours and quack medicine businesses might very likely be associated with Neptune in the second house.

With regard to his personal chattels, the Neptunian may be very unfortunate; they are likely to be lost and mislaid in somewhat inexplicable ways. His own carelessness in this regard will accentuate the effect.

In conclusion, the native must always be on his guard against fraud and deception in regard to financial affairs. He is particularly likely to lose money through trickery and chicanery in such things as the wording of the agreement. It will also be well for him not to undervalue trifles; the smallest incidents where Neptune is concerned often lead to the greatest results.

Neptune in the Third House

A great many of the remarks which were made about the first house are applicable to the third, but in a somewhat secondary sense. The tendencies which we have noted there are deep-seated and pertain rather to the ego itself than to any of its embellishments, but the third house dealing with the mentality must be considered as indicating the development of the mind through education and environment. This distinction is not so subtle as it seems. A person may have a very conventional personality associated with a very flighty mind, and an essentially eccentric person, on the other hand, may have a broad deep and well-balanced education. It is just such peculiarities that are best explained by astrology.

The Neptunian mentality is rather shallow. Very rare is it to find any intensity of scientific thought, or any ability to concentrate upon the business in hand. Quite small impressions and annoyances will cause the attention to wander. The task of education will probably have been difficult. The child will not have taken his work seriously, will have preferred to amuse himself with all kinds of fancies and if he takes up any study at all, that subject will probably have been fantastic and unpractical. It is true that most children collect stamps, butterflies or something for which it is hard to make out a good case, and which in any event, do not lead to mature development upon the same lines, but this tendency usually dies out at puberty, but the Neptunian intellect carries it on to adult life. It seems incapable of seeing things in due proportion and a man, instead of attending to his business, will be rummaging around the old curiosity shop in search of snuff-boxes.

In persons of a more advanced intellectual type, this characteristic is likely to appear in devotion to rather useless studies, and in the spiritually-minded, it will lead to a following out of false paths. In case of affliction of the planets, or if the horoscope be generally weak, there may be far more serious manifestations. One is likely to find imbecility, sometimes even idiocy in children, while those who pass through the early stages of life in a comparatively normal way, are likely to develop some of the milder insanities as they grow older. Possibly it would be fair to say that the general tendency is towards melancholia rather than mania. Delusions of persecution will not be uncommon and a bad direction of Mars or Uranus might bring about a tendency to suicide. In old age, dementia is very likely to occur.

It is very important in the training of a child who has this position of Neptune to endeavour to limit the mischief as closely as possible. The greatest pains should be taken to secure for it teachers and associates who will counteract this influence. The habit of mental discipline must be encouraged to the utmost and though it is improbable that complete success will be attained, yet a great deal may be done. The mind is more malleable than the personality. In following out this course of action, it must be remembered that with so strong a natural tendency to divagation, with this love of the unusual and useless, that a single bad influence may easily wreck years of careful training. The inherent tendency will always be there and the only question is whether it can be guided or not. In case it proves ineradicable, the wisest course will be to endeavour to attach it to other parts of the individual less afflicted. Considerations of self-interest should be brought forward and if this peculiar mentality manifests itself in some hobby, the endeavour should be to develop that hobby on such lines that it may be of practical use.

With regard to the more general qualities of the mind, there should be a dangerous degree of unreliability. You can never tell what such a person may do next, because you never know what he may think next. He will probably be unpunctual from sheer incapacity to understand the value of time. He will probably be unable to follow out any definite course, because of the power which every new impression makes upon him. He will go out to dinner and find himself going for a long walk in the country instead. The smallest matters attract his attention and he flies off at a tangent. He will be unable to follow the course of an argument. It is probable that in religion he will belong to one of those shallow, plausible sects which appeal to weaker minds. At the same time, he will probably not be a fervent believer in anything. His interest is too casual and interrupted. It is extremely likely that he is a good hypnotic subject. His mind, never strongly and sanely fixed upon any one subject, easily passes into a semi-conscious state. He probably spends his time in day-dreams. You will see him agape in the middle of his daily task. Long trains of disconnected thought pass through his mind in unwearying succession. Even in the middle of a conversation he is likely to lapse. As the saying is, 'his wits go wool-gathering'.

These qualities will naturally react, perhaps in a very marked manner on the social relations. People with the Neptunian mind wander in and wander out of other people's lives in a very aimless and erratic manner. They call on their friends for no particular reason at all and drift out again without having said or done anything. They are usually rather likable, there is a certain feeling of pity engendered in the normal man by their pleasant pointlessness. Such friendships, to abuse the word, often last indefinitely, for the very reason that they are themselves indefinite. It is quite impossible to quarrel when there is so little to quarrel with. Occasionally, one becomes extremely bored, but before one has time to protest, they are gone and when they turn up again, six months later, one is possibly quite glad to see them.

The third house also indicates the brothers and sisters of the native, and the general rule seems to be that any such will die in youth or else drift away in the course of a few years. Their character will, of course, be determined by setting up the horoscope with the third house in the Ascendant. They will therefore, be of the Neptunian temperament, but their influence upon the native is in no case likely to be great.

Another point to be considered is that of short journeys, by which is meant those undertaken in the normal course of life, as opposed to those which are the result of long fore thought and determination. Such journeys are likely to be productive of great annoyance, usually in small ways. The native will carefully pack his evening clothes, forgetting only the trousers, or he wrongly address his baggage. Again, he is likely to be unfortunate in getting into the wrong train or even if he is in the right train, it will probably be late. Sometimes these petty annoyances take on a more serious character, he may find himself involved in a railroad wreck.

There are likely, too, to be all sorts of difficulties in the small details of business – there may be trouble with accounts, correspondence will constantly go astray – papers will be filled out wrongly and various kinds of petty fraud are pretty sure to be practised. Unscrupulous people will certainly endeavour to take advantage of the native's easiness.

It will be very disadvantageous for the native to enter upon any serious business, such as a lawsuit for the flickering quality of his mind is unsuited to any occupation requiring long-continued application. It will be wiser for him to busy himself with matters which come to a head quickly in which he knows his gain or loss within a very few hours. For, if the critical period be extended beyond this, he is likely to be thinking of something else. His memory is not good enough, as a rule to enable him to pick up an affair at just the point where he dropped it.

In making these remarks, one does not forget that it is somewhat rare to find such a mentality as is described in its simple purity. The influence of the ruler of the third house will probably make great changes and a further modification is to be looked for from the influence of Mercury in his aspects wherever he may be situated in the nativity.

Neptune in the Fourth House

It is not particularly pleasant to be so low in the Heavens, but on the whole, he is not unsympathetic to Cancer, the natural sign occupying that position, and of course all planets are strong and angular.

With regard to the father of the native, he is indicated as being an eccentric person and perhaps worthless; very likely he took to drink or became insane. It is quite probable that his early life was rendered unhappy by the abnormal conditions prevailing in the home. As a child, the native is probably very much out of sympathy with his environment. Solitude will have presented much attraction. There will have been little inclination for the company of other children. The imagination will have been peopled with fantastic creatures of another world, invisible playmates, and the dreams were probably strange, fascinating and yet frightful. There was no fear of being left alone in the dark; on the contrary, the child will have felt that only when its parents left it to itself it was free to take up its individual life. The fairy world may have seemed entirely objective and any attempts to disillusion the child or to punish it for its strange ways, might result in serious mental damage. In some cases these tendencies may persist in adult life, though in a modified form. The native may possibly enjoy solitary, contemplative sports, such as fishing. His principal pleasure may consist in long, lonely rambles at night in deserted places. These characteristics, although unusual, are not to be regarded as in any way objectionable. Provided that the personality is strong and the mind well-balanced, such peculiarities may be very helpful. Much of the best thinking in the world is done under such conditions.

The fourth house of heaven refers also to the grave, and it may be found that people who have Neptune in this position die far from home in strange places and perhaps under very extraordinary conditions. Those acquainted with the secret history of the great know the amazing story of the death of President Felix Faure[75] who had this configuration. There is not necessarily any indication of violent death, but it is not unlikely that there may be mysterious circumstances – in one case it may imply a public funeral, in another a post-mortem, and in yet another a burial at sea.

Another matter connected with the fourth house is inheritance, and here one must regard Neptune as decidedly unfortunate, for Neptune is always tricky and the principal virtue of any inheritance is that it should come to you smoothly, and straightforwardly without any bother or worry. But if the native have Neptune here, particularly under afflictions of Mars or Jupiter, the inheritance may be contested on all sorts of flimsy and fantastic pretext, and delays, or even partial loss (in bad cases, total loss) may be expected.

All things pertaining to the earth itself and to those things which are hidden in the earth are also indicated by the fourth house, and here again Neptune is not propitious. The native is very likely to be tricked in any dealings which he may have with real estate, building speculation, or mining propositions. All such affairs, however open they may seem upon the surface, will have certain hidden disadvantages which only appear later, when the mischief is already done.

Persons born with Neptune in this position should be extremely careful not to play any tricks with the consciousness. They may suffer severely from insomnia, but they must on no account attempt to seek relief from narcotic drugs,

75. See note 150.

even those reputed most harmless, for there is a peculiarity in their constitution which may make a dose that the majority of people could take with immunity, fatal to them. Surgical operations, even of the slightest character, are also to be dreaded, more especially in Neptune is afflicted by Mars, or if Mars himself is weak in the horoscope. A mere scratch might bring on blood-poisoning and in the case of larger operations, the utmost precaution should be taken in the administration of anaesthetics.

The end of life is also described by the fourth house. Persons having Neptune in this position may expect a somewhat lonely old age. They will probably outlive those who are near and dear to them, and there may be a strong tendency to melancholy in consequence of this. The mental forces too may be impaired; in particular, the memory will become very weak and unreliable. The native is not likely to be settled in one place: he will move about aimlessly, actuated by the curiously childish impulses that are associated with certain types of senility but such gradual decay need not be unhappy. The second childhood will be full of pleasant fancies, possibly similar to those which characterized the early years of life, though naturally modified, to some extent, by the experiences of that life.

The fourth house also indicates the mother-in-law and the student may refer to what is said about the mother in the tenth house as similar remarks will apply.

Neptune in the Fifth House

The fifth house refers in the first case to the pleasures enjoyed by the native, and the influence of Neptune, while very peculiar, cannot be described as unfortunate, except in bad cases of affliction, or through the general weakness of the rest of the horoscope. The native is likely to find amusement in clandestine or, fantastic, pleasures. Conventional minds always associate such dispositions with moral laxity and this is entirely unjustified. One might instance the cases of Baudelaire and Maeterlinck, who both have this planet near the cusp of the fifth, and one may point to the very remarkable character of their poetry. No doubt in these cases, this poetry was a true reflection of the moral character.

Lord Byron again had this position and although his poetry was singularly sane, no doubt his pleasures were, to some extent abnormal, as viewed from the standpoint of orthodoxy. On the other hand, there is the case of Rosa Bonheur,[76] who dressed as a man and associated with men, but there is no suggestion that this, in any way, detracted from her uprightness; the force of her character was very remarkable. We know of another case through private practice, in which the native likes to disguise herself as a working girl and frequent dance halls in the less wealthy parts of the city where she lives, and she has spent the summer in the woods, cooking for a party of girl guides. Neptune is, however, strongly supported by the Sun, and these experiences have been no more harmful to her than those of Joan of Arc in history, Una and Britomart[77] in romance or many saint or virgin in the jester's sanctorum.

On the other hand, we have such cases as those of Marie Bashkirtseff,[78] who found pleasure in writing the most extraordinary diary that has ever been given to the world; Bulwer-Lytton,[79] who set the fashion of occult novels, and spent a great part of his life in fantastic experiences among Rosicrucian friends; and Bismarck, who, though of spotless moral character, sought relaxation in diversions unnatural to his station. It will be remembered that his favourite author was Gaboriau[80] and that he was usually to be found when not at work chatting with the students in beer-halls. A less favourable influence of Neptune is seen in the case of Lillie Langtry.[81] We may also instance Martin Luther, who tore a nun from the convent and in so doing pulled down the temporal power of the Catholic Church; and there is also

76. Rosa Bonheur (1822-1899), distinguished animal painter, born at Bordeaux of Jewish origin; she was known as 'Rosa Mazeltov', Hebrew for 'good luck'.

77. Cf. Spenser's *Faerie Queene.*

78. Marie Constantinova Bashkirtseff (1860-1884), singer, painter, diarist.

79. See note 40.

80. Emile Gaboriau (1833-1873), French popular novelist and father of the detective story.

81. Lillie Langtry (1852-1929), known as 'The Jersey Lily'. She was a mistress of Edward VII and a minor actress.

George Edalji, who was sentenced to many years' imprisonment for a series of maiming outrages upon horses and cattle, a campaign which was carried on in connection with a number of anonymous letters sent by him to the police.[82] He called himself Captain Darby, chief of the Great Wyrley gang, which probably existed only in his imagination. The anarchist Vaillant[83] also had this position of Neptune.

In many cases, however, the indication implies no more than a passion for art and music, or even more frequently, the theatre. From this alone one cannot judge whether there is much ability to create or even to interpret art; such questions must be decided both by the aspects to Neptune and by the tenth house, and the first, but the love of all such things is evident. It is unlikely that there will be much tendency to the enjoyment of outdoor sports, or of the pleasures of study. The indulgences will be rather trivial and transient. They will usually involve some kind of make-believe; nor are they likely to be particularly vigorous, still less violent, and they should fascinate temporarily, rather than create any serious interest.

The fifth house also refers to children and here Neptune may be regarded as decidedly unfortunate. Even with a fertile sign on the cusp of the fifth house and a well-aspected ruler, the native is not likely to have children unless Neptune itself be very well-aspected, or if there are children they will die in infancy. This is more strongly indicated where the native is a man; favourable aspects will of course remove this disability and in such a case, the children may be of the Neptunian type. This will make them adorable as children, but it is evident from what has been said with regard to the first house, that they will need the greatest care with regard to health and to education.

As Leo is the sign naturally pertaining to the fifth house, affairs of the heart are indicated thereby. By this one not only does not mean wedlock, but rather tends to exclude it. The native whose Neptune is in the fifth house will probably be very curious in the matter of love. He will fall in love with

82. A famous case of the time. Some (including Sir Arthur Conan Doyle) believed him innocent.

83. Edward Marie Vaillant (1840-1915), bomb-throwing anarchist.

strange and curious people, and he will manifest his affections in a very unusual way. Spirituality of love is particularly indicated in the best cases. As, however, this planet on which we crawl, has a habit of being very practical, these relations, sometimes work out in a manner far from satisfactory, and lead to more trouble than common and gross infringment of the conventional rules. In many natures, there will be a disinclination for any kind of love in the ordinary sense of the word. It is likely to take such forms as symbolism, fetichism, and other more or less harmless weaknesses and incapacities. There is also a liability to secret and solitary habits and in particular the native may be tempted to indulge in alcohol, ether, or narcotic drugs. There is probably no conviviality in such practices, the native prefers to enjoy his perverse pleasure in secret.

The fifth house also indicates speculation, but not so much those speculations which are undertaken on the large scale, and with a definite end in view. We are not to include under this house such questions as the exploitation of inventions, the establishment of large businesses or even any kind of gambling which is undertaken in cold blood for purposes of gain. It is rather when speculation is undertaken merely as an amusement that the fifth house indicates the fortunes of the native. Neptune in this position is decidely bad. The pendulum of luck will swing in a very violent and irregular manner. There may at times be large gains, but they will be offset by even larger losses. The native will have very little control of himself in this respect; he will enter the casino with a firm determination not to risk more than the amount he is carrying about him, but having lost it all in the morning, he will be cabling hysterically for funds in the afternoon. He will probably have a settled contempt for mathematics and a belief in all kinds of wild systems. He will wear his pockets out with mascots and irritate every hunchback in the neighbourhood by his assiduity.[84] Another danger with which he has to contend is that of actual cheating on the part of those with whom he gambles.

84. To touch the hump of a hunch-back is supposed to bring good luck.

Neptune in the Sixth House

In the first instance the sixth house refers to the servants of the native. In this category, one must include all people whose function is to serve, even if their social status and power are much greater than that of the native. For example, if we were to consider the case of a poor man employing a wealthy lawyer and a prominent physician, the character of the lawyer would be determined by the sixth house in so far as his relations with his client are concerned.

As the first virtue of servants is steadiness, reliability and freedom from any form of independence, self-will or initiative, it will follow that Neptune is very unfortunate in this connection. The servants of the native are likely to behave in a very erratic way. They may rob and cheat the master, though this will take, in all probability a petty and sporadic form, but they are certain to be unpunctual, disobedient, forgetful, careless and altogether unsatisfactory. It will be difficult to keep a servant in the house for any length of time.

In regard to servants in the larger sense of the word indicated above, the native is likely to find similar troubles. He may consult a doctor and discover later that the man is a quack or is suffering from some subtle form of insanity. If he consults a lawyer, he will probably get bad advice, be induced to enter into some litigation, in which he has no chance of success and find a large bill of costs run up against him into the bargain. Similar troubles will occur in every event of life where he is paying another person for service of whatever kind. It does not, however, apply to commercial transactions. If the native is an employer of labour, whether on a large or a small scale, he will meet with every kind of obstacle. His workmen will strike and he will be involved in all sorts of disputes. He may have to pay compensation for accidents and that, often, unjustly.

From what has been said, it might appear that these misfortunes are due to the character of the persons who serve. But it would not be right to draw such a conclusion. Every question has two sides to it, and in this case, there is no doubt that the master is equally to blame. His methods with servants will not be wise. It is certain that he will lack firmness – he will be slack and capricious. The most important quality in a master is that the servant should know exactly what to expect. He should be patient, kind, courteous and yet inexorable. He should be to the servant what the laws of nature are to humanity, and it is exactly in these points that any person who has Neptune in the sixth house will fail.

The health of the native, although to some extent indicated by the Ascendant and the position and aspects of the Sun, or the Moon in the case of a woman, depends principally upon the sixth house. Persons born with Neptune in this position will probably suffer from many obscure maladies of the nerves. In fact, insidious and wasting diseases of all sorts are often associated with this configuration. There is likely to be a general weakness and irritability in the constitution, which may manifest itself in hysteria and similar complaints. Painful and intractable, though not dangerous, disorders such as eczema and psoriasis may prove a continual torment. It is very important that the native should not fall into the habit of dosing himself. Of course, quack remedies are principally to be avoided, but there is some danger also that he may acquire a superficial and inaccurate knowledge of medicine. Medical books may fall into his hands and he may read them with avidity, understanding them, however, imperfectly, owing to his lack of a thorough training. He may then become his own physician; a good many of his ailments will be imaginary, but whether this is so or not he will try all sorts of medicaments. In his case this will be exceptionally dangerous, for anyone with Neptune in the sixth house is peculiarly susceptible to poisoning. Bromism, iodism, plumbism may follow the abuse. He may also acquire such a habit as that of arsenic eating. One must not, however, include narcotism; for if he acquire any of the ordinary drug habits, such as the abuses of morphia, cocaine, heroin, veronal, hashish and the like, he will do so not because of any idiosyncrasy – not with the idea of gaining new experiences and extravagant pleasures – but because he hopes thereby to obtain relief from the ill-health, real or imaginary, from which he is suffering.

The sixth house also refers to small animals, especially domestic pets. The native is likely to have rather curious fancies in these matters. Instead of being contented with a dog, he will have a monkey. An ordinary parrot will not satisfy him – he will require some very particular species, difficult to obtain and of no use when obtained. If he should attempt to breed small animals for profit, he must not expect any great success. Sickness will probably decimate his farm at the most unexpected moment. Sometimes when the ninth house indicates that the native will take long journeys, he will become a collector of rare species of animals and plants, and if Neptune should be well aspected, this life may be suited to him and prove, on the whole, successful; but even in such a case, he must expect plenty of strange adventures. Another matter traditionally referred to the sixth house, is that of ambassadors. By this we should understand negotiations involving personal interviews. Once again Neptune proves far from fortunate. There will be a trickiness and uncertainty in all such affairs. The native will come to an agreement and find subsequently that it has not been understood or that some hidden flaw vitiates it. There will be a general atmosphere of misunderstanding in the best case, and, in the worst, there will be a deliberate attempt to deceive, on the part of one or both persons concerned in the interview. If follows from this that unless there are afflictions of Mercury in the horoscope, it will be better to conduct all important negotiations by means of writing.

Another matter which is decided by the sixth house is intimate daily life of a rather trivial order and such questions as food and clothing are decided thereby. The native will prefer curious and unusual foods; a plain beefsteak will be abhorrent to him, and he will decide to dine upon food which is neither nourishing nor digestible. At times he will find it difficult to make up his mind as to what to eat. The whim of the moment will be his only rule. His appetite is thoroughly morbid; he is likely also to eat at unusual times. He will get up in the middle of the night and feed upon tinned salmon, jam and beer. The indigestion from which we have already suggested that he may be suffering is hardly likely to be helped by such irrational habits. He is especially liable to attacks of ptomaine poisoning, and even greater misfortunes may befall him in case his mental qualifications are not first class. He may become a food faddist and experiment seriously with all kinds of ridiculous diets. He may be very fanatical about these, while they last, but they will not last long. He will go from one to another in a way which is the despair of those friends who may wish to entertain him.

With regard to clothes, he will be equally a nuisance. In mild cases, this may amount merely to eccentricity, just sufficient to make the ordinary man a little doubtful of whether it is desirable to be seen in the street with him. But once more, if the mind is weak, he may have settled convictions that it is dangerous to wear wool or a hat or boots. He may thus constitute himself a public nuisance. Cases have been known in which this position of Neptune combined with those configurations which show moral degeneracy has led it to manifest as exhibitionism.

The last of the important subjects which are covered by the sixth house is speculation, in a restricted sense of the word. We have already spoken of speculation under the fifth house, but the natural position of the sixth house is Virgo and Virgo is the sign which deals more particularly with the earth, especially the fertile earth. Virgo is ruled by Mercury and Mercury is also exalted in Virgo. For this reason, the type of speculation covered by the sixth house is entirely mercurial. It is sheer, cold drawn gambling, where no sporting element is implied, and such speculation is likely to choose for its field the food of the people, and similar commodities, particularly wool, cotton and other materials of clothing. The gambler should conceive vast combinations, but they will all turn out unfortunately, owing either to his own wildness or to unexpected circumstances beyond his control.

Neptune in the Seventh House

The seventh house governs the marriage of the native. The presence of Neptune in this house is, on the whole, not to be desired. In the first place, the partner selected is likely to possess most of the qualifications of a person born with Neptune rising, and while these cannot be described as wholly bad, yet the average person does not select for a lifelong partner anyone so doubtful. What is really sought in wedlock is the negation of adventure. Wedlock is the spectre at the banquet of romance; matrimony is the tomb of love, and therefore what is most favourable for pleasure is most fatal in those affairs in which settlement is the object aimed at.

The attitude of the native himself to marriage will also partake of the Neptunian taint. He will probably contract some rash alliance on whimsical grounds, or through some extraordinary accident. Permanent relations should always be based upon considerations well thought out and approved by the reason and judgment, not only of the contracting parties but of those who have their interests at heart. Any such relation which may be entered into by a person with Neptune in the seventh house is likely to prove eventful. Many small things of a disturbing character will occur, and the general atmosphere of the house will probably be that of disquiet. It is probable that the matrimonial adventure will end in open quarrel, but this quarrel is not likely to be a plain, single issue. It is rather incompatibility of temper that is indicated than anything more definite. Infidelity to the marriage vows on the part of both the husband and wife seems assured, but such incidents will only be trivial factors in the general discontent. The whole attitude of the parties toward the marriage state will be extremely unusual. There may be all kinds of fantastic theories of the relation, based not upon the sober experience of humanity, but upon idealism, which have little to recommend them beyond the enthusiasm and the *bona fides* of their advocates. It is no doubt unfortunate that human nature is not wholly divine, that that which ought to be so often is not, that we are imperfect beings living in an imperfect environment, that practical considerations continually interfere with our ideas of what is right. But such is the situation, and it is the first thesis of all biology that the happiest and most prosperous individual is the one who accommodates himself most cleverly to his environment. The Neptunian is, therefore, handicapped in a world where grosser planets hold the greatest sway, and while in his own curious realm of dream-delight he may be king, he must expect to meet with continual obstacles which will bring him down to earth, often with an unpleasant crash.

Unless the financial position of the native is assured in other ways, he must expect tribulations of this kind from the outset. Even if he be well off previous to marriage, he will, in all probability, suffer hardships subsequent to and in consequence of matrimony for nothing is more certain than the fact that he cannot take marriage seriously. He does not conceive of it as an affair of settlement, of inheritance, of domesticity. It appears to him as a mere romantic adventure. He surrounds it with glamour; it is but a figure in a cotillon, and when the practical questions of increased rent and bills for food and medical attendance and such things arise, he will be disgruntled thereby. The dawn has come, the dancers remove masks and dominoes; and as they step from the garish lights of the ballroom on to the dewy grass, they feel the chill of the morning air. It is probable that a person in this position will be thoroughly discontented with his marriage, and cast about him for ways and means to break the link. He will embark on a series of rather futile intrigues which he does not prosecute with energy or ability, and which usually go wrong. Very likely he will slip from one marriage into another with the same results. He is not at all fitted to undertake so serious a responsibility. He has not the necessary heroism, the fixity of purpose, the patience and the long-suffering required to make marriage a success.

These remarks do not apply at all to the love-affairs of the native, which are judged by the fifth house. It is only when the intention is a permanent settlement and partnership under legal and conventional guarantee, that the seventh house is implicated.

The seventh house implicates the business partner and all public contracts and arrangements, including lawsuits. All these affairs are likely to be as unfortunate as marriage itself for the same reason. The thought behind all such matters is that Neptune, shedding as it does the rays of a spiritual plane, is peculiarly unsuited to any thing definite or binding. His influence is to upset the physical world by bringing into it ideas of a higher and finer order, and if this be considered from the lower standpoint, the result can only be described as disastrous. In business, the partner is likely to be of the Neptunian temperament. Perhaps easy enough to get on with in a general way, but unpractical and arbitrary, unaccountable, fitful, eccentric and unbusinesslike, as regards the affairs of the firm. Such a partnership is likely to terminate in exactly the same way, *mutatis mutandis*, as we have already indicated will be the case in marriage. There will be a subtle feeling that everything is going wrong; and yet it may be difficult to put one's finger on the sore spot. There is some indication too, that the partner may ruin the business by wastefulness and caprice. There will probably be a great deal of trouble over accounts, and profits are likely to disappear in a very extraordinary manner, which may seem suspicious.

In the matter of lawsuits, too, similar considerations apply. The native will probably be involved in many such, and they will be of a dragging, tedious character. He will neither win nor lose outright. The thing will go on interminably like Jarndyce v. Jarndyce[85] and nobody will be a penny the better. In the same way it will be difficult to get any business through of any kind. People will miss appointments. Contracts will go to and fro for revision, and, very likely, after months of arguments the whole thing will fall through. One should be careful in doing business with anyone who has Neptune in this position.

The seventh house also indicates the open enemies of the native; and, in this respect, the indications are not so unfavourable. For these enemies themselves will be vacillating and without energy to prosecute their assaults. A great deal of trouble may arise, but it will be of a somewhat petty character. The attacks upon the native will be futile, fatuous and carry in themselves their own condemnation. However, from time to time they may be exceedingly annoying; but in the long run, not much harm will be done. The only liability to long-continued and bitter enmity would be in case of a transit of Uranus or Saturn over the planet's place.

In conclusion, one may remark that this and the fourth house are, on the whole, the worst positions for Neptune. Generally speaking, he should not be low in the heavens; the higher he is placed, the more kindly is his influence, as will be seen when we come to treat of the tenth house or *medium coeli*.

85. Cf. Charles Dickens, *Bleak House*.

Neptune in the Eighth House

The eighth house refers to the subject of death. The presence of Neptune in this house is very peculiar in its indication. In the first place, the consciousness of the native may be on the borderland between life and death. He may be liable to fall into trances, lethargies, catalepsies, and the like. It would be wise for him for to have standing instructions as to what to do in case of his apparent death as otherwise he may run some risk of being buried alive. Not only should he acquaint his friends and relatives with the circumstances, but he should carry a paper on his person which could easily be read by any stranger who discovered him with all appearance of death.

In any case, the manner of his death is likely to be very singular. If the cusp of the sixth house be occupied by a watery sign and its ruler be afflicted, he will drown. If a fiery sign, he may be burned to death or die in consequence of a fire. In an airy sign, he might die from mental shock, and in an earthy sign, it is possible that he might be killed in a mining disaster or through the fall of a building.

It is not, however, necessary to draw such conclusions except in extreme cases. There is also to be considered a more normal means of exit from life. Possibly some long wasting disease, some obscure malady of the nerves or of the cerebral-spinal fluid, may be the cause of death. The actual circumstances surrounding the death may also be very strange. In some cases, it may come very suddenly, a chronic illness of many years' standing might develop some fulminating form. Most probably of all, the native may not know that he is ill, or if he does so, he may find that the doctors entirely fail to diagnose his disorder. The death itself may prove inexplicable, even on a post mortem examination and be ascribed to 'the failure of the heart's action'. There is also a possibility that death may be caused by poison.

The views of the native with regard to death are likely to be very original. He may hold some fantastic theory on this subject. His mind will tend to dwell habitually upon it. He may regard it with extraordinary aversion, or, on the other hand, it may possess a morbid fascination for him. He may be addicted to some form of necromancy as spiritualism, and the subject will rarely be absent from the 'back of his mind'.

People born with this position of Neptune should be exceedingly careful not to dose themselves with any drug which has a direct action upon the consciousness. They hold to life by too delicate a thread.

A friend of the author's was walking in the forest of Fontainebleau with a pupil, and was explaining to him how perfect freedom was compatible with perfect obedience. 'I do not threaten to shoot you, if you disobey,' he said. 'I do not take you by the throat and strangle you.' To emphasise his remark he put his hand to a thick woollen scarf which the other was wearing, not however exercising any marked pressure. However the man lost consciousness and was only restored to life by prompt measures. He has Neptune in the eighth house.

The condition called *status lymphaticus*[86] is sometimes associated with this position.

The eighth house refers also to the goods of the dead. The native may probably benefit through legacies, but he will do well to beware of trickery on the part of the executors, and he must be prepared for all sorts of small disappointments and delays in connection with this matter. These remarks do not apply to questions of direct inheritance, such as may be expected in the normal course of events, as from the father.

The goods of the partner in business or life are also indicated by the eighth house. Here again, the native must expect a certain vagueness, and possibly deception and disappointment. He will be very foolish to marry for money, for if he did so, he would almost certainly fail to obtain it, either through some chicanery or through the property being lost wholly or in part shortly after marriage. Similarly, on entering into a business partnership, the capital of the partner should be regarded as a very doubtful element.

The native must also be very careful in regard to making his own will. He should see to it that no loophole is left for any disputes subsequent to his death, and he should also take the greatest care that his will is safely in the hands of reliable

86. A condition of the body characterised by excess of water leading to obesity.

persons who will know where to find it at his death. Nor should he be lax in the choice of proper executors.

Neptune in the Ninth House

The ninth house refers to science and religion. This house being exalted in the heavens, Neptune has a more proper influence than in houses not placed so highly. Unless badly afflicted, therefore, it may be considered as almost entirely benefic. The native will have an extraordinarily pure and lofty conception of God and nature. His aspirations will be strong, so strong that they may carry him away completely from this earth, and induce him to devote the whole of his life to the most arduous and subtle researches into the glories by which he is surrounded. It may be, to some extent, a defect that he misses the sense of actuality; the enthusiasm which fills him may lead him to think far in advance of his period; he may fail entirely to realise that the human race, as a whole, is not in line with him. A striking instance of this is the poet Shelley, who had this position. His ideal of the human race not only has not been realised, but is generally recognised as being unrealisable. For this reason he is pre-eminently the poet of the adolescent, in whose beautiful virginal mind, the whole world appears tinctured with the light of the divine creative force, with which the recent development of sex has endowed it.

'A beautiful and ineffectual angel, beating in the void his luminous wings in vain' is a perfect description not only of Shelley, but of almost all persons in whose horoscope Neptune in the ninth house is the dominant influence.

Of course, in affliction these indications may take an undesirable turn. The detachment from the facts of life may lead to superstition, psychism, faddism, crankiness and all such abominations.

The intuition will probably be very highly developed – it may be almost uncanny. At the same time it may be untrustworthy in this way – that the intellectual stability of the native may not be adequate to enable him to discriminate between the true intuition which arises spontaneously and unbidden, and the false intuition which is false or invoked and which nearly always deceives.

The influence of Neptune may also show itself in dreams of a semi-sacred or mystical character. The native may have strange presentiments and queer ideas. It is to be hoped that he will not allow these to lead him away from the realm of commonsense; he may be tempted to act too readily upon belief, and visions, and he may become the prey of malicious and interfering entities who may drag him to his destruction.

In a well-behaved horoscope, this position is admirable for mystical and spiritual progress. There is no height to which the native may not expect to attain. Nor will it be necessary to force his inclinations. He is a natural seer; and, by the operation of good judgment, he may make the most extraordinary spiritual progress.

In the domain of science, the native is nearly as fortunate. He will have a pure understanding of the truths which lie hidden in nature; and if he has the ability to work them out properly, he should not merely make his mark on humanity, but add substantially to the world's knowledge, and assist its progress in a notable degree. His danger will be that he is so sure of these truths that he will fail to understand the necessity of bringing them down to the level of the intelligence of common people, of proving to the world at large, by arduous investigation, what he knows intuitively to be the truth.

The ninth house also refers to long journeys, particularly those which involve a sea voyage. Here the influence of Neptune is by no means so favourable. Strange adventures are certain to occur, many of these of a trivial yet annoying type. There is a decided danger of accidents – it will be remembered that Shelley himself was drowned, while upon just such a voyage. It is also possible that long journeys may be disappointing for another reason – the native may be induced to make a journey on false pretences, and when he arrives at the end of the passage he may discover that it had been undertaken in vain.

The ninth house refers also to the family of the partner in life, and to the mental equipment of the partner in business. The outlook on these points is not particularly favourable. One need not enter in any detail into these matters – it will be sufficient if the student refers to what was said about brothers and sisters and mentality, in the third house.

Neptune in the Tenth House

The tenth house, or *medium coeli*, refers primarily to the business career or occupation of the native, and whether Neptune in this position will be propitious or not depends very greatly upon the nature thereof. This will depend naturally upon the sign which rules the cusp of the tenth house, and its planet. In the ordinary affairs of life, Neptune is likely to bring about a great deal of embarrassment for reasons like those indicated in regard to previous matters of a similar kind. The career may be very strange and eventful, but it is not likely to be smooth or free from interruption. Neptune, and this remark applies to almost all that has hitherto been said, causes the native to suffer lapses. The inspiration which he implies is said to be distinguished from a steady flow of energy. It comes and goes without much apparent cause. The native may have brilliant ideas in regard to his business. He will carry them out with great vigour, but only for a time. Then he will forget all about it, only to begin again later on. As business depends so largely upon application, the effect is on the whole, unfortunate. There is also to be considered a good deal of risk from the nature of the business itself. This is likely to be of a queer and unusual character, and there will be many loopholes for fraud; also it is to be presumed that it may be a little difficult at times to keep track of the business. Profits will be irregular and uncertain. There will be a number of bad debts; and the business may also suffer from the occurence of apparently trivial circumstances, totally unconnected with it. There does not seem to be much risk of a definite smash. The indications are rather those of vicissitudes. The native may feel inclined, again and again, to give it up for something steadier but he will find it hard to relinquish it.

The tenth house further refers to the mother in a man's horoscope and father in a woman's, who is indicated as a person of the Neptunian type. The eccentricity may take any of the forms previously described as characteristically Neptunian, but there is probably a special tendency to religious fanaticism of an ascetic type. It is very rare for the native to remain on good terms with his mother; there may be a great deal of natural affection, but it will be partially inhibited by the incompatibility of temper which is shewn.

The tenth house, moreover, describes the fame or reputation of the native, and this is, of course, in the horoscope of important people, the chief point to consider. Fame, too, being not altogether of the earth, is a particularly Neptunian matter. When this planet is free from interference by others highly placed the fame should be starry and world wide. At the same time it is likely to be of a somewhat extraordinary character. Jupiter in the tenth house gives fame, but in matters more generally recognised, more in touch with the common life of mankind. There may be certain sinister elements connected with it. The name of the native may be involved in strange legends. He will appear to men under a thousand masks; and even time itself may fail altogether to unveil him. We need only instance the cases of Shakespeare and Michael Angelo. Both of these men were big in the best sense of the word. Humanity, much as it may admire them, may fail fully to recognise the grandeur and universality of their genius, unless they, too, be under Neptune. It is difficult to add a third name to these two, even by going back to the Greeks. Goethe had Neptune in the ninth house near the cusp of the tenth. Their comprehension of human nature was so vast that they stand unrivalled. Many other artists have excelled them in execution, in aim, but there are no others who have attempted work of anything like the same importance and also attained the same general level of excellence. (It is further to be noticed that there is something a little unfair in the way in which their fame has developed. They were entitled to it and they obtained it, but they seemed to have obtained it under false pretences. They were originally praised for quite the wrong reasons.) Another example is that of Nostradamus;[87] in the Middle Ages, there

87. Learned physician and astrologer who, in an extensive letter to Henry II of France, dated 27 June 1558, foretold the great historical events of the next five hundred years, including the French Revolution and the rise of Hitler. It was published in the Amsterdam edition of 1667 as *Vrayes Centuries et Prophéties de Maistre Michel Nostredame.* 'Then in the beginning of that year ye shall see a greater persecution

were thousands of astrologers fairly celebrated in their day; but history has picked out the name of Nostradamus without any adequate reason. He was no more distinguished than any of the others, but for some reason legends gathered about his personality, and he passed through history as his rivals passed into oblivion. Another case of quite undeserved reputation is that of Mary Queen of Scots. This lady was, after all, a very ordinary queen – her morals were no better and no worse than those of any other queen – her fate was shared by dozens of monarchs, and though, no doubt, she was beautiful, there is no reason to suppose that she was much more beautiful than twenty others of the rulers of her period. And she has won a fame almost as equal to that of Helen of Troy. She has inspired poets, not only in her own country, but all over the world. She was the darling of Goethe's imagination; Swinburne devoted twenty years of his life to studying her life, and he made it the central figure of an entire period of his work. To take yet one more example, we have the Kaiser.[88] (There is no doubt that however the war may end, he will stand out as the one figure of heroic stature in modern Europe.[89] It may again be remarked that in his case also his character has been totally misunderstood by his contemporaries.) A final example is Sir Humphrey Davy,[90] who was a very great chemist, but not more so than fifty others – yet the name of Davy has become more popularly known than that of almost any other chemist. Even his greater pupil, Faraday, is always connected in the mind with Davy.

In lesser cases, the fame indicated will partake on a smaller scale of the same characteristics. A person with Neptune in the tenth house will constantly make talk in his circle. He

---

against the Christian Church than ever was in Africa [where Islam arose] and it shall be in the year 1792 at which time everyone will think it a renovation of the age . . .' See C.G. Jung, *Aion*, 1959.

88. See note 50.

89. This sentence was written in the beginning of 1918. Crowley was in America at the time. He had either not interpreted the Kaiser's horoscope correctly or he was mistaken on political grounds.

90. The famous chemist and Fellow of the Royal Society who invented in 1815 the miners' safety lamp. He was born in 1778 and died in 1829.

will be somewhat of a mystery. He will be misinterpreted – perhaps, even in a very sinister sense; yet in spite of this or because of it, his name will become widely and more widely known. People will invent stories about him – good, bad and indifferent but all strange and either baseless or totally inaccurate.

In matters of ordinary reputation, Neptune is still less favourable. Where the general character of the native is such that he is not capable of attracting general attention, Neptune will stand for petty scandals – everything the native does will seem peculiar. The merest trifles will be passed round as dainty bits of gossip – no malice is implied. Perhaps the reader has sudden attacks of self-consciousness in a room in a public place, anywhere where people are, he may discover to his great embarrassment that for no reason at all, everybody is looking at him. Although there is nothing to cause it, he is the focus of attention. There is nothing peculiar in his appearance, yet people turn in the streets to look at him. It may be very painful to him to attract notice in this way – he may pay infinite attention to his appearance, endeavouring to make it conventional and yet he may fail.

It may also occur that the native changes his name or perhaps does business under an assumed name. This will probably suit the circumstances very well and success is to be expected.

The tenth house also indicates the employer, superior or master of the native. In spiritual matters, this position is the most favourable that is possible. He should find a teacher of the highest order, and if he follows out the instructions described, his spiritual advancement should be rapid and assured. He should reach the greatest heights that are possible to humanity. But where the career is more conventional, Neptune is not very good. The employer may be tricky, undependable and difficult to deal with, because of his being elusive. He will not be steady-going and matter-of-fact. The relations with him will be continual ferment. People with Neptune in the tenth house should be very careful not to take any chances with the law or the government of the country. To do so will have, perhaps, a quite uncanny fascination for them, and they will no doubt be very clever in keeping out of trouble, but if they were to take any chances at a time when the house was afflicted by direction or transit, they might find themselves in serious trouble.

Neptune in the Eleventh House

The eleventh house refers to the friends of the native, and the society in which he will move, generally speaking Neptune in this position will cause him to attract, taking it by long and by large, Neptunian persons. He is likely to associate with actors, artists, and among women neurotic persons and those of ill repute. He will not be very tenacious in friendship – he will be very capricious in his dealings. He will probably take an extraordinary fancy to a person and cultivate him violently for a little while and then leave him just as suddenly, without any quarrel or other definite reasons. It seems as if there were no deep root in affections of this character. He will be somewhat unfortunate, too, in his acquaintances, for it is really rather absurd to speak of them as friends. They will treat him as cavalierly as he does them. It is not unlikely that these relations will result in a very great degree of unhappiness, for as a general rule, the emotions are not sufficiently deep-seated. There are, however, cases in which definite misfortune may result. For example, Nell Gwynn, who had this position, was left to starve by all those who had courted her in the days of her prosperity.

The element of treachery is, however, decidedly marked. One may instance Napoleon – who was betrayed by his own Marshal.[91] His fall was certain, owing to the presence of Saturn in the tenth house, but it is Neptune in the eleventh that indicates the manner of that fall. It is but rarely that this position must be taken so seriously. In the average case it means little more than the trivial troubles described above, but wherever the horoscope indicates greatness, every aspect and position therein is emphasised, and becomes significant of far more important events than if the nativity as a whole is

91. Napoleon was betrayed by most of his Marshals. Crowley is thinking of Marshal Marmont, Duke of Ragusa, who is pilloried as the figure of treachery in Rostand's play, *L'Aiglon*.

weak. In the case of a person like Napoleon, practically every detail of the life is found accurately mapped by the planetary position. In the case of lesser men, there is such a superficiality that the forces of nature seem hardly .to care to condescend to arrange their affairs, or perhaps it would be better to say that the material on which they operate is too muddy to produce clean-cut effects.

The eleventh house refers also to the wishes and hopes of the native. These may be fantastic and lack the sense of actuality. He may be always, as the phrase goes, 'wishing for the moon', and he will not be very stable and enduring. He will take up a matter with enthusiasm and drop it without regret. This, however, may be called day dreams. The main moral purpose of his life may be perfectly firm and clear, but it is certainly probable that a man who has Neptune thus placed will want more than he is ever likely to get. Still as Browning says:

> Ah, but a man's reach should exceed his grasp,
> Or what's a Heaven for?

Neptune in the Twelfth House

The twelfth house in the first place relates to prisons, by which we mean to include any kind of restraint that is placed upon the freewill of the native. With regard to the probabilities of actual confinement, Neptune is not particularly good or particularly bad. In some cases, it might, perhaps, mean that he was liable to continuous small distresses of this kind, and if there were extremely bad aspects, a long and wasting imprisonment might possibly be expected, but with regard to what may be described as interior restraints, the effect is extremely irritating, especially if Neptune be well on in the twelfth house, near the cusp of the first. In such an instance, it might well be that the native was constantly dominated by his own whims. Its action might interfere seriously with the general purpose of his life. The twelfth house is itself a restraining influence, and it is possible that a bad aspect from the ruler of the mind or of the will might imply completely moral imbecility.

The twelfth house also refers to the secret enemies of the

native, and to the intrigues which may be aimed at him. Here the influence is rather favourable, for the enemies are not persistent, but they may cause a great deal of annoyance before they evaporate.

Another matter, with which the twelfth house deals is that of secret associations, and here the influence of Neptune is as good as possible. A person with Neptune in this position should be extremely successful, not only in carrying through any . . .[92]

92. There is a lacuna here in the original manuscript.

III

Uranus

Ouranos, Uranus or Heaven, is said to have been the father of Saturn, who, jealous lest another son should appear, annihilated him with his scythe. This legend is but an apologue of the nature of this planet, often called 'Herschel' after the man who rediscovered it.[93]

This planet swims lonely in the awful abyss that separates Saturn from Neptune. If we have compared Neptune to the outpost, we may continue by saying that Uranus is the moat of the fortress, and its secret passages. And if we have called Neptune the Soul of the Sea, then Uranus is the essence of Volcanic Fire. There is no planet so strange, so sinister, so occult and mysterious or so contradictory.

For this is in the story of Uranus, the principle of heaven bereft of fatherhood by the jealousy of Time. It is a god who is no longer love, a god whose pleasure has become only cruelty, whose occupation but dark intrigue. It is intellect divorced from benevolence; it is the madness of a noble mind. The proper purpose is baffled, and the will turns to perversion.

But like all gods, Uranus in his happier days was incarnated upon earth under the name of Pan. And this Pan, suffering by sympathy, is not only the first god of music and science, but the Satyr god. He protects the husbandman, but also he delights in things abominable. He is cynical in the old sense of the word, and his comedy is hideous tragedy. Thus, while his brows are noble, they are horned, and from his thighs he is a goat.

93. The planet Uranus was discovered by William Herschel, the private astronomer of George III, in 1781. Crowley is hinting at an ancient awareness of the planet's existence but he gives no details.

It is in Pan rather than in his archetype that we recognise the doubtful ray of Uranus. We must think of his pursuit of Syrinx, of her mad flight, and her transformation into a reed on which the god might play. We must think of the Panic fear which sometimes seizes man, and often multitudes. Then we shall understand.

This planet is the planet of genius, the planet of the secret magical power in man that lies (according to the Indian mythology) coiled at the base of the spine like a snake,[94] ready to strike up and illuminate the whole, or downward to damnation.

Men, common men, are always stricken with the panic fear when genius blazes on them. Always they mistake it for madness until it justifies itself by its effects. And often indeed this never takes place. Unless genius be buttressed by a thousand virtues, it is truly madness. But why is this? Because genius is easily thwarted; it even tends to thwart itself. It is so absolute (by the purity of its truth and logic) that in a relative world, a world of compromises, there seems no place for it. Genius may break; it will not bend. So it rushes forth, hits its mark standing, is diverted from that high aim into desperate courses. It enters the dark paths, pursues them to some dreadful goal.

Gilles de Rais,[95] de Sade, Caesar Borgia[96] were men of genius, just as truly as Michael Angelo and Isaac Newton. All genius desires the infinite, and the infinite is one, not many. Only the mediate steps are diverse. Darwin regretted his limitations as bitterly as did Alexander; and the love of Christ equally with the malice of Satan would destroy the world were each not thwarted by that world's inertia.

The essence of genius is this occult, but overmastering lust of achievement in practical and material shape. If Neptune makes the saint or hermit, Uranus makes the magician, the man who calls forth from the unseen, not only its peace but its power. The dream of the Uranian is universal dominion by

94. Kundalini or the Fire Snake of the Hindu and Tantric tradition.
95. See note 74.
96. Caesar Borgia (1476-1507), fourth son of Pope Alexander VI. Every species of crime has been ascribed to him, but among his subjects he was regarded as virtuous and just.

and for his Idea. This Idea may obsess him, blind him to all else, ruin him by narrowness. He rarely understands that Being must take Form before it can be perceived, and he misses his opportunities. He does not known how many veils must be thrown over the splendour of his Virgin before men can bear to gaze upon her without going mad.

All genius is equally 'good', but unless it be accompanied with utmost breadth of sanity, with moral strength as of a god, and above all with humour, it thickens, it ferments, it turns to deadly poison.

He that began by wishing to save men continues by secret murder. The man perhaps sees chastity as the salvation of the race, and instead of living and letting his light shine before men, becomes mad and assassinates some man whose influence he deplores. It is characteristic of the infatuation with an idea that all sense of proportion is lost. Even so a diplomatist plunges his country into war at the cost of millions, both of men and money, in order to gain an advantage of negligible worth; one remembers the comments of Hamlet on the expedition of Fortinbras.[97] So also Uranus is the particular planet of all secret vices that tend to usurp the whole nature of a man. From religious fanaticism to indulgence in dangerous drugs the gamut runs; and because of the obsession of the one idea, the defiance or neglect of circumstance attending it, we find what we call fame or infamy as our bias determines. There is no good or evil absolute; to one man Caesar is a hero, to another a fiend; the Puritans destroyed cathedrals; others even today hate pictures and statues. One critic thought Shelley a devil specially incarnated to plague mankind, another calls him a beautiful but ineffectual angel.

Any genius thwarted, as Uranus was thwarted, in the beneficient purpose of his life, turns either to horrible self-indulgences, or to revenge. '*Maudite race!*' exclaims the starving man of genius, whose great heart only willed to burn itself out on the altar of art that he might bring men Truth and Beauty from the gods. 'I wish that mankind had but one

97. King of Norway, whom Hamlet the Dane slew in the war between their countries. See *Hamlet*, I.1.

head that I might top it at a blow'.[98] The anarchist throws his bomb in the spirit of philanthropy. Unless all this is fully understood, it is useless to try to judge mankind for every man has this Uranus in him, strong or weak, subtle or gross, fortunate or unfortunate, and this is the Royal Snake of Egypt,[99] the giver of life and death. If you will not allow him to create, he will devour. And your own snake has his own ambition; busy yourself with that and do not waste time on criticising others.

The most important thing in the life of any man is to discover the secret purpose of his incarnation and to follow it with wariness as well as with passion. Astrology has no more useful function than this, to discover the inmost nature of a man and to bring it out into his consciousness, that he may fulfil it according to the law of light.

The Uranus in us is the Sacred Lance of the Legend; in the hands of the Holy King it built the Temple of the Grail; in those of Klingsor,[100] the Garden of Evil Enchantments. Genius may be fertile or sterile, radiant or self-consuming; the one is White Magic and the other Black. But the force is the same, and being thus double it is of the utmost importance to direct it aright. The purity of a strong noble Neptune is the greatest safeguard to this force; and the Sign of the Cross in its fullest, holiest, most Pagan and most Christian sense is its warrant. For it is not only the Redeemer, but it must itself be redeemed.

Uranus in the Zodiacal Signs

We have already explained concerning Neptune that this planet represents the soul. But it is static; with regard to its position in the Zodiac we see it in its relation to the *Zeitgeist*; and the quality of the individual soul must be determined by its mundane position and by its aspects. But this soul is sensitive and passive; as we said above, static. If we wish to see how this soul can heap itself up as it were and issue forth

98. Caligula.
99. The Uraeus Serpent crown worn on the brow of the Pharaohs.
100. See note 24.

flaming at will, we must look to Uranus.

Now, this is the doctrine, that every living soul has a purpose in incarnation; and that purpose is single. Not one in a million, perhaps, is conscious of that purpose. We seem for the most part to be a mass of vacillations. Even the main career of an individual cannot be considered as necessarily an expression of the interior will.

Now, Uranus indicates this will; and the reason why he is so explosive and violent and upsetting to men is that he represents this real intention, which, lying deeper than his conscious purpose, often contradicts it. The outer and the inner are in conflict; and whenever battle is joined the inner wins. To the outer this must naturally appear as disaster; for he does not recognise the force as part of himself, or if so he regards it as a disturbing entity and loathes its dominion.

Uranus is the Royal Uraeus Serpent[101] in Egyptian Symbolism, slow yet sudden Lord of life and death. It takes a great deal to move him; but when once in motion, he is irresistable. This is why, to the normal mind, he appears so terrible. Occasionally too, this is no mere illusion; there are certain forces represented by Uranus, of which it is better not even to think. Most fortunately it is rarely necessary to do so. In any case, this subject is too subtle, difficult and deadly to discuss in general terms; and it will be sufficient if the student is referred to what we may call 'the literature of the Abyss', using that term in the special technical sense known to initiates.[102]

From what we have said with regard to the character of Uranus it will be seen that his force is peculiarly sympathetic to the Cherubic Signs Taurus, Leo, Scorpio, and Aquarius. He represents (to flash a vivid and illuminating, if not pedantically accurate thought) the spirit of the Cherubin. We shall see in the course of this paper how his action is modified in each

101. See note 99.

102. A reference to Crowley's *Liber 418* ('*The Vision and the Voice*') in which the ordeal of the Abyss is described. The Abyss is the gulf between the actual and the ideal, or in Qabalistic symbolism the worlds of Briah (the Creative World) and Atziloth (the Archetypal World). Crowley's Order of the Silver Star taught the means of crossing the Abyss.

of these signs, the Aquarian *menstruum*[103] bringing out his emancipating and scientific qualities, since Aquarius is the man-Cherub; the Taurine exhibiting him as the fearful personification of earthquake and upheaval, since Taurus is the Bull; the Leonine emphasising his revolutionary and fighting qualities; and finally the *barathrum*[104] of Scorpio manifesting him as the Death-star, or as the treacherous and subtle power of poison, or as the eagle which, although it cries 'The House of Death', makes whole the spirit. For Scorpio always best and worst of the signs quintessentialises Uranus more strongly than ever Leo or Aquarius, being indeed in some sort flux of these.

Now, as has been seen, the deeply interior purpose of any being is nearly always obscure and undecipherable but there is an indication or hieroglyph of it which is usually very significant. One can hardly call it more than the artistic expression of the purpose; and this appears a very good way to describe it. We call it the Temperament. It does not define the will, but it sets limits to the sphere wherein the will may work.

Now we have already assigned the personality to the sign of the Ascendant; and to this must now be added a consideration of the sign in which Uranus may be situated. Where these two factors are harmonious, we get a character with unity or moral purpose; where otherwise, a self-tortured waverer. It might be cited as an objection to this that those with Uranus rising are usually eccentric characters; but the argument is on the other side. Such eccentricity is temperament in its highest development; it shows the entire overruling of the superficial qualities by this deep-seated turbulent magical will. It is only to others that the person with Uranus rising appears so eccentric; to himself he seems profoundly, lucidly, rational and if properly understood, he is so. Herschel himself is perfectly in accordance with the higher law; he is only a law breaker in the same sense as, when the civil law is superseded by martial law in times of

103. Crowley uses the word '*menstruum*' in the sense of a 'vehicle' or 'transmitter'. The Astral Light is the *menstruum* of thought forms and other subtle impressions.

104. 'A pit, gulf' *Oxford English Dictionary*.

grave crisis, the officer who at another time dares not lift his cane orders the firing of a murderous volley.

We are now in a position to investigate the truth of these purely *a priori* assertions by the study of the horoscopes of famous persons.

We shall class these under the signs in which Herschel is situated, as this is the purpose of this paper, to isolate his influence in the Zodiac from other considerations, and to this end we must look always at the rising sign in order to see whether that influence modifies it and in what direction.

Uranus in Aries

Uranus in Aries gives a character intrepid, dauntless, fiery and indomitable, whether for good or evil.

Flaming, headstrong, hot-tempered, impetuous, self-willed and obstinate is the type; but sometimes the native will make a sudden and complete *volte-face*, and purpose a new and contradictory course with the same energy as he did the former. Nor, as a rule, will he be capable of seeing that he has changed in any respect. There is nothing particularly constructive in this type of energy. A strong example of this temperament is found in Annie Besant,[105] Aries the rising sign; in Pope Alexander VI[106] the same qualities are apparent; but here Capricornus is rising, and although Mars is exalted in Capricornus, and so not inharmonious with the Aries temperament, yet a Saturnian element is super-added, with the most unfortunate results.

People with Uranus in Aries are always so firmly convinced that they are right that opposition to their wishes appears to them as something positively Satanic, and they are therefore entirely unscrupulous in crushing that opposition. Sometimes this masterful quality is confined to legitimate lines, as in the case of Edison. Scorpio is rising, and its lord Mars is softened by the conjunction of the Moon in the third house; thus the powerful will implied works mostly on the mental plane, where the enemy is only stubborn nature; and in

105. The fiery labour leader who turned Theosophist after one meeting with the dying Madame Blavatsky. She immediately became the head of the Theosophical Society. She died in 1933.

106. See note 227.

bending to his will by the force of his genius, he has earned the thanks of humanity.

Contrast this with the case of 'Bloody Balfour',[107] whose name will go down to posterity with that of Cromwell as an oppressor of the Irish people. Here Virgo is rising, with its lord Mercury in square to Uranus. Hence we find Balfour not a strong, but only a violent man, alternating pusillanimity and ferocity; the dominant characteristic in the whole conformation being the heartlessness and a sexuality which so often goes with the Mercurial type.

Lord Rosebery,[108] on the other hand, has Aries rising, or rather 28 degrees of Pisces. At least Uranus occupied the Ascendant and so we find a fair uniformity of disposition. But his career has been interrupted by his sudden laying down of things and equally sudden resumption of them.

Anna Kingsford[109] has Uranus in Aries, but it occupies the eighth house. Here as in the case of Balfour, Virgo is rising, but its Lord Mercury is in his own house and exaltation in conjunction with Venus, and the Ascendant is further dignified by the presence of Sol and Mars in conjunction. Here we find, then, a great example of the driving force of these configurations, for Anna Kingsford, despite all mental and moral disqualifications, disposed of an initiating force sufficient to transfigure the thought of half the world. It is her work which made Theosophy and its analogous cults at all possible. She was the head of the battering-ram that broke in the gates of Victorianism and the materialistic philosophy of the time.

The Earl of Strafford[110] and Oliver Cromwell both had

107. Arthur James Balfour (1848-1930), British Conservative Statesman, dilettante and philosopher, now remembered principally for his 'declaration favouring a national home for Jews in Palestine', 1917. He earned the soubriquet 'Bloody Balfour' during his tenure of the Irish chief-secretaryship in the late 1880s.

108. Archibald Philip Primrose, 5th Earl of Rosebery (1847-1929), British statesman, succeeded Gladstone as Prime Minister in 1894.

109. Dr Anna Kingsford, M.D., (1846-1888) mystic, anti-vivisectionist, vegetarian, author of *The Perfect Way; or the Finding of Christ*, and other works.

110. Thomas Wentworth, 1st Earl of Strafford (1593-1641), statesman. His ruthless methods in Ireland led to his impeachment and ultimately his execution.

Uranus in Aries, and it should be most instructive to compare their nativities. Each had an iron will, an unscrupulous determination to have his own way at any cost, but Strafford has Virgo rising, like Balfour. He prepared a plan for dealing with Ireland called 'thorough' which was to legalise massacre even more effectively than did the Coercion (Crimes) Act of the Victorian statesman. But he was not strong enough to carry it out. He hung fire. Cromwell, with Aries rising, simply went through Ireland like a new Attila. There is no passion in Virgo to do any such act.

Robert Louis Stevenson has Aquarius rising, but Pisces is cut out in the Ascendant, and Uranus is just within it. There is no great harmony between Aries and Aquarius, but their presence together gives harmony. So indeed we find Stevenson, despite terrible ill-health, executing a series of masterpieces. Critics of literature will attribute to Aquarius the curious gentle profound psychology and to Uranus in Aries the passion for bloodthirsty incident which reveals him in his work. Saturn is also in the Ascendant, just above Uranus, and this adds the tinge of melancholy which so increases his incomparable charm.

Another example is Ludwig II of Bavaria.[111] Here Uranus is in the tenth house. Cancer is rising, weak, feminine, and receptive, and assorts ill with the violence of Uranus in Aries. So we see a dreamy, easy, pleasure-loving temperament, which burst out at times into maniacal enthusiasms and extravagances. The lack of harmony between these two configurations is the essential gulf within the personality which ultimately manifested itself as madness.

A final example is Abbas Effendi.[112] As in the case of Stevenson Aquarius is rising, and Herschel is just within the second house. Here is the same gentle profundity as Stevenson's. But Neptune is rising, and instead of the tremendous

111. Ludwig of Bavaria (1845-1886), the 'mad king', patron of Wagner whom he invited to settle in Munich and for whom he built an opera house.

112. Abdul Baha (1844-1921), known as Abbas Effendi, Persian religious leader and head of the Bahai faith. The tenets of this faith are the unity of all the major religions, racial equality, disarmament. Jesus, Moses, Buddha, Mohammed are considered as prophets of the one God.

will which enabled the writer to rank with the greatest masters of all time, there is but a soft and somewhat indefinite personality, its will interior and not externalised, owing to the forces that oppress it being too strong to overcome, and to the inhibitory influence which Neptune exercises on all continuous activity.

Uranus in Taurus

This position is highly favourable for Uranus, for his great energy is set to honest constructive work. One can immediately instance such empire-builders as Napoleon, Cecil Rhodes, and Wilhelm II: and on the higher plane, we find two persons who actually invented new theogonies, which philosophy declares to be the highest creative work possible to the human intelligence. We refer to Dante and Swedenborg,[113] whose conceptions of Hell still hold sway over the minds of great masses of men. Such empires endure long after earthly thrones have crumbled.

Swedenborg has Sagittarius rising, and his Uranus is on the cusp of the fourth house: Dante has Gemini rising, and Uranus well above the horizon in the twelfth. Both these signs are far from material, Sagittarius more mystical, Gemini more intellectual; and accordingly we differentiate between the types of work which they were able to accomplish.

Wilhelm II[114] has Cancer rising, and accordingly he is blamed by his own subjects for that obstinate devotion to peace which delayed (and thus made more uncontrollable, ultimately) the outbreak of the Great War.

Rhodes[115] has Sagittarius rising, with Jupiter its lord just above the horizon; Swedenborg's Jupiter was exactly trine to Uranus, emphasising the religious bias; that of Rhodes is squared by Neptune, which would tend to remove those qualities from Jupiter, and bring out his force on more terrestrial lines.

113. Emmanuel Swedenborg (1688-1772), Swedish scientist and mystic, who had the gift of second sight, i.e. the sight of the third eye, or clairvoyant vision. He unfolded the geography of the Celestial Kingdom in his *Arcana Coelestia*, 1749-56.

114. See note 50.

115. See note 30.

Napoleon had Libra rising, and his Uranus is in the seventh house; but Libra and Taurus are sympathetic through the fact that Venus rules both; and Venus is sextile to Herschel and culminating. There lies the explanation of his extraordinary sense of justice; the *Code Napoléon* ranks with the laws of Manu[116] and the Li-King[117] as supreme among legislative efforts.

Yet another example of Uranus in Taurus is the Prince Imperial;[118] but for reasons indicated in another place, the life itself was cut short, and its will consequently aborted.

Tom Mann[119] has this planet in the Ascendant, but Aries is on the cusp. The two signs are contrary in nature, so there is a lack of harmony. His will-force is occupied entirely with Taurus in its lowest form, that of labour; the sextile of Neptune to Uranus lends eccentricity to the ideas involved, and Aries rising makes the temperament violent and abrupt. Uranus thus assumes its most explosive form, and the result is an ignorant and unbalanced agitator.

A superficially most dissimilar case is that of Charles I. Here Leo is rising, and Uranus is on the cusp of the tenth house, always a dangerous position for a malefic. Leo gives the good-heartedness characteristic of that unfortunate monarch, but Neptune rising made his temperament unstable. This combined with the obstinacy of will shown by Uranus in Taurus, gave a disposition which could only bring about disaster.

116. *Lawbook or Code of Manu*, a Brahmanical work ascribed by some scholars to the 5th century B.C., by others to the 2nd century B.C. According to the Code of Manu, 'the root of all law is the Veda and the traditions of those who know the Veda', i.e. the traditional lore or scriptures of the Hindus.

117. *Li-King*, the 'Book of Rites', is one of the ancient books accepted by the Chinese as classics. The Rites are those of the Imperial Dynasty that was reigning in the time of Confucius (551-479 B.C.) and was founded in 1122 B.C. The *Li-King* was in part edited by Confucius and his disciples.

118. The Prince Imperial, only son of Napoleon III and the Empress Eugénie, was ambushed and killed with the British army in the Zulu campaign of 1879.

119. Labour leader and socialist, born 1856, died 1941.

Here is a very cognate example in Asquith,[120] whose obstinate patience (and nothing else) has kept him at the head of a most unruly majority in the House of Commons. Here Cancer is rising, making him tactful and pliable on the surface; Uranus in the house of Friends enables him to conceal beneath that apparent amiability a determination of steel.

A case of very similar persistence in a woman is furnished by Lillie Langtry.[121] In a feminine horoscope one naturally expects to find the venereal side of Taurus brought out fully, especially as Libra is rising. So the career is marked as singularly successful; the constructive form is able to develop itself without too great hindrance, especially as the Sun is rising, sextile to Jupiter. No doubt this aspect determines the character of the object of her will; for example, had Saturn and Luna been in the Ascendant, she might have become a worker among the poor.

Finally, we have a large group of writers. We may pair for convenience Bernard Shaw and Havelock Ellis.[122] The Uranus of the latter being in the third house caused his mind to occupy itself with very unusual subjects; Aquarius rising gave a scientific turn to the personality, the result we know.

Shaw, with Gemini rising, has Uranus just above the eastern horizon: the unusual character of the man is thus made emphatic; but the moon, on the very cusp of the Ascendant, makes it vacillating and even self-contradictory. Gemini rising adds to the airy lightness of the personality, and conceals the tremendous driving force of Uranus. For beneath the mask of easy wit and paradox, Shaw has done more to upset conventional ideas than any other man in England, except Swinburne, since Shelley.

120. Herbert Henry Asquith, 1st Earl of Oxford and Asquith (1852-1928), British statesman and Liberal Prime Minister from 1908 to 1916.

121. See note 81.

122. Henry Havelock Ellis (1859-1939), author of *Studies in the Psychology of Sex* in six volumes, a work so filled with details about normal and abnormal sexual activity among the peoples of the world that it aroused the wrath and disdain of Victorian and Edwardian society and became consequently a bestseller. His wife, a lesbian, died mad.

Among novelists we have Guy de Maupassant[123] and Mabel Collins.[124] It is hardly too much to say that the former created the 'short story' in France. Here is Virgo rising, with Venus on the horizon in conjunction with Mars. This violence of passion, with Uranus in the eighth, presaged his melancholy and appalling death; but before this effect could take place on the physical plane, it must first produce that miraculous labour whose fruit is still so sweet in our mouths.

With this we may compare the horoscope of Oscar Wilde. Here Uranus is again too near the tenth house to make for permanence. Virgo rising has its lord Mercury near the opposition of Uranus; a careful consideration of the differences in these dispositions will mark most significantly the variation of his career from that of the great French writer. But we must once more point out that Uranus in Taurus cannot fail; Wilde's work, shallow, insincere, and stolen as it was, yet produced a tremendous, and we are bound to admit, a not altogether desirable effect upon the younger generation, especially among the half-educated.

There is also Mabel Collins, who did much to make the success of the theosophical movement by some rather interesting writings. As in the case of Lillie Langtry, Libra is rising; but Saturn being in exact conjunction with Uranus, Venus trine to them and Neptune sextile with Jupiter in the Ascendant, the career is less material; the direction of the will is more to power of a subtler and more permanent sort.

Lastly, we have two very singular poets, Coleridge and Philip Bourke Marston.[125] The former has Sagittarius rising, which adds its element of shy suddenness to the personality; it is refined and beautiful like a deer. Uranus in the fifth gives that mystic tinge which is the essence of the beauty of his poetry, but alas! when it worked down to the material plane made him the slave of his pleasures. The pre-Raphaelite poet [Marston], on the other hand, has Leo rising, and was generous, frank and free. Uranus in the ninth house gave

123. See note 249.
124. See note 72.
125. See note 66.

another kind of mysticism. Both these men, were, however, strongly determined by Uranus in Taurus. Their work is patient steady and constructive. Coleridge had it hampered by the exact square of Jupiter, and the blindness of Marston no doubt prevented his will from coming to full flower; but the determination in both cases, is most evidently there.

Uranus in Gemini

The sign Gemini is by nature singularly unsympathetic with Uranus; for its force is dispersive and gentle, easily moved, but not persistent in motion; and the influence is accordingly weak. We shall find persons indeed pre-eminent for driving force of will. Their power will be mainly that of idea; and unless the rising sign be thoroughly harmonious, and both its lord and Uranus himself, well-dignified, we may expect examples of failure rather than of success.

We have, however, three great religious teachers, and all are distinguished for the gentleness of their doctrines and suavity of their methods. These are the founder of the Christian religion, Swami Vivekananda,[126] and Dr Rudolf Steiner.[127]

In the first case, Libra is rising, a sign peculiarly harmonious with Gemini – Jupiter is ascending squared by Sol, which is in exact conjunction with Mercury and in direct opposition to Mars and Neptune. Uranus himself is on the cusp of the tenth house. This makes Uranus by far the strongest planet in the figure, so much so that we may regard his influence as paramount and unchecked, thus summing the career insofar as the will is concerned in the one word 'emancipation'.

The Hindu adept [Vivekananda] has Capricornus rising, with the Sun and Venus, and these are square to Mars. Uranus is in the eleventh house, and this made his doctrines readily acceptable to many minds. But there is no great harmony between Gemini and Capricornus, so that the complete temperament is not nearly so efficient as in the case previously considered.

The German mystic [Steiner] has Scorpio rising, which

126. The principal disciple of Sri Ramakrishna, the Bengali saint. Vivekananda was the first to popularise Yoga in the West and to establish the Ramakrishna Mission in countries outside India.

127. See note 67.

adds great scientific accomplishment to the Uranian vector, Mars, too, its lord, is exactly semi-sextile to Uranus; but the latter is squared by Sol, gravely diminishing the general potency of the planet, which is, moreover, in the seventh house, by no means a powerful position in such a case.

We now come to a group of notoriously weak personalities. George V, the Duke of Clarence and Avondale,[128] Alfred Dreyfus,[129] Don Carlos of Spain,[130] Florence Maybrick,[131] W.B. Yeats,[132] Marie Bashkirtseff[133] and Vaillant.[134] Every one of these may be classed as a failure in his or her own line of life, and one need look no further into the horoscope to discover the reason.

A more successful type is Maurice Maeterlinck,[135] but here Scorpio is rising with its lord Mars in sextile to Uranus. Consequently, the driving force of the one compensates the weakness of the other.

We have an even better example of this in Lord Brougham,[136] with Libra rising, and Venus in her own house just above the horizon. The influence is still mental; Gemini can never act on the material plane directly; but Uranus is in the eighth house, and so the great lawyer became what he was through dealing with the minds of the dead by his study of precedent. Libra, again, in material matters implies the

128. The eldest son of Edward VII, a psychopath recently claimed to have been Jack the Ripper.

129. See note 37.

130. Don Carlos (1848-1909), Prince of Bourbon, claimant to the Spanish throne. See Crowley's *Confessions* for an account of Crowley's connection with Don Carlos.

131. Florence Maybrick was alleged to have poisoned her husband with arsenic extracted from fly-papers. She was tried and convicted in 1889 and sentenced to death, but she was subsequently reprieved and served a long term of imprisonment. At the time there was grave doubt about her guilt.

132. See note 46.

133. See note 78.

134. See note 83.

135. Maurice Maeterlinck (1864-1949), Belgian poet, dramatist and essayist, author of *Pelléas et Mélisande*, 1892, which Debussy made into an opera, *The Blue Bird*, 1908, and *The Life of the Bee*, 1901.

136. Lord Brougham (1778-1868), famous statesman and lawyer. He designed and gave his name to a four-wheeled, closed, horse-drawn carriage.

judicial faculty, and Mercury the mental ruler is just below Venus.

An even more strenuous politician is John Burns.[137] Once more the forceful Scorpio is rising, implying iron determination. Uranus in Gemini here gives the limit and the means. His trust is in his eloquence, and Uranus being trined by Mars makes him a great fighting orator. Both he and Brougham display the same dogged will, but the difference between them is most clearly characterised by the difference between Libra and Scorpio; the one adroit, supple, weighing every word, the other hacking through.

Not dissimilar to either, indeed a sort of mean proportional between them, is Theodore Roosevelt.[138] Here Sagittarius is rising and Uranus is in the fifth house. There is a sort of boyish pleasure in the will, a spontaneity in the eloquence, which appealed immensely to the great hearted children of the Republic. The breeziness, the spirit of the vast deserts that they have wrung from the bison and the Indian, was in his words. The affliction of Jupiter by the opposition of Venus makes the temperament somewhat rash and tactless; and when the people were not swept off their feet by the first gust, there was no reserve of fact to influence their second thoughts. Here then, in this simple configuration of three planets, we read the whole secret of his success and of his failure.

Not so far removed, either, from this category is the preacher, Billy Sunday.[139] Once more, Scorpio is rising,

137. Socialist politician and labour leader. He was born in 1858 and died in 1943. He led, with Ben Tillett, the great London dock strike of 1889.

138. See note 47.

139. A Philadelphian revivalist who was at the height of his powers during the time this book was written. In Crowley's *Commentary on The Book of the Law*, written in 1921, appears this passage: 'In Latin countries, where Sin is not taken seriously, and sex-expression is simple, wholesome, and free, drunkenness is a rare accident. It is only in Puritan countries, where self-analysis, under the whip of a coarse bully like Billy Sunday, brings the hearer to "conviction of sin", that he hits first the "trail" and then the "booze". Can you image an "evangelist" in Taormina? It is to laugh.' Crowley also wrote a brief essay on Billy Sunday, which was published in *The International*, New York, October 1915.

Mars and Jupiter in close conjunction just above the cusp of the ascendant, and once again we see the brutal thrust of the personality almost blatant, breaking through all obstacles to attain its ends. And here again the effort is upon the minds of men. But there is nothing subtly persuasive; the only weapon is the bludgeon. He liberally bullies men into belief or what for the moment passes for belief.

Another vigorous personality is that of the suffragette Mrs Pankhurst,[140] with Aquarius rising, but its lord Saturn in some trouble on the cusp of Leo, his own decan, whose name is strife.

Aquarius and Gemini are friendly enough however, and thus we observe that within the narrow limitations – Mercury is afflicted by the conjunction of Saturn in the sixth, a most unfortunate house for the mental ruler – her will has produced remarkable results.

Turning to music and the arts, we have the composer Richard Strauss, with cancer rising, and Uranus not far above the Orient. The Moon, lady of Cancer, is in the third house, in Virgo; thus the mind and the temperament are in tune; and Cancer is a sign most delicate and pleasing, receptive of harmonious impulses from without. The Sun too, lord of Music, is with Uranus, and Venus stands, the morning star above them. How beautiful a picture of the temperament of the composer of *Electra* and *Salome.*

The painter J.M.W. Turner is another most excellent example of this thesis. One may ask where lies the peculiar force of Gemini; but a further investigation of the horoscope will justify wisdom of her children. Capricornus is rising with Saturn in close trine to Uranus, thus harmonising the personality, while Uranus himself is modified by the conjunction of Venus, the Planet of gracious form and brilliant colour. A certain ruggedness and power is added to these by the square of Mars.

Far less amicable dispositions are found in the nativity of

140. There were two suffragette women called Pankhurst, mother and daughter. Crowley presumably means the daughter, Sylvia, who was active during the time he was writing and who founded a militant suffragette movement in 1903. She died in 1960.

the poet Thomas Moore.[141] Scorpio is rising, and there is the successful man, no doubt, especially as Mars is in his own house, just above the eastern skyline. But he is sorely weakened by the conjunction of the moon and of Saturn, while Uranus is squared by Jupiter. Hence the extremely narrow limit of his art, and the monotony of his melody. Uranus, too, is in the seventh house, and it is never well for the will to conflict with the personality. Moore was consequently but a feeble singer; his ambition was never equalled by his achievement; and his best-known work is not as vital and elemental as with happier configurations it might have been. Even more than William Morris,[142] he is 'the singer of an empty day', the least brilliant of that extraordinary galaxy of genius which dazzled the eyes of men a century ago.

One of the greatest chemists that ever lived was Sir Humphrey Davy.[143] He, too, has Scorpio rising, but its Lord Mars is in exact trine to Uranus, in Libra, giving him that noble devotion to justice, in Nature, which made him so perfect an observer. Here then is a temperament of ideal balance, and the will worked freely at its gigantic and most honourable ambition. It may be objected that Mars is in his detriment, but the trine of Uranus fully compensates for this weakness. Scorpio gives the inquiring mind, and the position of Uranus in the Zodiac could not but operate freely with such assistance. With Neptune and Jupiter in exact conjunction in the House of Fame, the will was assured not only of success but of recognition.

Uranus in Cancer

So passive, so placid, so receptive, so mutable, so conservative, a sign as Cancer cannot be expected to accord with the active, violent, creative, determined, revolutionary rays of

141. Thomas Moore (1779-1852), prolific and popular poet, friend and executor of Byron. To his eternal shame, he agreed to the destruction of Byron's *Memoirs* which were considered too frank for the time.

142. William Morris (1834-1896) British poet, Pre-Raphaelite, utopian socialist, architect, printer, designer and protagonist of the arts and crafts movement.

143. See note 90.

Uranus. It will tend to dissolve his violence, rather as water mingles with sulphuric acid, generating fierce heat perhaps for a moment, but leaving a diluted substance, the qualities of both, for good or evil, quenched and dissipated. Yet there may in favourable conditions be found a modification and expansion of the force, just as some violent perfume needs to be spread out into a greater volume before the olfactory nerves can perceive it with pleasure. We shall then expect to find the power of Uranus neutralised by Cancer, and whether this leaves a residuum potent and yet pleasant will depend far more than in other signs upon the Ascendant, and upon the dignities and aspects of the lord thereof, and upon those of Uranus himself.

We shall certainly not expect to discover many people who have revolutionised their age, who have dominated their contemporaries in any radical manner. We shall not expect any real strength of will, any true masterfulness of temperament.

The facts bear out this prognosis. There is Savonarola,[144] to take out best available example first, but his Uranus is in 29 degrees, and its influence extends therefore to the cusp of Leo. In his case, moreover, Aries is rising, with Mars exalted in Capricornus; and his Uranus is trined by Jupiter. Mars is weakened by the conjunction of the Moon, but the square of Saturn adds determination, and somewhat embitters the configuration, while Mars, being in the tenth house, dominates the entire figure. There is therefore, much force in the personality; the temperament is directed to religion and confined within those limits by the aforesaid trine of Jupiter who is in his own house, Pisces, just above the horizon.

In 28 degrees is the Uranus of Byron, and here, too, perhaps Leo has something to say in the matter. But Cancer is rising and its lady the Moon is in close conjunction with Uranus. The temperament is therefore harmonious within itself, but easy-going, pleasure-loving, artistic, sensuous, eccentric and mutable. The power of the character comes rather from Mars – in his fall on the cusp of the Ascendant. This configuration seems admirably to describe the best and

144. See note 57.

the worst of the poet. Strong-willed and self-willed he was, yet unable to persist in will; he was at once weak and violent, stormy and querulous; with all his advantages and his talents, his rank and his reputation, he died a disappointed man, having sought in vain that victory which comes only from virtue.

Another hot-tempered individual was Queen Elizabeth I, whose Uranus is with Saturn, Lord of the Ascendant, Capricornus, in the house of marriage and of public enemies. Here is a fatal opposition of personality and temperament. The whole substance of her will was bound up in the seventh house, and arrogant and masterful as her personality was, she could never secure dynasty. In spite of all the glories of her reign, its true essence and tragedy – and the tragedy of England, the beginning of her decline and fall was her failure to save her house. From a Tudor to a Stuart, from a Stuart to a Guelph, from a Guelph to a Coburg,[145] is a decay longer drawn-out, yet no less certain than the downgrade in Imperial Rome from Augustus to Tiberius, to Caligula, to Nero.

There are two other persons of importance in their day who have this position of Uranus: Alfred Harmsworth[146] and Rudyard Kipling, both journalists, one in the wholesale and the other in the retail business. Kipling has Uranus on the very cusp of his Ascendant, and unquestionably there was never a more self-supporting personality. He struck an excessively definite note, and rose at times to extraordinary heights. He is the only author who has really succeeded in understanding and portraying the ruling class of England. The conjunction of Sol and Jupiter, and that of Mercury, Mars, and Venus, have much to say to this; but this is a digression, the point here to be emphasised is the unique personal note struck by Uranus in the Ascendant, and its resolution in artistic form by the fact of that Ascendant being Cancer.

With Harmsworth, the case is different. Jupiter is rising in Sagittarius, and the Uranus in Cancer becomes of secondary

145. By 'Guelph' Crowley seems to mean, in a derogatory way, the House of Hanover, which instituted the Royal Guelphic Order of Knighthood. The Coburgs, or Saxe-Coburgs, were the family of Prince Albert and his descendants.

146. See note 63.

importance. It merely ties him down to a method, that of working upon the people, by publicity. The suddenness and fierceness of his schemes is determined by the rising sign.

Sir David Wilkie[147] is a good example of this position. Gemini is rising, and its lord Mercury weakened by the opposition of Mars, so that the influence of Uranus in Cancer comes out strongly. Uranus is in trine to the Sun, confirming the artistic predisposition conferred by Cancer. Thus he was a sensible successful painter, with a fine sense of beauty, but with nothing in him to set the Firth of Forth on fire.

With him we may place Sir Henry Wood,[148] a good, capable, conservative conductor, who would have been as faithful had fate placed him on a street car as in a concert hall. Gemini is rising; Uranus on the cusp of the third house, and Mercury is squared by Jupiter. It is the same cause, a weakened personality, with the same effect, the undisturbed action of the placid Cancer mentality. Four planets in Pisces confirm the tendency to expression in artistic form.

Another example is the Tsar Nicholas II.[149] Virgo is rising, as passive and quiescent as Cancer itself, and Mercury is in close opposition to Saturn. Venus is in almost exact conjunction with Uranus in the tenth house. From such a configuration what good can be expected? The native happened to be born to the throne of all the Russias. Oh, unfortunate nation, to be punished with so weak a ruler at a time when a Caesar or an Alexander could hardly have averted the impending catastrophe.

Our last example is Madame Steinheil.[150] In this nativity Aquarius is rising, but there are no less than five planets in

147. Sir David Wilkie (1785-1841), Scottish genre and portrait painter.

148. Henry Joseph Wood (1869-1944). For over half a century he was the conductor of the Queen's Hall Promenade Concerts in London.

149. Tsar Nicholas II (1868-1918) came to the throne in 1894 and was assassinated by the Bolsheviks, together with the Tsaritsa, Tsarevitch and other members of the Imperial Family, on 16 July 1918.

150. The President of France, Felix Faure (1841-1899) died of a cerebral haemorrhage during sexual intercourse in his study in the Elysée Palace with a lady called Madame Steinheil. Steinheil afterwards married Lord Abinger, the grandson of General Scarlett who led the charge of the Heavy Brigade in the Crimea.

Aries, all just under the Ascendant, and the lord Saturn is trine from the tenth house to all of them in general, and Neptune in particular. Here then is the insatiable ambition, limitless and indomitable, except that being in the fifth house, it gave her the temperament of pleasure, and laid down the lines along which she worked to aggrandise her vaulting personality. Saturn in the tenth house laid his scythe to the root of her tree in the very season of its blossoming.

Uranus in Leo

There is a particular sympathy between Uranus and Leo, not only because of the cherubic quality of the sign, but because it is a Solar sign, and Uranus is the secret generative force by which we call the Sun Father. Leo, too, by the Yetziratic[151] attribution of the Qabalists, is a snake as well as a lion, and the magical image of his first decanate is a crowned lion with the body of a snake. Now Uranus himself combines very closely the force of these two animals. Fierceness and subtlety alternate in his mode of action; he is weighty in his onset and yet dangerously sudden; he is the giver of life and death. In fact, it is through Uranus that we are led to recognise the extremely close correspondence between Leo and Scorpio. One is the Lion, the other the Eagle, of the alchemistic philosophy; both possess the secret nature of the snake; and in their evil and averse aspect one is Cerberus and the other the Black Dragon of Putrefaction. Those versed in alchemy will behold and wonder at the beauty and lucidity of this symbolism.

There is however one serious drawback to this position of Uranus; this, that the very sympathy with the secret part of the Solar force creates a danger. Apollo is called 'creator and destroyer'; the Lingam[152] is addressed by the Greeks as 'all-begetter, all-devourer' and this force is now seen to be concentrated in Uranus. And unless the Sun in any male horoscope be reasonably well-dignified there is no danger to the life of the native. Now the presence of Uranus in the

151. Yetzirah (the World of Formation), the name given by the Qabalists to the astral plane.

152. Lingam, the phallus, an emblem of the god Shiva, a form of adamantine, or 'diamond', consciousness.

house of the Sun is itself an affliction of the Sun, on the material plane, and so we must have Sol well-dignified in other ways or the native is liable to die before the occult power of the planet has time to manifest.

There is accordingly a great paucity of examples of the thesis which we have put forward as to its natural action when isolated; since from the nature of the case, such isolation is rather rare. Shelley is our one great exemplification; and his case is fortunately very perfect. We see the revolutionary influence at work in Greatheart;[153] the rebel against the fetters that bind humanity, overflowing with solar force and love, blazes on high, melting the cold passions of age and experience with his flaming jets of white-hot vapour of gold. Such works as *Prometheus Unbound* and *The World's Tragedy*[154] are pure Uranus in Leo. Shelley was saved from early death through illness by the conjunction of the Sun and Venus; six degrees from Uranus Sagittarius is rising and its lord Jupiter is in conjunction with Mars and Neptune. Unfortunately, Uranus being in the eighth house, a violent death was indicated. However, he had done his work; he had sown a new seed in the field of humanity, one of the most fruitful ever planted.

Another case of the most promising talent cut short is Edward VI,[155] admittedly the most accomplished scholar of his period. At an age when most boys are still struggling with the elements of Latin, he spoke fluently not only that comparatively easy language, but also Greek and Hebrew. Here again, however, the Sun is only seven degrees from the square of Uranus, and is himself squared within one degree by the Moon. The lord of the Ascendant Virgo, Mercury, is squared by Mars again within one degree. With such aspects it

153. Shelley did not write a poem called 'Greatheart'. There is a poem of that title by Kipling, written on the death in 1919 of Theodore Roosevelt. Great-Heart is a character in Bunyan's *Pilgrim's Progress.*

154. Crowley also wrote a book with this title, published in Paris in 1910. 'Privately printed for circulation in free countries. Copies must not be imported into England or America.'

155. Edward VI, only son of Henry VIII, reigned from 1547 to 1553.

was impossible for the promise of youth to be redeemed by the achievement of age.

Another superb example of the seductive, fascinating temperament given by Uranus in Leo is that of Mary Queen of Scots, as she stands out from all other queens for beauty and tragedy,[156] not because these were so much greater than the others, but on account of the temperament itself, which has the faculty of inspiring the most amazing extremes of attraction and repulsion. There is never anything half-hearted about the feeling with which such people are regarded. With Shelley, half the world made him Apollo incarnate; the rest thought, and even wrote, that he was in sober truth not a man at all, but a devil sent specially from hell to plague humanity. So with Mary Queen of Scots. She had Taurus rising and Venus in semi-sextile to the Moon, Sol is trine to Uranus; but being in the eighth house, a violent death was presaged as soon as the direction permitted, which duly came to pass.

Rather similar is the case of Cleo de Mérode,[157] whose fascination may be held to match that of the unhappy Stuart. It has the same serpentine quality. Here Pisces is rising and its lord Jupiter is culminating. The life is made secure by the trine of Mars to the Moon, and there is no incompatibility anywhere to hurt the native.

Another example of the fascination, this time in a man, is Winston Churchill, the one really attractive personality in English politics. At an age when most men, even if they start with his advantages of birth and wealth, are just taking their seat for the first time in Parliament, he was a Cabinet Minister, holding the most responsible portfolios. Scorpio is rising, a most harmonious circumstance and Sol is in the Ascendant, sextile to Saturn, so that the life is protected. However, Uranus is rather near the cusp of the tenth house and a sudden fall, such as took place in 1915, was only to be expected.[158]

156. She was executed in 1587.

157. Belgian courtesan, flourished about 1900, a friend of Edward VII. She held court at the famous Paris restaurant, Maxime's.

158. Crowley did not see, in Churchill's chart, his later rise to unheard of heights.

Sometimes the temperament of Uranus in Leo confers unique powers in some obscure direction. One may instance Datas[159] with Cancer rising, the sign of memory and the Moon in opposition to Uranus, limiting the mental powers to this peculiar faculty of remembering dates.

Like him is Houdini[160] with unequalled dexterity in one very small and unusual accomplishment. The square of Mars to Uranus indicates the special line in which the temperament is displayed. A third case is Pélissier[161] who scored no special success until he did something original and unique, producing a new form of entertainment. Here Leo is rising, Uranus in the twelfth house squared by the Sun. Hence the success was sudden and all too short.

Our last example is George Edalji.[162] Here Scorpio is rising and Uranus too near the cusp of the tenth house to be pleasant, especially as Mercury is in exact opposition to him. An exact semi-sextile of Venus to Sol saves the life and Mars the ruler is in his own house. But there is no great help to the career and therefore we need not be surprised at the tragedy of the life. If he was guilty, we may consider that the Uranus in Leo position conferred dexterity in crime almost unparalleled in history; and the nature of the crime is very characteristic. But in any event, the fascination of the personality is evident; for his case excited the continuous interest of many of England's leading publicists, so much so that ultimately not only his pardon but his reinstatement as a solicitor was obtained from the King.

Uranus in Virgo

So earthy, mercurial, passive a sign as Virgo can have little in common with the fire and activity of Uranus. Sometimes the

159. William Bottle, 'The Memory Man', born 1875, died after 1938.

160. American entertainer and escapologist, born in Appleton, Wisconsin in 1873. His forte was escaping from locked chambers. Keenly interested in psychical phenomena, he was so adept at creating them that he was hailed by spiritualists as a medium, despite his own protestations.

161. Harry Pélissier, actor and theatrical manager, founder of *The Follies*, first husband of Fay Compton, the actress. He died in 1913, aged 39.

162. See note 82.

influence, as in the case of Cancer, becomes harmonised and fixed; but this will only be in special cases. For the most part the temperament will be meanly marked; one is likely to find eccentricity and mental instability, and it is improbable that any great driving force will be developed.

However, there is the case of Balzac, presumably the greatest novelist that ever lived. Here Leo is rising, and Uranus, though just within the second house, has no planet between him and the horizon. The Sun, lord of the Ascendant, is in conjunction with Jupiter in the tenth house. There is no lack of harmony between the personality and the temperament, except for the mercurial touch given by Virgo, which made the master personally very eccentric in manner and somewhat unaccountable in his actions; at least, so it appeared to the majority of his contemporaries.

A person of great learning was Pico de Mirandola.[163] Here Libra is rising, and Uranus is in opposition to Sol. This gave him a love for obscure branches of knowledge; the temperament, although bound to study by its mercurial side, was further limited by opposition.

Mercury having much to do with the minor, executant, sort of music, it may be that the temperament turns in this direction. We have the pianist Wilhelm Backhaus, and the violinist Maud MacCarthy with this position. Each excellent technically, lacks any creative power such as we see in great composers.

With Brigham Young,[164] however, Uranus is rising just within the second house in exact sextile to Mars and within 4 degrees of the conjunction of Jupiter. Mercury the lord is in close conjunction with Sol. This combination gives that tremendous energy and ability which he had, and which the mere position of Uranus would have denied him.

Far more characteristic of the isolated action is Miss Lind-af-Hageby,[165] with five planets in Virgo, and Libra

163. See note 42.

164. See note 44.

165. Emilie Augusta Louise Lind-af-Hageby was born in 1878 in Sweden and became British by naturalisation. She was an anti-vivisectionist, a women's liberation champion, and author of many books on humanitarian subjects.

rising. Venus, the lady of the Ascendant, is less than seven degrees from the conjunction of Uranus. The temperament and personality are therefore united, but Virgo has full sway, and so the character is somewhat cold, sexless, and logical. A trine of Jupiter and Sol give enthusiasm, but this lies within the arid plains of knowledge. Despite its humanitarian object, one feels nothing very human in the work.

The influence of Virgo at its worst is seen in Miss Violet Charlesworth,[166] of the imaginary motor-car accident and scarlet cloak and momentary music-hall engagement notoriety. Here Mercury appears as the boyish trickster; and Uranus makes the trick fantastic and explosive.

This sort of thing is much more to be expected from the Uranus in Virgo of the ordinary person, than anything of a constructive, creative, or even emancipatory or revolutionary character.

Uranus in Libra

Owing to the exaltation of Saturn in the house of Venus, there is something sinister and subtle about the sign of Libra. Its own nature too, is the balance; and when that balance is upset by such a flaming sword as Uranus being cast into the scale, we may expect very astonishing results. Where Venus is afflicted and Saturn strong, we shall find that the influence is often excessively dangerous; but good dispositions and dignities of Venus, and an harmonious rising sign and happy aspects to Uranus himself, may bring about the development of the most useful forces. The freedom of Libra, an airy sign, will give play to the impulses of Uranus; in fact, one might almost say that he is never more himself than when he is in this sign.

Taking first some rather unfortunate examples, let us consider the nativity of Joseph Smith.[167] Note, however, that it only appears unfortunate to us insofar as we may happen not to be mormons, and we must recognise even those forces of genius with which we are not in sympathy. It will, however, be lawful for us as astrologers to give planetary reasons for thinking this prophet to have been mistaken. At

166. A well-known soubrette of the day.
167. See note 33.

his birth Cancer was rising, a very proper sign for the reception of inspired knowledge; unhappily, Luna, close to Mercury, is in exact opposition to the cusp of the Ascendant, in her detriment, and square to Uranus, which is conjoined with Saturn. Libra itself is not very harmonious with Cancer, and though there is much power developed, such power is bound to work in a disordered manner. There is no help from the bright planets, Sol, Jupiter or Venus, and so the operation of the temperament issues in the putting forth of the most unreadable books ever written, dull, stupid, disconnected and pointless, for the records of truth.

There is much tragedy in the horoscope of James II[168] of England. Here Uranus is in the third house, with a sextile of Luna and a semi-sextile of Sol, but squared by Jupiter. Sol is Lord of the Ascendant, Leo, but he is in Scorpio; and Mars is rising in his own, the third, decanate of Leo, which represents unsuccessful struggle. Uranus, too, is in the third house, so that the mentality is eccentric. The whole outlook was gloomy in the extreme, and it is easy to predict an increasing tension, due to tactlessness and ill-temper, qualities which indeed cost him his throne.

Contrast these positions with those of Louis XIV, 'le grand monarque'. Here Scorpio is rising, its lord Mars sextile to Uranus. Instantly we perceive a harmony of temperament, of the ambitious type, not very amiable, perhaps, but singularly strong and without inhibitions. The reign of such a monarch could not but be successful, as the world judges success.

A case of great misfortune is the Crown Prince of Portugal, shot, with his father, in Lisbon some years ago.[169]

Here Uranus on the cusp of the twelfth house, opposed by Mars in Aries and squared by Saturn in his detriment, Sol and Mercury going to the conjunction of Mars, could only mean violent death. The temperamental quality bestowed by the position of Uranus is therefore masked by his direct malefic action on the material plane.

168. See note 187.

169. Luiz Felipe who was assassinated with his father, Dom Carlos, in 1908. His younger brother, Dom Manoel, ascended the throne. In 1910, Portugal became a republic and Dom Manoel settled in Richmond, Surrey.

The severe quality of the vision of Dürer is determined by the conjunction made by Saturn with his Sun, Lord of Leo, the Ascendant. Uranus is in the third house, making possible such pictures as 'The Astrologer' and 'The Four Witches'. But there is a strong friendship between Leo and Libra, and the temperament is a most musical symphony of these signs and planets.

A more Venusian type of artist is Sir Joshua Reynolds.[170] Here Virgo is rising, but in 29 degrees, so that Libra occupies almost the whole Ascendant. It is therefore to be taken that his influence is singularly free from admixture. A sextile of Jupiter and Saturn to Uranus lends him exceptional force, and it is to be noted that Sol, Venus, Mercury and Luna are all in the tenth house, and thus bear rule over the entire figure. It may be remarked here that when there is any dispute, so to say, among the other planets, the tenth house assumes primary importance.

In literature we have a figure analogous to that of Reynolds in painting: Sir E. Bulwer-Lytton.[171] Here Cancer is rising, causing him to prefer antiquity to modern times, to write historical novels rather than modern, and even when he wrote of modern times, as in *A Strange Story*, to introduce the ideas of the past and make them more prominent than those of the present. The Moon is on the cusp of the Ascendant, or he might have gone even farther than he did; as it was, his personality was diffuse, his tendency was to play first at magic, next at politics, then at literature. Were Cancer more appropriate to Libra, the result had been happier; but the truth is that nothing goes well without a dash of fire somewhere in its composition. But in any case this dispersion of interests is somewhat characteristic of Libra.

The influence of Uranus in this sign at its best and most judicial is seen in Sir William Hamilton,[172] who may be

170. Sir Joshua Reynolds (1723-1792), founding member and first President of the Royal Academy. He was a prolific protrait painter, a friend of Dr Johnson and a member of the famous dining club which included Gibbon, Burke, Garrick, Sheridan, Goldsmith and others.

171. See note 40.

172. Sir William Hamilton, Bart. (1788-1856), Scottish philosopher whose doctrine of 'natural realism' was attacked by John Stuart Mill.

considered on the whole as one of the six greatest metaphysicians that Britain has ever produced.

Here Gemini is rising, and Mercury is in his own house Virgo in conjunction with Venus. This gave the mental development full play, otherwise Uranus in the fifth house might have caused trouble. The perfect harmony of the two airy signs, and the good dignity of Mercury, allow full play to the better side of Uranus. Hence we find him probing deeply into the most recondite mysteries of existence, and displaying the most even judgment as well as the subtlest power of analysis.

In the case of Petrarch, we find on the other hand that emphasis is to be laid upon the fact that Venus rules Libra, Leo is rising, giving him a large and warm heart, especially as Sol, its ruler, is close under the cusp of the Ascendant, while Mercury, exactly on it, adds keen intellect to the personality. Venus is trine to Uranus, and lends tenderness and beauty to his fierce and passionate rays. Is further explanation needed of the circumstance that he challenges even Dante as the Poet of Love, twin lamps of glory in the darkness of the Middle Ages?

In the horoscope of Erasmus, Uranus is in 9 degrees of Libra, just above the cusp of the Ascendant, while Venus is rising just below it. But Uranus is opposed by Saturn, making the temperament cold; Mercury, too, is ascending, and the Sun is in conjunction with the Moon and Neptune in Scorpio, diminishing his glow. Here then is the great scholar as opposed to the great lover.

A very incarnation of passion is to be found in George Sand,[173] with 27 degrees of Aquarius rising and Saturn sextile to Neptune. The temperature is harmonious enough, and the intellectual side of the woman is clearly indicated by the points given above, but Uranus in the seventh house disordered the marriage relation, especially as he is squared by Sol from the fifth house. These configurations soon became dominant, for by direction Pisces soon became the Ascendant, and Herschel reached the radical place of its lord,

173. George Sand (1804-1876), prolific French romantic novelist whose list of lovers is longer even than the list of her published works. She was an early advocate of women's liberation.

Jupiter. The result is clearly to be traced in her volcanic career.

George Borrow[174] has Uranus exactly rising squared by Sol and Mercury, while Venus, the lady of the Ascendant, is squared by Saturn. This fully accounts for his queer sardonic temperament, its flashes of genius and its strange outbursts of passion.

In the nativity of Victor Hugo,[175] Scorpio was rising with Mars in Aquarius not specially strong, high or well-aspected. Aquarius is friendly to Libra, however, and as after all Mars is within 5 degrees of the trine of Uranus, the personality and temperament go well enough together. In fact, one may conceive that this combination gave the extraordinary power of work which the great poet and novelist possessed.

The cynical voluptuary Sainte-Beuve[176] has Pisces rising and Jupiter in Scorpio in conjunction with Venus, and Neptune, a very apt description of the personality. Uranus has the conjunction of Saturn, squared by Mercury, and there is the temperament, and the tone of his life's work criticism.

Dumas has Leo rising with the Sun just above the horizon, sextile to Uranus. Here again is a splendid harmony and its dominant note is the rich boyish glow always conferred by Leo, unless the Sun be most sorely afflicted, or Saturn present in the sign.

174. George Borrow (1803-1881), linguist, novelist and agent of the British and Foreign Bible Society, author of *The Bible in Spain* and *Romany Rye*. He introduced the gypsies into English literature.

175. Victor Marie Hugo (1802-1885), French poet, novelist, dramatist and leader of the romantic movement in France, was one of the great figures of world literature.

176. Charles-Augustin Sainte-Beuve (1804-1869), French literary critic. 'He is a short, tubby little man, stockily built with a peasant's neck and shoulders, dressed in a simple country manner, rather like Béranger, without any stylish touches. He has a high forehead, a bald white head, large eyes, a long, inquisitive, sensual nose, a wide, crudely shaped mouth, a broad smile which reveals a set of white teeth, prominent cheekbones like a pair of wens: altogether a somewhat batrachian face with a pink, well-fed complexion. To judge by his hale and hearty appearance, his white forehead and his rosy cheeks, one might take him for an intelligent provincial coming out of a library, a cloister of books, under which there was a cellar of rich burgundy' (*Pages from The Goncourt Journal*, tr. Robert Baldick).

Two very successful young ladies on the London stage are Phyllis and Zena Dare,[177] both of whom has Uranus in Libra. The former has Libra rising, Venus on the cusp of the Ascendant trine to Neptune; the latter with Pisces rising, has Jupiter in conjunction with Uranus in the seventh house, that of marriage. The former was more famous than her sister for her personality; the latter married into the British aristocracy.

Uranus in Scorpio

The nature of Uranus is so singularly like that of Scorpio, so far as his less humanitarian and uplifting aspects were concerned, that we may anticipate his presence in this house to be so strong as to dominate the personality, even where that is of an opposite character. The excellence of this position will depend largely upon the aspects of Uranus, more so than in the case of other signs. It has been generally alleged that Uranus has a special affinity for the sign Aquarius, and some innovators have gone so far as to call it his house. To such a position, breaking up as it does the entire septenary system of correspondences, it is impossible to assent. Neptune and Uranus represent forces far beyond the plane on which that system operates; and it is useless to destroy the old unless the new is demonstrably better. We prefer to assign Uranus to all the Cherubic signs, Neptune to all the passive signs, while the *primum mobile* may be properly considered to rule over the Cardinal signs. By this method, we not only retain the septenary system but complete it by assimilating it to the Qabalistic tenfold system of the Tree of Life, without the smallest disturbance. We retain the twelvefold Zodiac, and the attributions of the Tarot, and a thousand other systems which are irrevocably interlocked with these; and we remain in perfect communion with the thought of the Ancients. This appears a wiser and more rational course than to exhibit our ignorance of the necessity of the septenary in order to show off our knowledge about Uranus.

177. Phyllis and Zena Dare, distinguished actresses, born 1890 and 1887 respectively.

To return, Aquarius is in any case a sign interchangeable with Scorpio; the eagle of Scorpio is the water cherub, and the man of Aquarius the air cherub. We also see the intermixture of air and water in the attributions of the Pentagram,[178] and in an hundred other ways, all methods of Truth which conceal important mysteries.

Let it not be a reproach, therefore, if we emphasise strongly the affinity of Uranus to Scorpio.

With some aspects, the scientific inquiring side of Scorpio will be brought out very strongly, with others the treacherous subtle-witted function of that mysterious sign, while in a third group we may find sensuality and passion most deeply marked.

To begin with men of science and philosophy, we have three emancipating intelligences of the highest order; Copernicus, Newton and Immanuel Kant.

The first of these great men, has Virgo rising, with Mercury in the ninth house trined by Luna and only 8 degrees from the trine of Mars. Uranus is in the third house near the conjunction of Neptune, and is trined by Saturn. It is impossible to imagine a more perfectly harmonious disposition of the planets for intellectual and scientific eminence.

Sir Isaac Newton had Libra rising, giving the balanced judgment so requisite in scientific investigation and Uranus himself is within the Ascendant, and is trined by Jupiter in his own house Pisces, Jupiter himself being only 6 degrees from the conjunction of Saturn. Here the interest is somewhat broader than in the previous example; on the whole, the difference well describes the larger aspects taken by Newton's investigation.

In the horoscope of Kant we find Taurus rising but in 29 degrees, so that most of the Ascendant is occupied by Gemini. Mercury, its lord, is in exact conjunction with the

178. The five-pointed star of magic. It is used in the ritual invocation of spirits and forces, each point of the star being assigned to these realms: (from the topmost point in clock-wise direction) the realm of pure spirit, attributed to the Sun; the sphere of Scorpio, attributed to the element water; the sphere of Leo, attributed to fire; the sphere of Taurus, attributed to earth; the sphere of Aquarius, attributed to air.

Sun, and these are trined by Luna in Virgo. It forms an admirable picture of the pure intelligence, introspective, philosophical and metaphysical.

More of the revolutionary phase of Uranus is found in the nativities of Gladstone and John Bright.[179] The former has Capricornus rising and Saturn is conjoined with Neptune, with 2 degrees, and with Venus within 9 degrees. It is easy to see that the interest must be mainly human and political, for Jupiter trines this conjunction and is in Aries, near the cusp of the third house.

The temperament is not very harmonious with the personality in this case, though both are powerful; and in this dividuality we see the possibility of trouble. In fact, we note that his career was tumultuous, and that he would suddenly reverse his policy in an arbitrary and, as some thought, unwarrantable manner.

The career of John Bright, not so astoundingly successful or so tempestuous, was yet simpler and clearer. Here Cancer was rising, the Moon conjoined with Venus, close to Neptune and Uranus is in conjunction with the Sun. Cancer and Scorpio being friendly signs, the man was always himself and attained the highest reputation for suavity and for integrity.

We might also pair Dickens and Tennyson. The former has Uranus rising in Scorpio sextile to Mercury. Mars is squared by Saturn and this makes the temperament stronger than the personality. Hence the man's work was more important than himself.

Tennyson, with Gemini rising, was of a coldly intellectual and rather priggish type, Mercury suffering severely from the square of Jupiter. Uranus, too, is in conjunction with Mars. Venus is rising, sextile to Jupiter, which is in the eleventh, and so it is easy to understand that this is more important than either the personality or the temperament. The fame of Tennyson was due to his adroitness in pleasing his sovereign, rather than to any quality inherent in himself or in his poetry.

Another Victorian was Sir Isaac Pitman,[180] with Libra

179. British radical statesman and orator, born 1811, died 1889.

180. Sir Isaac Pitman (1813-1896), English educationalist, and inventor of a shorthand system which bears his name.

rising, Venus is not specially strong in any way, but it is on the cusp of the third house, within which is Mercury. The inventive genius, therefore turns naturally to developing ease in matters connected with writing, in other words, to the construction of the system of shorthand which is associated with his name.

Before we proceed to the domain of art, let us look for a moment at the nativity of Caesar Borgia.[181] Virgo is rising, with Mercury on the cusp of the Ascendant, giving a cold, shrewd, nature. Uranus, on the cusp of the third house, gives a somewhat horrible turn to the mind, for he is squared by the moon. Mars and Saturn being in conjunction with Leo, we can figure to ourselves the icy, violent, unscrupulous, qualities of the man, while the Sun rising sextile to them assumes ambition, and success in attaining it.

In art, we have a brilliant trio of musicians, Wagner, Chopin and Schumann. Schumann has Capricornus rising, Saturn and Neptune semi-sextile to Uranus, near the square of a conjunction of Mars and Sol. There is no great warmth in any part of this disposition, but there is no lack of harmony, except in the signs themselves; though one may urge that they are at least both cold. It well describes his music.

Wagner has Gemini rising, which accounts for the literary quality in his work; even in his operas this is the case; the *leit-motif* is literature, not music. But he was a voluminous writer on all sorts of subjects. Mercury is square to an opposition of Mars and Jupiter which explains the violent and brilliant qualities of the man. Uranus is squared by Venus, and the whole figure represents strife and turmoil. Venus close above the eastern horizon in her own house, in conjunction with Sol and sextile to Jupiter is on the whole the most important feature in the figure. It gives the intense humanity, the great dramatic and artistic feeling, especially for pictorial effect for Wagner's music has always a visual value, and it assures success.

Chopin is far more like Schumann. Virgo is rising, the Moon about to rise. Mercury sextile to Jupiter is otherwise not very strong. Saturn and Neptune are sextile to Luna; it is

181. See note 96.

another example of the cold, dreamy melancholy temperament, especially as Uranus is in the third house.

More like Wagner, in another line, is Michael Angelo. Here Pisces is rising, Mercury and Venus conjoined on the cusp, with Sol not far below them. They are trine to Uranus and Luna. Pisces and Scorpio are friendly; it is the ideal harmony of nature which permits a man to turn out apparently unlimited quantities of the finest work.

For a final example, Alfred de Musset[182] offers himself as a contrast. Here Aquarius is rising, Saturn in conjunction with Sol and Mercury in the tenth house, with Neptune only 9 degrees away. The personality goes well with the temperament, though Venus being in Capricornus, her hated house, and Jupiter close to the opposition of Uranus, the whole make-up is bound to be of cynicism and disappointment. The square of Mars and Venus adds some violence of passion; but this is not well regulated. In spite of brilliancy of talent, even genius, in spite of great achievement, one can only rank him sadly with those who are not quite immortals.

Uranus in Sagittarius

In the sign of Sagittarius lies much of the nature of the horse and of the deer, timid, delicate, proud, courageous and swift. Only the suddenness of its action in any way resemble our typical Uranus force; but the sign itself, if Jupiter be happily aspected, may have much power to overcome much that seems hard and coarse and cold in the planet. Cold, say we, for the cruelty of Uranus is calculated and deliberate, the cause of a joy no less sinister than divine, while that of Mars is the hot cruelty of far more 'human' passion. But Sagittarius never fails to give liveliness to the temperament; it is as Celtic an Ascendant as Leo or Pisces, more so, in fact, than the latter; thus we find in him what one might humorously call a 'reformed' Uranus, etherealised, sublimised. But of course, as before, bad aspects and an inharmonious Ascendant will weaken and corrupt these qualities. For example the horoscope of Queen Victoria shows arrogance and petulance, impatience of contradiction. Gemini is rising, a totally

182. See note 36.

opposed sign, and Neptune is within 5 degrees of Uranus in the seventh house. Saturn squares them, but fortunately Venus is trine; else had the situation been hopeless. It just supplied the missing element of fact. Mercury is in the twelfth house, and not particularly strong, undoubtedly temperament plays a much larger part than personality.

George Eliot has Scorpio in the Ascendant, and Sol, Venus, Mercury, Uranus and Neptune are all in the east, not far below the horizon. Mars is in Leo, trine to Venus, but opposed by Jupiter. The result is naturally a highly confused mass, for which no single true resultant emerges; a stormy life, and a mixed career of joy, sorrow, failure, and triumph are effects of this complicated chain of causes. Naturally, on such a sky no eternal repose, starry, can shine; the native was bound to be submitted in the end.

Sir Richard Quain[183] is an example of the contrary, a placid and successful career, with no great wealth of dramatic incident.

Here Leo rises, and Sol is between Mars and Jupiter, within 18 degrees all told. Venus is exactly semi-sextile to him and approaching Uranus which is in the fifth house. Here there is nothing very important; but what there is, is pleasant. There is no obstacle to overcome.

Now let us consider the horoscope of Shakespeare, with Virgo rising. Mercury is in Aries, and has no notable aspects, though it is within 6 degrees of the trine of Uranus. There is no planet ascending; Uranus is in the fifth in opposition to Neptune, a world-shaking aspect; Venus is with Neptune within 5 degrees, and sextile to a conjunction of Saturn and Jupiter. Here then we see a tremendous temperament, and a negligible personality; and we find this diagnosis confirmed by a study of Mr Frank Harris' admirable book on the subject.[184]

Another master-mind was that of Herbert Spencer.[185] Uranus is on the exact cusp of the Ascendant, 28 degrees of

183. British physician, author of *A Dictionary of Medicine*, 1882.

184. *The Tragic Life-History of the Man William Shakespeare*, 1910. It received a long and laudatory review by Crowley in *The Equinox*, vol. 1, no. 3.

185. See note 27.

Sagittarius, and Neptune is rising only 2½ degrees below him, again a tremendous aspect. Hence the epoch-making character of his philosophy. The man himself was retiring. Jupiter in Pisces softened by the square of Venus – and there is no conflict of any kind indicated; the work was everything.

Bismarck, again, has the lord of his Ascendant (Leo) squared by Luna and very near the trine of Uranus; here is again excellent harmony, save that the Moon gives some brusquerie. On the whole, it is a disposition likely to afford the best results, from the standpoint of a career.

Still more earth-shaking is the colossus Luther. Leo is rising once more, but Sol, Saturn and Mercury are in conjunction of Venus, Mars and Jupiter. Thus both personality and temperament are tremendously strong and harmonious with the other. The result we know.

A far calmer figure is that of Cornelius Agrippa.[186] Virgo is rising, and Mercury in the second house, not specially strong. Uranus is near the square of the Sun and within 9 degrees of the opposition of Mars. But there is nothing fulminating in the figure, and so we have scholarship and deep thought without any further manifestation than the acquisition of a great and not very well-deserved reputation as a magician, and some books rather curious than revolutionary.

Ruskin is a very difficult person. He has the critical Aquarius rising with Sol close to the cusp – temporary success, no more. Uranus is squared by Saturn so that his ideas were foolish, and Luna and Mars close to Mercury are in opposition, making him quarrelsome and weak, violent and obstinate, but without clear vision. A lamentable wreck of good material! Of course, the obvious incompatibility of Sagittarius and Aquarius will already have occurred to the reader. An interesting example of temperament is seen in Nell Gwynn, with Capricornus rising, and Uranus exactly conjoined with Neptune on the cusp of the eleventh house. Here is a tremendous force to work through friendship, as she did,

186. Henry Cornelius Agrippa (1486-1535), Counsellor to the Holy Roman Emperor Charles V, and author of the celebrated three books of *Occult Philosophy and Magic*, which were translated into English and published in London in 1651.

and as the Lord of the Ascendant, Saturn, is trine to Sol, she had the force of character to make use of it.

William III[187] of England has Luna rising in Leo, trine to Mercury, with Sol in conjunction with Jupiter. Uranus and Neptune are exactly conjoined – this, by the way, often stands for Great Opportunity – and the whole figure is very favourable, so that, from a petty princeling, he became the King of England. Mars is square to the Neptune-Uranus position; no effort of his own was necessary to his success.

The Tsar Alexander II[188] is a very remarkable type. Once again Leo is rising, and Sol is trine to Jupiter, sextile to Mars, the two latter planets being in opposition. Saturn, too, is sextile to the Sun. On the other hand, Uranus receives no great help from any quarter. Hence the personality of the man was strong and courageous, but he was brought to ruin by his work. However, he did at least achieve it, and if he could not control the storm that he aroused, who shall blame him, since the tempest-blast that overturned his bark was the breath of Liberty.

Uranus in Capricornus

It is very pleasant to the astrologer when those rare occasions arise on which he can sum up the potentialities of any force in one succint phrase. Such an occasion is here. The explosive force of Uranus counteracts completely all that there may be of sluggish Saturn in Capricornus; and we get 'an he-goat also, against whom there is no rising up'.[189] The man with Uranus thus placed is, in Kipling's phrase, 'a first-class fighting man'. The examples of this are so convincing that they need only to be announced. The power evoked is so great that no troubles with the personality appear to daunt it, unless they are extraordinarily evil. The magical will of the man, his mission

187. William III (1650-1702) a Protestant Dutchman invited by the English to replace the Catholic James II. He landed at Brixham in 1688 with a large army and was crowned the next year. He married James' sister, Mary, with whom he ruled as joint sovereign.

188. Alexander II (1818-1881), emperor of Russia, liberator of the serfs. While out driving in St Petersburg, he was killed by bombs thrown by nihilists who called themselves the 'People's Will'.

189. See *The Book of Lies* by Aleister Crowley.

in the world, are everything to him.

We have, to begin with, the poet Baudelaire, who despite all persecutions, revolutionised French thought, and by adopting Swinburne as his spiritual first-born son,[190] revolutionised English thought as well; we have Louis Pasteur, who revolutionised surgery in the teeth of the deadliest opposition; Huxley, who battled for science against orthodox religion, the most Homeric and spectacular combat of the Victorian period; Wallace one of his principal colleagues in the fight; Kruger, who broke the power of the British Empire, and staggered humanity by the dour fight that his handful of burglars put up against the overwhelming hosts of the oppressor; Grant who smashed Lee; Cicero, who smashed everybody in sight, from Catiline to Varro; Burton, the most desperate fighter in private and in public life, that England ever bore;[191] and Tolstoy, who went out into the snow of a Russian winter, to die in a wayside railway station, so bitter, even in extreme old age with the hand of death upon his shoulder, was his hatred of 'home' and 'comfort' and the normal life of man.

Then we have Rosa Bonheur,[192] whose life was one long battle against her own femininity; and finally George III (whom we must have regarded merely as a symbol of the race which he ruled) who broke with dogged courage and endurance the power of the great Napoleon. But even in himself we can see the fighting quality; it was his obstinate bull-dog stupidity that lost to his crown these United States of America.

Uranus in Aquarius

In this sign Uranus appears most clearly as the emancipator. Aquarius is the sign of the Man Cherub, not so spiritual as the Eagle, but with the clear light of reason luminous in his eyes.

Nor is it without significance in this connection that the Tarot trump corresponding to Aquarius is 'Hope'.[193]

190. The French poet Charles Baudelaire 'adopted' the English poet in a metaphorical sense.

191. A hint at Sir Richard Burton's bi-sexuality and open curiosity in all sexual matters, unusual in a Victorian. See note 35.

192. See note 76.

However, the sign is too harmonious to the planet to produce the great emancipator every time. It requires some special excitement before it becomes operative in its fullest extent, and it is rendered commonplace by an easy going personality.

Thus in the cases of the Emperor Maximilian,[194] and of Lords Roberts and Wolseley,[195] we find no marked humanitarian or revolutionary impulse. Roberts has Pisces rising, with Jupiter just under the cusp, in opposition to Saturn and Mercury. Uranus is 'in prison' just within the twelfth house, with no help anywhere. There is therefore nothing sufficient to arouse those deeper and stronger spiritual forces to which we have learned to look for the revolutionary ideas which sway mankind.

Wolseley has Aquarius rising with Saturn in Virgo not particularly strong. Uranus is near the cusp of the Ascendant, giving him the peculiar personality, which, harmonising so well with the temperament, brought him so much honour, as it was close to the sextile of Jupiter. Once again, however, there is no deeper force at work; the career was conventional.

The unhappy Emperor Maximilian of Mexico is an example of feebleness and lack of unity. Sol and Mercury were rising in Cancer; but the Moon is in Nadir, in opposition to Mars; Uranus, too, receives no help; it is a fine illustration of how mere good fortune, unaided by personal strength, fails to keep a man from mischief.

There are two humorists with this position, Du Maurier,[196] very shallow, and Lewis Carroll, very deep. The

193. Some years after writing this sentence, Crowley revised his ideas about the Tarot. The trump he here calls 'Hope' was, in the light of his researches, renamed 'The Star'. See his *The Book of Thoth*, 1944.

194. The ill-fated emperor of Mexico, brother of the Austrian Franz Joseph. French troops kept him on his throne. When they were withdrawn, the country was invaded by Juarez who captured and shot him in 1867.

195. Garnet Joseph Wolseley, 1st Viscount Wolseley (1833-1913), British field-marshal, Commander-in-Chief of the British Army. For Lord Roberts see note 38.

196. George du Maurier (1834-1896), British illustrator, caricaturist, and author of three successful autobiographical novels, the most famous of which was *Trilby*.

former has Uranus on the cusp of the Ascendant, with nothing better than a semi-sextile of Luna to assist him; Saturn is in opposition to Mercury. It is a feeble display.

The latter, on the other hand, has Sagittarius rising, and Jupiter is close to Uranus near the cusp of the third house. He has benefit of a semi-sextile of Neptune – here is the subtle yet sacred character of the humour – while Venus and Mars rising in conjunction, lend passion and power to the personality. Sol, too, is only 8 degrees from Uranus. A most fortunate figure, on the whole, but at the same time, nothing revolutionary to be found in it.

President Garfield[197] has Virgo rising, with Mercury not very strong but in the third house. Jupiter is in conjunction with Uranus; Saturn has just risen. There is evidence here of a clever, even, nature, likely to move harmoniously enough, but without that quality which overturns faiths and empires.

General Gordon[198] is a wilder type. Aries is rising, with Mars sextile to Jupiter. Uranus is 10 degrees only from Sol well above the eastern horizon. One can understand the impetuous and romantic and adventurous disposition; and there are also indications of great emancipatory ideas. But there is hardly sufficient force to carry them out. Uranus being in the twelfth house, is hampered sorely.

Compare with this the nativity of Joan of Arc. Scorpio is rising, and Mars is semi-sextile to Jupiter, and trine to Saturn, and trine to Venus. Here is an all-conquering personality; Uranus giving the revolutionary idea, is content with his achievement and the work is carried out by the ego. Hence, to some extent its instability.

Consider a true empire-builder, Franz Josef of Austria,[199] who, from a congeries of races who detested each other

197. James Abram Garfield (1831-1881), the 20th President of the United States, elected in March 1881, and assassinated in July.

198. Charles George Gordon (1833-1885), known as 'Chinese Gordon', made his name by leading the Imperial Chinese Army which suppressed the Taiping Rebellion, 1860. He was killed in Khartoum in the Sudan during a revolt led by the Mahdi which he had been sent to suppress.

199. See note 71.

mutually, made a nation strong enough to bear the shock of the greatest war in history.

Libra is rising, giving the even judgment and sound balance necessary for any such work, and Venus has the semi-sextile of a conjunction of Sol, Luna and Saturn. She is opposed by Neptune, which led to certain set-backs, but failed to inflict permanent injury. Uranus, too, has the sextile of Mars. It is the great strength of Venus (in her beloved sign Cancer) situated in the tenth house that gives all its great political future to this figure.

A very different type of emancipation is Goethe, with Scorpio rising, and Mars exacted in Capricornus, trine to Mercury and Sol. Uranus has the square of Saturn, which is on the cusp of the Ascendant.

It is a magnificently harmonious picture, and a great one; for with such a sign rising, and such large planets involved, there must always be big things on the carpet.

With this compare Rossetti, a very similar mind, but less original and less cosmic. Gemini is rising, Mercury with Luna in the twelfth house, sextile to Venus and to Uranus. Venus is trine to Jupiter. All this is as harmonious as Goethe's figure, but not nearly so big. The forces involved are all conventional and commonplace.

Another great mind was that of H.P. Blavatsky,[200] with Cancer rising and the Moon trine to the conjunction of Jupiter and Uranus. Sol is in the Ascendant giving success. But the other combination gives the real force of the character, the dreaminess, the religious impulse and the occult impulse all working together.

Her chief of staff, Colonel Olcott,[201] has a much more

200. Helena Petrovna Blavatsky (1831-1891), the leading occultist of her day. She founded (with Colonel Olcott) the Theosophical Society in 1875. In spite of the fun that Crowley poked at her, he regarded her as a high adept of the grade of Master of the Temple, and her greatest work, *The Secret Doctrine*, as part of the foundation of his own magical system.

201. 'He [Solov'yov] describes the Colonel as a man fully fifty years of age, of medium height, thickly built and broad, but not stout. There was a large bald patch in the usual place on his head, but his face, framed in a magnificent silver beard, was handsome and pleasant. Moreover, his energy and the liveliness of his movements showed that

idealistic temperament, but lacks the explosive force. Libra is rising, and Venus is conjoined with Sol; but the square of Mars makes these less effective than they might have been without it; Uranus, too, is in opposition to the Sun. Naturally with such a figure, one should anticipate but second-rate qualities. The trine of Mars and Saturn makes them efficient, such as they are; he did his work right well.

The great sage and mystic of antiquity, Proclus,[202] the neoplatonist, has this position. Here Uranus is in conjunction with Sol and Venus, Saturn and Jupiter are square to them. Aries is rising, Mars exalted in Capricornus. Here once more is the double gift of the gods, the preoccupation with great things and the power to execute them.

Melanchthon,[203] the friend of Luther, is a milder figure. Virgo is rising, Mercury not very strong. Uranus has the sextile of Mars and Jupiter; but it takes a great deal to pull up a weak Mercury when Virgo is rising. He was all very well in his place, like Olcott with H.P. Blavatsky, but alone he would never have set the Rhine afire.

Our last example is the unhappy Chatterton.[204] Here Uranus is in 29½ degrees of Aquarius, so that one is tempted

---

he was far from being an old man, a description which Solov'yov caps by asserting that the Colonel possessed great strength and sound health. He wore glasses which, to some extent, concealed the sole defect in his appearance, a defect which Solov'yov, quoting a Russian phrase, calls a spoonful of tar in a barrel of honey. "One of his eyes was extremely disobedient and would turn in all directions, sometimes with a startling and very unpleasant speed. As long as the disobedient eye remained still, you had before you a handsome, pleasant and kindly, but not especially clever man, whose appearance aroused your sympathy and inspired your confidence. Then suddenly something twitched, the eye tore itself from its place and darted off suspiciously and knavishly, and confidence immediately vanished." ' See *Madame Blavatsky* by John Symonds, 1959.

202. Neoplatonist philosopher of the fifth century A.D.

203. Philip Melanchthon (1497-1560), Professor of Greek at Wittenberg, helped Luther translate the Bible and adopted his theological views.

204. Thomas Chatterton (1752-1770), poet. He poisoned himself with arsenic and opium after three days' starvation and was buried in the paupers' pit of Shoe Lane workhouse. His collected works in three volumes were edited by Southey and Cottle in 1803.

to relegate him to the next section, Cancer is rising, the Moon imprisoned in the twelfth, Uranus squared exactly by Sol, and not much assisted by being within 10 degrees of the trine of Mars. Luna has a sextile of Jupiter, and no other aid of importance. It is all feeble in the extreme.

Uranus in Pisces

On the surface, there is not much sympathy between this planet and this sign. The only point which they seem to have in common is the suddenness; but the suddenness of Pisces is that of the will-of-the-wisp, a better word might be elusiveness. Pisces is an exceptionally receptive sign – there is no driving force in it. It is the precise antithesis to the aggressiveness of Uranus. There is, of course, a great deal of subtlety in Pisces, but this is a different kind of quality to the secretiveness of Uranus. We shall consequently not expect to find very many men of the first-class with this position of Uranus. Occasionally, the dispositions of the planets may be such that it is completely dissolved in, and its influence spread throughout, the sign, and where this occurs there will be an extension of the occult influence of Uranus in the psychic *menstruum*[205] of Pisces. There is fortunately one example of this in its perfection – William Blake.

Here Cancer is rising with the lower edge of the Moon touching the cusp of the Ascendant, semi-sextile to Neptune and trine to Uranus, but in opposition to Venus, which is sextile to Uranus. We have often pointed out that the opposition of two planets is very much mitigated by the presence of a third, trine to one and sextile to the other. The personality is therefore extremely well suited to the temperament. The general influence is, of course, watery; and Uranus being in the ninth house, it is only natural that religion, and particularly that extremely personal and true religion which takes the form of direct vision, should be the key-note of the career.

Curiously enough, Swinburne, who discovered Blake and introduced him to his own blind countrymen, has the same position of Uranus. Cancer again is rising 3 degrees earlier

205. See note 103.

than that of Blake, and Uranus is 12 degrees earlier than Pisces, but still in the ninth house. The Moon of Swinburne, however, is in close conjunction with the Sun in the tenth house, and Mars occupies the Ascendant in conjunction with Jupiter. Uranus receives no more assistance than the semi-sextiles of Venus, Mercury and Neptune and the Ascendant is evidently much stronger than the ninth house. We have a personality of extraordinary force and violence, far more creative than that of Blake, but entirely without inspiration in any sense in which Blake would have understood the word. The sympathy between the two poets is confined to the Ascendant and the position of Uranus, and this proved strong enough to get one to appreciate the other. But in spite of the warmth of the appreciation, there is not the remotest trace of Blake's influence in the work of Swinburne.

As an example of the visionary quality of thought produced by this position of Uranus at its worst, where it is little better than muddle-headedness, we may look at the horoscope of Sir Edwin Durning-Lawrence.[206] Here Sagittarius is rising, with Jupiter near the conjunction of Mars, squared by Saturn, and in opposition to the Sun and Mercury. Uranus is near the cusp of the third house and can show nothing better than the semi-sextile of Neptune to help him. The mental disturbance is consequently well-marked, and the personality is shown as eccentric, obstinate, violent and lacking in all sense of proportion. It is a lamentable figure.

An even more unfortunate example of the weakness and flabbiness and sponginess of Uranus in Pisces is Henry VI[207] of England. Here, Taurus is rising with the Moon, and Venus is in the house of her abomination, Capricornus, sextile to Uranus. The Moon is afflicted by the opposition of Mars, and there is nothing whatever to set off against these disabilities. There is no lack of harmony between personality and temperament, there is not enough strength in either to create any unpleasantness. Uranus, too, is in the twelfth house.

206. See note 31.

207. Henry VI (1421-1471), inherited the kingdoms of England and France as an infant. During his reign the English were driven out of France. He was founder of both Eton and King's College, Cambridge, and died a violent death.

Thus his influence is not great. The Lady of the Ascendant being in the ninth house in a Saturnian sign, we get a form of religious devotion not far removed from Melancholia.

Another unfortunate monarch of very similar temperament was Louis XVI. The weak Virgo is rising, with Mercury imprisoned in the twelfth, and Mars just under the cusp of the Ascendant. Jupiter and Sol are in close conjunction with Mercury, but although these planets are benefic, in such an instance it may be held that they rather overpower the planets. A trine aspect would have been far preferable, especially as Uranus is close to the opposition of his conjunction, and though he is benefited by the trine of the Moon, this is not sufficient to make him really strong, when he is in a watery sign. It needs some warmer planet to kindle his fire. Hence we see, the temperament of a mild-mannered person who passed his time making watches, while his throne crumbles beneath him; and when it came to the point where his personality was put to the test, it proved entirely weak, and unable to cope with the situation. His no less unfortunate Queen has Cancer rising, Mars in the Ascendant, and the Moon squared by Saturn. Uranus has a trine of the Sun and Venus and is situated in the tenth house, Sol and Venus being in the fifth house. We get a somewhat faded though voluptuous type, intensely pleasure-loving and causing scandal through this quality. The pamphlets written against his queen, Marie Antoinette, did more to bring about the revolution than almost any other single issue.

A little better is the horoscope of Tchaikovsky. Here Cancer is ascending, and the Moon though near the cusp of the third house, has nothing between her and the Ascendant. Uranus has a square of Saturn, which is not altogether bad, and a trine of Jupiter which is distinctly good, and he is also helped by the sextile of the Sun and Mars in very close conjunction. The Moon has no particular dignity but that of her mundane position, and even that is not very strong. The result is a rather insignificant man, turning out great work. Uranus and his aspects are all-important in his horoscope.

The greatest singer of our times Adelina Patti,[208] has also

208. See note 56.

this position of Uranus; Leo rising, the Sun in conjunction with Neptune, trined by the Moon; and although squared by Mars may be counted strong, since Mars has the trine of Uranus. On the whole, however, the temperament is stronger than the personality; a supreme artist with no interference from any eccentricity or self-will.

We may now consider two writers, singularly sympathetic to each other, Alphonse Daudet[209] and Thomas Hardy. Daudet has Scorpio rising with Mars in his detriment in Taurus in the seventh house in conjunction with the Sun. Uranus, on the other hand, has a square of Saturn, which is one of the better aspects of these planets, and he is near the cusp of the fifth house. The temperament is consequently very powerful and it expressed itself naturally in an artistic form.

Thomas Hardy has Libra rising with Venus in Taurus, near the conjunction of Mercury and Mars, but otherwise not particularly strong, nor is the eighth house altogether a desirable place for her. As with Daudet, Uranus has the square of Saturn. This aspect will have to be taken to indicate the clear-sighted and philosophical realism which is to be discovered in the works of both authors.

To return for a moment, to the Middle Ages, let us look at the horoscope of Nostradamus. Here Aries is rising, with Mars in no way assisted by aspect or dignity. Uranus is in the twelfth house, giving a great secretiveness, and the only thing which can be called help to him is that he is pretty close to a trine of the conjunction of Jupiter and Saturn. The man is accordingly much less than his prophecies. With Sol on the cusp of the mid-heaven and Neptune occupying it, his fame was assured, and considering the trine referred to above it has been perhaps not altogether undeserved.

We shall now proceed to a consideration of the nativities of a pair of very clever, successful and unscrupulous politicians, one born to a throne and the other to a screw factory, Edward VII and Joseph Chamberlain.[210] The late

209. Alphonse Daudet (1840-1897), French writer, known best for *Lettres de mon Moulin* and his novel *Sappho*.

210. Joseph Chamberlain (1836-1914) prominent British statesman and imperialist, one of Churchill's 'Great Contemporaries'.

King of England has 28 degrees of Sagittarius rising, with Jupiter just touching the cusp of the Ascendant. It is square to Uranus, but the latter has a trine of Sol, and Jupiter has a sextile of Venus, all of which things make for success. The subtlety and astuteness with which he engineered the Triple Entente and isolated Germany will long be remembered in history, as the principal cause of the Great War.

In the horoscope of Joseph Chamberlain, on the other hand, we find little beyond chicanery and selfishness. There is no indication of true statesmanship or enlightened patriotism. He changed his politics as another man would change his neck-tie, and he did it so successfully that, in spite of the intense hatred and distrust with which he was regarded by the more intellectual classes of his countrymen, he always managed to be on the side of the majority. Cancer is rising, with the Sun on the cusp of the second, Mercury on the cusp of the Ascendant, the Moon exalted in Taurus, square to Neptune, which gives a certain trickiness, for which indeed he was celebrated. Mercury is trine to Uranus, and is exactly on the cusp of the Ascendant. Thus we see an extraordinary degree of concentration on the aggrandisement of self, and the marvellous skill in engineering schemes to attain purely personal objects.

Our next pair should prove exceedingly instructive. Here the influence flows to a purely financial channel, and we see emphasis laid upon the fact that Pisces is the house of Jupiter. The pair consists of Jay Gould[211] and J. Pierpoint Morgan.[212] The former has Gemini rising with Mercury just below the cusp of the Ascendant, very strong in his own house with a trine of the Moon and Saturn. This is a very cold and heartless combination. There is no warmth from any source. The Sun himself is imprisoned in the twelfth house and forms a square with Uranus. It is the very picture of a greedy, calculating, cold-blooded, unscrupulous financier. Venus and Jupiter being in the second house turn the affections towards money, and assure its gain. The affliction of Uranus removes all trace of constructive intelligence from that planet, and as he is situated in the tenth house, it is easy

211. See note 48.
212. See note 4.

to understand that the financier could not escape from the reprobation of his fellowmen.

J.P. Morgan has Leo rising and the Sun is in very close conjunction with Mercury. He is exalted in Aries, and culminating, which renders him suddenly powerful. There is no particular help to Uranus, but on the other hand he suffers no damage. The personality is far finer and nobler than that of our last example, not nearly so concentrated upon pure gain and in no way inhibited from undertaking constructive work.

In France, we have already had two persons prominent in the political world, and we now strike a whole group, equally prominent though not born to the purple. They range through all degrees of failure and success, probity and improbity. It should be well worth our while to examine their nativities in detail.

General Boulanger[213] – here Cancer is rising with the Moon in Aquarius, within 9 degrees of the conjunction of Uranus, which is on the cusp of the tenth house. Beyond a sextile of Sol and Venus and a semi-sextile of Neptune, which applies to Uranus rather than to Luna, there is no particular assistance. We find, in fact, that it was the personality of the man which failed him; at the critical moment he wavered and broke down.

Contrast him with the great Gambetta,[214] who has Scorpio rising and Mars in his own house Aries, quite close to the conjunction of the Sun and Mercury. Saturn is rising within 7 degrees of the trine to Mars. Uranus is in conjunction with Venus in her exaltation but in opposition to Jupiter. The personality appears extraordinarily forceful –

213. George Ernest Jean Marie Boulanger, French general and politician, born 1837. He fought successfully in various wars, was appointed War Minister in 1886, and resigned the following year. He was taken off the active list for insubordination, entered politics and made it obvious that he was intending to establish a dictatorship. Failing to seize his opportunity in 1889, he committed suicide on the grave of his mistress in Brussels in 1891.

214. Leon Gambetta (1838-1882), French statesman, who opposed Napoleon III and declared the Third Republic. When Paris was besieged by the Prussians in 1870, he escaped by balloon and organised resistance in the provinces.

the temperament not so markably so. In fact, his work was an obvious one. It was merely that of rallying the French in the hour of their defeat, an idea which might have occurred to anyone. The amazing energy and success with which he carried out his task are due to the great power of the Ascendant and the good aspects of its lord. It will be noted, of course, that the affliction of Uranus led in this instance to a manifestation upon the material plane – violent death.

The three very commonplace politicians are Presidents Carnot, Faure and Loubet.[215] Carnot has Capricornus rising with Saturn, semi-sextile to Mars and trine to Uranus. No planet is ascending except the latter. There is consequently great harmony between the personality and temperament, but there is no development of any extraordinary force. There is success but only ordinary success.

President Faure has Libra rising and Venus is within seven degrees of the conjunction of Uranus. Venus is squared by Saturn and Uranus by Jupiter, and though there is no particular lack of unity involved in these configurations, they are not strong and the presence of Mars in the Ascendant, would seem to outweigh them. There is energy and capacity shown, but once again, no very great tendency towards any development of the Revolutionary qualities of Uranus.

Emile Loubet is an even softer type. That he should have permitted himself to be publicly smacked upon the face at a race-course is not indicative of a force of personality such as commands universal respect, more particularly in a ruler.[216] The passive and easy-going Cancer is rising, the Moon is touching the cusp of the Ascendant, with the lower edge of her silver orb, and she is almost exactly in opposition to the Sun and Venus. She has the trine of Uranus and this assures that general harmony of character of which we have been speaking. It also assures success, but that kind of success

215. Marie Francois Sadi Carnot (1837-94) became President of the Republic in 1887 and remained in office until he was stabbed by an anarchist on 24 June 1894. Emile Loubet (1838-1920) was President from 1899 to 1906. For the luckless President Faure see note 150.

216. The smack on the face was from a virulent anti-Dreyfusard. President Loubet, who succeeded Faure in 1899, re-opened the Dreyfus case.

which comes to a man, as an Irishman or a philosopher might say 'through no fault of his own'.

The last of our group will be found to remind us far more of Joseph Chamberlain than of any other. It is Robespierre. Here Aquarius is rising, Saturn just under the cusp of the Ascendant and Uranus a little below him. Saturn has the semi-sextile of Venus and the square of Mercury, which indicates a successful and plausible lawyer with a sense of reality, but no load of scruple sufficient to hinder his march toward power. Uranus receives only the doubtful assistance of a semi-sextile of the Moon, and though Jupiter is in the tenth house, in his own house Sagittarius, trined by Mars, we can only regard this as adding executive force to his ambition without making, in any way, a harmonious combination with it. Here is a picture, one may almost say a clinical picture, of a cold, harsh, overbearing, ambitious, unscrupulous man, and so, as in all the cases that we have been considering, we find the clearest possible witness of history through the truth of astrology.

Uranus in the Twelve Houses of Heaven

In dealing with Uranus generally and in his position in the signs it has been necessary to emphasise his interior effect, his influence upon character, his position in the houses of heaven, though still to some extent important in this regard, is less so than his external effect.

Having defined Uranus as the interior, subconscious, magical will of the native, so far as it refers to himself, it follows that this planet as applied to the non-ego will represent its will. Uranus may consequently be called the planet of destiny. It is consequently very shallow to class him crudely as fortunate and unfortunate. At one time the native may be in complete harmony with his surroundings and he will naturally describe himself as 'lucky'. At another time he will be entirely out of unison and complain accordingly of his misfortune. Either view is, of course, prejudiced and unworthy of a philosopher. There is, however, no doubt that Uranus more than any other planet, produces the most extraordinary vicissitudes. Sometimes he may occasion death, but not often. His force is too vital, and one might also say spectacular, to bring about anything so banal as the mere fall of the curtain. Where he does bring death, it is usually of a catastrophic and tragic kind, but for initiating critical events in the career and for determining the whole tone thereof, he has no equal. The influence of Neptune is so subtle and obscure that even though it be more truly profound it does not strike the eye in the same way. The tragedies of the soul are invisible, except to the eye of the poet and the philosopher.

The incidence of the operation of Uranus depends entirely upon the house in which he is situated. In his case, as in that of Neptune, the problem is not complicated by any question of the sign upon the cusp of the house, because these two planets are beyond the zone of the Sacred Seven[217] and do not possess the same close correspondences with the signs as the lesser planets. Pertaining as they do to the operations of the inscrutable Will of the All-Father, they have not the same dependance upon the lesser laws of the universe. The Seven are much more mechanical and calculable in their action. Perhaps it would be at least useful as an explanation of certain difficulties in interpreting the action of the two greater planets, were we to suggest that they are not so simple and constant as the others. It is quite conceivable that from time to time they receive new and varying influences of force from the higher planes, and if so, however far we might advance in the science of astrology pure and simple, there would always be a possibility of our calculations being upset by some such cause of disturbance. This hypothesis is, to a certain extent, supported by the already discovered characteristics of both these planets. In each case there is a peculiar uncertainty about their action which we, living as we do, mostly upon the material plane and upon a planet comparatively close to the Sun, are apt to call tricksy, or at least unaccountable.

217. The seven planets of old – Mercury, Venus, Mars, Jupiter, Saturn, Sol and Luna. In the language of initiation, 'seven' stands for the highest stage, out of which comes the 'eighth', or 'height'. In the Christian Mysteries, the number 8 was attributed to Christ. See *Aleister Crowley and the Hidden God* by Kenneth Grant.

To return from this digression, let us repeat that the actual effects of Uranus upon the career of the native will depend almost exclusively upon his mundane position. The exception to this rule will be in the case of his possessing some important aspect to the ruler of the sign upon the cusp of any given house. Instances of such action are given in the chapters upon the aspects of the various planets. Our present purpose is to demonstrate the exact effects of the mundane positions.

Uranus in the First House

The essential dignity of Uranus should first be regarded by reference to the sign in which he is situated and to his aspects, before his influence in the house is investigated; for his nature must be modified by these circumstances. *Ceteris paribus*, however, he will be more influential in the Ascendant than most other planets for the reason that he is not tied down as they are by zodiacal considerations.

People who have him in this position are nearly always of an extremely independent and original turn of mind. Their point of view is almost always different and radically so from that of the mass of mankind. Such people are invariably what their friends call 'characters'. But when this is at all accentuated or when the surroundings of the native are ultra-conventional a certain antagonism may develop and he may be described as eccentric or even something stronger.

In any case, from the point of view of common sense, these criticisms are usually justified. In all ordinary circumstances, the best way to get on is to follow the line of least resistance, and if a person with Uranus in the Ascendant even does such an obvious thing as this, it does not strike him in that light at all. He regards it as a wonderful discovery of his super-subtle intelligence, and in any case is not likely to carry it out with any persistence. For the rule of the Uranian is above all to strike out a new line. He is in nearly every case a thoroughly emancipated thinker. Conventional ideas are quite beneath his notice; tradition has no weight with him; he always goes to the root of the matter, decides everything on first principles and even with regard to these principles is more inclined to idealism than to realism. To take a concrete example, it will appear quite obvious to him that the only possible way of running the world is by mutual forbearance and love. He is then apt to assume that it is so run. This quality is likely to be manifest whenever Uranus acts upon the mental plane, so that in the third and ninth houses its effect is as conspicuous as when in the Ascendant.

The general effect of this tendency of Uranus is to make the native a solitary, not in the least as Saturn does, as it were by nature, but on the contrary entirely against nature. The Uranian detests solitude, seeks the sympathy and companionship of his fellows and his life is rendered only too often extremely unhappy by the failure of his contemporaries to sympathise with his ideas. It must not be supposed, however, that he is likely to find this sympathy even with other Uranians. He will like meeting such people and find their company for the time refreshing, because of the originality of their ideas, but those ideas will probably not be the same as his own and even where they are he will most probably be jealous. His striking personality is, however, likely to make him extremely attractive to the hero-worshipping type of individual and he will often find brief solace in their caresses. Yet all the time a serpent will be gnawing at his heart and he will say to himself that he is utterly lonely because even those who adore him do not understand him. In this he will be right, on the surface. His error arises from the fact that he is really out of touch with the spirit of his age. In fact he is sent into that age as one born out of season to implant in it the seeds of those ideas which may be good and generally accepted a hundred years later. He must learn to be content to plow a lonely furrow, for the benefit of those who are to follow. He must sow in tears that others may reap in joy.

Occasionally Uranus is sufficiently strong to overpower, at least temporarily, the spirit of the age itself. Where great executive ability is shown and where the general horoscope predicts greatness, the native may become supreme in his section of the universe. Thus we find Cromwell overthrowing not only the king on behalf of Parliament, but Parliament itself as soon as it showed divergence from his own ideas. It may here be remarked that Uranus rising sometimes declares itself by facial characteristics. It is well known that Cromwell had warts on the nose. Another example of conspicuous success is Disraeli; here the eccentricity shows itself by his fantastical dandyism, but the extreme power of the personality is demonstrated by the fact that it was only a few years before his elevation to the position of First Commoner in the British Empire that the political disabilities of Jews had been removed.

In the case of Robert Louis Stevenson, the eccentricity shown by Uranus rising is modified to shyness and gentleness of character. This is readily explained by the fact that Uranus is trined by Venus. Herbert Spencer shows more the recluse in his nature; it will be remembered that he had plugs made for his ears, so that he should not be distracted by the conversation of people at the dinner-table.

In the case of Sir Isaac Newton, again, the reader will recall the fact that he would seek mental relaxation by endeavouring to balance peacock's feathers upon his nose and that people who discovered him engaged in this manner described him as eccentric. One does not, however, remember the names of those people. In nearly all cases Uranus stamps the face with some subtle peculiarity of a kind that tends to inspire the average individual with a kind of dread.

Occasionally, as with Cromwell, Uranus takes a menacing and destructive turn. Add to his name those of Robespierre and Annie Besant,[218] but these lacked Cromwell's capacity, and the element of destruction began to manifest itself almost as soon as the success of their revolutionary efforts. Cromwell's influence at least lasted while his life did.

The student will note the very peculiar facial appearance of Mrs Besant, especially the lips, while in the cases of Robespierre, the nose is equally characteristic. The student is also referred to Carlyle's account of his personal appearance and character.

Those persons with Uranus rising should never lose hope. They are inclined to pass from action to reaction with a strain of suddenness and periods of absolute despair may be the penalty which they pay for their exhilaration, but fortune for them is ever on the turn. When things are at the

218. See note 105.

worst, they mend as suddenly as they collapsed. As a rule it is not good policy for such people to attempt to fit themselves in with their surroundings; failure is only too likely. It is a wiser policy to accentuate their unlikeness to the rest of mankind, so that they may achieve the toleration which is ultimately extended to all those who, while they are distrusted as being evidently not of the herd, are yet respected and feared by the sheep. The unknown animal may be a wolf or a lion!

Uranus in the Second House

With regard to material possessions of the nature of ready money, earned money and money acquired in business, Uranus may be considered fortunate or otherwise very much in accordance with the nature of the business. He is certainly bad for steady businesses, such as that of the grocer, or the baker, but for businesses which are gambling from first to last, like publishing, he may not be so bad. For the sudden vicissitudes which he brings are all in the day's work if you are playing poker, and to win a jack-pot with four threes against an ace fully compensates for a hundred hand that were not worth drawing to. People with this position of Uranus go on making nothing for a long time, and then make a lot. Very likely they lose or spend it almost as soon as they get it. But in whatever straits they may find themselves, they never actually starve. Something always turns up at the last moment. For people whose personality is conventional, this state of things will be extremely depressing; the artist's temperament or the gambler's temperament or the temperament of the religious man soon accomodates itself to the fact. We have four very striking examples of people with this position. Edward VII, until he became king, was in constant straits for money. He gambled desperately and put himself in the hands of the money lenders. It will be remembered that his difficulties even led him to accept invitations which one in his position should hardly have done. The Tranby Croft scandal and the Gordon Cumming trial[219] which nearly

219. Colonel Gordon Cumming of the Scots Guards, a prominent social figure in the Prince of Wales's set, was accused of cheating at baccarat, played at Tranby Croft. He sued his accusers for slander and

wrecked the monarchical system in England may be regarded as directly due to this position.

Sir Richard Burton[220] is another case in point. He made very large sums of money from time to time by the sale of his books. He netted twelve thousand pounds sterling straight off from *The Arabian Nights* alone, yet fortune constantly played traitor to him. He was another of those rich men who are always hard up. Stranger still is the case of Byron, who received thousands upon thousands of pounds from his publisher, Murray, yet who felt so bitterly the slings of poverty that he sent Murray a bible for a present with the sentence 'Now Barabbas was a *publisher*', for 'robber'.

The same story is true of Balzac, but with him he was always in actual extremity, ever on the point of being sold out, although receiving at frequent intervals sums almost beyond the dreams of avarice.

It is not necessary to describe Uranus as malefic to explain these facts. It is all part of the psychology of gambling. When you sit down and do a week's work and receive a year's income in return for it, it is only natural that you should feel wildly optimistic, and when for the next week's work you only get six month's income, you become unreasonably depressed. 'Easy come, easy go' too is a very good rule about money. It is only natural that one should value a little what one obtains without great effort. More than this, extravagance is definitely one of the Christian virtues. 'Take no thought for the morrow', said the Saviour; 'consider the lilies how they grow'. 'Are ye not of more value than many sparrows.' 'Freely have ye received, freely give'. All direct incitements to unthrift.

Sometimes, however, these qualities are modified and appear rather as a tendency to adventure money in pursuance

---

lost the case, thereby ruining socially himself and his family. The case caused great scandal because the Prince of Wales, afterwards Edward VII, was one of the gamesters and was called to give evidence in the case. The Prince was honorary colonel of a German cavalry regiment, and the Kaiser, Wilhelm II, who had a continuous feud with Queen Victoria and her son, as his senior officer, officially rebuked him for gambling with his juniors.

220. See notes 35 and 191.

of a great idea; thus, Sir Isaac Pitman was constantly in the direst straits for cash, not because he failed to earn it, or because he squandered what he had, but because with him every interest was subordinated to that of establishing his system of shorthand.

Those people with this position who are engaged in business of an ordinary and conventional kind must be constantly on the watch for altenations of fortune. It is particularly when everything appears to be going well that disaster is likely to fall upon the native, and it will usually be from the most unexpected quarters. Every kind of insurance against this type of calamity should invariably be made.

When disaster has actually occurred, there is no occasion to be down-hearted. It is, as a rule, not best to attempt to meet the storm during its height. Wait for a lull and take the ball on the rebound. People with this position of Uranus very often have a strong premonition as to whether any business which they may undertake will turn out successfully. This is much more reliable than similar psychic faculties usually are, and it should be followed. Never put a business proposition before a man unless you can do so with a kind of interior confidence that he will agree. All those forms of business in which the element of chance most enters, are likely to suit the temperaments of the native. The scientific character of Uranus makes it probable that the exploitation of invention or the manufacture of chemicals or even the backing of research might prove fortunate. Similarly, the influence of Uranus upon governing bodies of various kinds makes it suitable for the native to link his financial fortunes with those of such corporations. There is a very unfortunate tendency to irregularity in Uranus, where that planet is set to rule things which depend entirely upon strict adherence to conventional order, such as book-keeping, where the quality of imagination is out of place. People with this position are probably quite incapable of calculating their weakly expenditure. Such things bore them by what appears their triviality.

To illustrate what we mean, a banker engaged in negotiating war loans might congratulate himself on having this position of Uranus, but he would be very unwise to engage a cashier whose horoscope was like his in that respect.

In life, it is always necessary to play the game according to the rule, but there are many games and in some of them the rules are that there are no rules. If you have Uranus in the second house, try and select one such game for your business.

Uranus in the Third House

This is one of the most interesting mundane positions which Uranus can hold. Browning says: 'Our interest is on the dangerous edge of things'. The number of accidents and adventures that can occur on the physical plane is after all rather limited, and there is such a tendency to monotony, but the mind knows no such restrictions. Uranus in the third house, which primarily governs the intellect almost invariably produces the most extraordinary effect. One may say that its empire is practically without limit. There will certainly never be any blind adherence to convention and in such horoscopes as indicate general weakness, the nativities of common-place people, Uranus may be expected to stand for eccentricity of thought, just as in the Ascendant he stood for eccentricities of personality. When he is badly aspected and also if there are no planets between him and the Ascendant, this influence may be so accentuated as to constitute actual mental disturbances, or even disease. But of course such cases are exceptional. In the average case, however, we need expect no more than curious and unusual tendencies of the mind with regard to its occupation, and also with regard to the manner of its thought, the logical processes are likely to be very dissimilar from those of ordinary people. A somewhat extreme example of the effects of this position is Sir Edwin Durning-Lawrence,[221] who devoted amazing ability and energy to the foolish problem of the authorship of Shakespeare's plays. But there can be no question that the same qualities of mind directed in saner channels would have constituted superlative distinction.

We find once more such a mind attached to the criminal temperament in the case of Caesar Borgia,[222] whose intrigues stand out in the Middle Ages with overwhelming

221. See note 31.
222. See note 96.

force. In all history there is hardly an equivalent example of brain power misapplied. His imagination was immense and his combination subtle and profound.

Another mind no less extraordinary is that of Joan of Arc. Here we have extreme simplicity and piety of disposition, combined with a mind equal in scope to that of the greatest seers, and, as it turned out, to executive power of a high order. The essential factor in her greatness is of course the quality of the mind. There were hundreds of other people equally good and equally strong, but unless she had been fitted to apprehend the operation of superior claims to the intellectual she could not have saved France. Here we see Uranus in his best avatar; he enlarges, emancipates, revolutionises. We should also note the tremendous opposition which he excites on the part of minds not tuned to his vibrations. This quality of inspiration, as we may call it, is very characteristic of Uranus, when well-dignified, especially by such aspects as the squares and opposition of Saturn and trined to and sextiles of the Sun.

In matters of science, which has been for the last century the principal means through which the emancipating thought manifests upon the physical plane, Uranus is particularly good and powerful. We find Louis Pasteur and Dr Wallace[223] with this position. It is to be noted that the personality of both these men was quite conventional; they are to be contrasted with such as have Uranus rising. It was only the mind which was exalted through work in so exceptional a manner. In this connection, too, we should mention Goethe, who was in one sense the pioneer of science. He represents the transition; he was the first poet who ever understood the importance to humanity of the scientific method. Previous bards rather resented the introduction of precision. He, on the other hand, welcomed science with open arms. However this may be, there can be no question as to the very

223. Alfred Russell Wallace (1823-1913), naturalist. In 1858, while lying ill in the Moluccas, the idea of the evolutionary theory of man and animals occurred to him. He transmitted it to Charles Darwin who was just about to publish his *Origin of Species*. Shortly afterwards, a paper by the two men on the subject was read to the Linnean Society in London.

extraordinary character of his mind. In this one respect he may be said to have no rival whatever. To the true observer of the human intelligence, Shakespeare and Dante appear commonplace when compared with him. Their limitations were those of their period. Goethe was much more cosmic than either of them. If he did not understand the human heart so fully as the former and was not so exalted a mystic as the latter, he was yet more prophetic than either of them. He anticipated the modern spirit. The same unusual quality of mind is also to be seen in Dürer. Almost every other artist of whom we can think has what we may call family relations with others. Leonardo and Raphael and Michael Angelo and Rembrandt are much more like each other than Dürer is like any one of them. He thought, and with an artist that is the same as saying that he saw, in a manner entirely unique.

With regard to the lesser indications afforded by the third house, Uranus does not operate on so grand a scale. In the matter of writings, for example, he is not likely to produce any wonderful effect, except in so far as the writings may be the crystallisation of the mind which produced them, as in the cases of Goethe and Dürer for drawing is a kind of writing cited above. There is a tendency rather to some eccentricity and trickery. It may be due to this position that Dr Wallace in his old age took up with the ideas with regard to astronomy and spiritualism which were quite out of keeping with his former eminence in science.

In the case of the average man, Uranus in this house will probably stand for trouble and annoyance. Letters are likely to miscarry and even fall into the hands of the last person in the world whom the writer would have wished. In the matter of brothers and sisters, once more, the indication is unfavourable. It may mean in bad cases that one of them is mad or at least very queer in every way. No kind of harmony with such relations is to be expected, and the native will probably do well to avoid them as much as possible.

In all matters of short journeys and communications of a minor nature generally, there is the same feeling of uncertainty and unrest. The native will probably be unable to rest; he will flit about from place to place, never knowing where he may be from one day to another. There will always, too, be misunderstandings and confusions, with regard to all such affairs.

There is a special application to what we have said about the quality of the mind. In most cases when the turn is toward science or religion, there will be found a fascination for occult subjects. It will be noted that in every case cited above, with the exception of Pasteur, there has been a strong inclination to dive into the unknown. This being the case where the mind has been of such extraordinary calibre and one might think so largely occupied with other matters, we may assume that in the minds of more ordinary calibre, the total contents being less, there is more room for development of such ideas. This, on the whole, is not to be regarded as entirely fortunate, for the study of the occult is always dangerous, unless the mind is based so broadly upon general knowledge that there is no danger of it being upset or obsessed. The lure of the unknown is terrible, and unless the path of the student is fully lighted, it is likely to cause the native to follow false trails, in which case life may be ruined. 'Narrow is the way and strait is the gate and few they be that find it.'[224]

Uranus in the Fourth House

Uranus in the fourth house possesses no such importance in moulding the character or mind as in the first, third or ninth. It seems to be busy with more material affairs, and as is always the case with the planet, his operation is much better on the higher than on the lower.

With regard to the father, there is likely to be any amount of trouble. It is not unlikely that he may commit suicide or become mad. In any case, he will be a very queer character and it is improbable that the native will get on well with him. The house will in no case be a good environment. To go away from one's house in an astrological sense, does not necessarily or always mean to quit the locality, it may imply what is after all a much more radical departure, a change in the mode of life from that which might have been expected from the environment of infancy. A child is not likely to succeed in

224. Matthew 6, v.14.

that line of life for which his parents designed him, when he has this position of Uranus. Everyone of the people whom we are considering has this element of disturbance.

Shakespeare ran away from home; Joseph Smith[225] created immense trouble in his township; Bismarck broke away entirely from the position of his early environment; so did Bulwer Lytton. Rhodes spent most of his life and died in a foreign land. The lives of Chopin and of Petrarch were spent, so to speak, in exile. Baudelaire passed much of his life in distant climes, and besides was totally out of sympathy with the idea of home. His prose poem 'Anywhere, anywhere, out of the world' and several others expressed magnificently the nostalgia indicated by this position.

One may also see traces of the same thing in the paintings of J.M.W. Turner. Such gorgeous and flamboyant colouring is as unsuited to the grey skies of England as Baudelaire's exotic poetry to the gentle sunshine of France. From England one can expect Constable and Whistler;[226] the extravagance of Turner is more suggestive of Algeria.

Examples of domestic disquietude caused by this position, the undesirability of remaining in the home, is shown not only by Lytton (mentioned above in another connection, but now in regard to his unhappy domestic broils) but by Alexander VI[227] who lacked conspicuously that sublime repose which one would naturally attribute to his position as the vicar of Christ, and by Henry VIII. The troubles of this monarch were as Froude[228] showed, not at all due to his

225. See note 33.

226. See note 7.

227. Crowley believed that Alexander VI, the brilliant but apolaustic prelate, was a previous incarnation of himself. The accusations of murder, incest and piracy, made this pope especially appealing to him. One of Crowley's treasured possessions was a gold sequin which had been struck by Alexander: on one side was his papal and family arms, on the other the Gospel story of the miraculous draught of fishes. Crowley used this coin as his 'disk' or talisman in his magical operations for getting gold.

228. James Anthony Froude (1818-1894), English historian, disciple and biographer of Carlyle. His *History of England from the Fall of Wolsey to the Defeat of the Spanish Armada* (1854-1870) was an apologia for Henry VIII.

own temperament; they sprang entirely from the necessity in which he found himself of establishing his dynasty. This unfortunate monarch has been shamefully misjudged by the unthinking. It is too often forgotten that he was the first monarch since Edward III who had any sort of secure seat upon the throne of England. Every single one of the intervening monarchs had been involved in civil war, with the brief exception of Henry V[229] and the trouble which had brought England into ruin, laid waste her fairest provinces and slain her noblest sons were entirely dynastic in character. His father, Henry VII, had only obtained his throne as the result of England's complete exhaustion, and it was pre-eminently the duty of the King of the nation to see that no further trouble of this sort arose. All the policies of Henry VIII were consequently, and rightly, subservient to the one policy of having a son to succeed him. As we shall see in another paper, Saturn was on the cusp of the fifth house, which governs offspring, and this position was unfavourable, but the presence of Uranus in the fourth was even worse. It caused eternal turmoil in the affairs of the State, which is, so one may say, the house of the King and it was also unfavourable for the end of the matter, which is also governed by the fourth house. So indeed it turned out. None of his three children, though they occupied the throne successively, was able to continue the dynasty, which accordingly passed to a remote branch, not even English. No better example could possibly be found of the fatal influence of Uranus at his worst. Had it not been for the trine of Mars, he would, in all probability, have been unable to score even a temporary and apparent success.

The case of Theodore Roosevelt is also very instructive. His early environment was evidently very unsuited to him; he was extremely delicate and threatened with very serious diseases so that his medical advisers were afraid that he would not survive adolescence. All this trouble disappeared as soon as he got away from home and adopted that free, open-air life which he subsequently made so famous.

229. The most popular of English kings, Henry V came to the throne in 1413 won the battle of Agincourt in 1415 and died in 1422.

With regard to the other matters indicated by the fourth house, it may be stated, as a general rule that the native is likely to be influenced by people much older than himself and also by people of great importance or engaged in affairs connected with governing bodies or large corporations.

The fourth house also indicates the end of the matter, and here the caprice of Uranus is particularly manifest. All of the concerns of the native are likely to terminate in an unexpected and probably a dramatic manner. Affairs may drag for a considerable period and then come to a head almost catastrophically. Whether this last word is to be interpreted in a favourable or unfavourable sense will naturally depend upon the directions to Uranus and transits.

The close connection of Uranus with the will indicates that in some cases, advancing age may bring with it certain ailments of such a nature that the will is interfered with. Exactly what form these may take will depend upon many things. For example, the sign in which Uranus happens to be placed – his direction and his transits. To take a concrete example if Uranus were in Gemini, an affliction of him might mean aphasia, since Gemini is particularly connected with the organs of speech, while if he were in Capricornus, the tendency might be for paralysis of the lower limbs. It is unnecessary in this place to enumerate all the possibilities which are reserved for the special chapter dealing with ill-health.

Sudden and violent death is not indicated by this position of Uranus, so much as when he is in such houses as the eighth or twelfth.

People with this position often possess the 'wander-lust', are fond of adventure and enterprise. Anything settled in their lives does not appeal to them. They should not struggle against this disposition, but endeavour to harmonise it, so far as may be with their general welfare.

Uranus in the Fifth House

Uranus in the fifth house is not at all favourable, so far as children are concerned. As a general rule there are none, but where this is not the case, either the first-born is destroyed by some accident of gestation or its non-viability or it turns out very peculiar in character. They are likely to be extremely independent and difficult to manage, and must be treated accordingly. It is quite possible that they possess genius or something very like it, and in order to bring out their best qualities, it is necessary to give reason for the course of action taken much more than would be the case with ordinary children. It is not sufficient to give the reason 'because I say so'. This advice is not intended to imply indulgence. The child would be apt to regard it as an insult. What is wanted is the establishment of a feeling of mutual respect and affection. Such children should be treated as responsible beings and appeal made to their better natures.

With regard to the pleasures of life, more particularly those involving the question of sex, Uranus exercises a very full influence. There seems to be no limit to the violence of the temperament indicated. It is not so capricious and fantastic as when Neptune is in this house, but it is more passionate and violent and it is more likely to lead to violations of conventionality. With some people this may amount to crime. The affections are subject, in any case, to sudden and constant changes of the spirit of revolt against conventionality and even against the bonds of love itself will be extremely strong. It does not necessarily follow that the irregularity of the *vita sexualis* will imply the upholding of any unusual theories. The mind of the native may be perfectly conventional and his violations of rule may cause him extreme mental disturbance and regret. Whether this is so or not will depend principally upon the first, third and ninth houses, their rulers and aspects.

With regard to other pleasures, the same tendency to caprice and extravagance will be evident. Very often such pleasures will take an undesirable form. The fifth house itself is connected with gambling, in so far as gambling is undertaken for excitement and dissipation rather than with any clear idea of gain; and when Uranus is there situated, he will accentuate the tendency of the native to indulge in this respect. In fact, he will probably be a somewhat desperate and violent gambler, whether fortunate or unfortunate will depend upon the aspects to Uranus, and so on, as usual.

In milder form, this position may imply what is sometimes

known as 'a taste for low company', and it is certain that the native will never find any pleasure in the ordinary amusements of his own class. Dinners and dances will bore him to distraction; he will prefer to wander about congested districts of the city in which he lives and exchange his views of life with loafers or policemen.

Addiction to drugs or drink is not shown so strongly as when Neptune occupies this house. It is only to be looked for when Uranus is in a watery sign or afflicted by the Moon. When it does occur, it is likely to be more violent and fatal than in the case of Neptune, for there is a continuity of purpose, a desperation about this planet which Neptune does not possess, and where he turns to evil, he is far more to be feared.

In the best condition, the unusual nature of the heart's love will show itself in mystic longings. This is to be distinguished from the preoccupation of mystical subjects given by Uranus in the first, third or ninth, just as the mind differs from the heart. Coleridge, Dickens, Swami Vivekananda,[230] Savonarola[231] and Luther all had this predisposition, and it is to be contrasted with the mystical speculation of Goethe, who had it in the third house, and with the mystical aspirations of Blake, who had it in the ninth. In the one case, it is the mind which was interested; in the other, the soul. But with the five people mentioned above, it is the affections of the heart that are involved. The very peculiar form which this took in Savonarola is explained elsewhere by the aspect of Venus, but the sex irregularity of Luther is fully explained by this position itself, if the reader will refer to the general remarks upon the subject made above. The ordinary irreligious reader of the present day can hardly realize how startling it must have been in the Middle Ages for a monk to marry a nun, and he will find a better example in the career of Madame Steinheil,[232] which is extremely characteristic of Uranus in this house at his most efficient.

230. See note 126.
231. See note 57.
232. See note 150.

It is to be understood that where the temperament of the native is scientific or philosophical, some of these forces will either not operate at all or else their operation will not become manifest. Consider, for example, Sir William Hamilton,[233] who has the purely intellectual sign of Gemini rising, with its lord Mercury upon the cusp of Virgo not very far from the cusp of the fifth house, and squared for greater coldness by the Moon. Saturn, too, is in the fifth house, only 6 degrees from the conjunction of Uranus. It would be absurd to suppose that the pleasures of such a man could exhibit any similarity with those of Savonarola with Aries rising and Saturn and Venus in conjunction squaring him. Neglect to consider such details is a constant pitfall to the unwary student of this science.

To return for a single moment to what was originally said with regard to children, it will be remarked that only two of the seven people named had any children.

The fifth house has a special connection with public appearances in connection with amusements; many people with this position of Uranus become public entertainers and often acquire the greatest distinction in this line. Their careers, however, are likely to be even more checkered than is usually the case, even with this profession.

The native should always be ready to receive shocks in the matter of his pleasures. Great good-fortune is likely to come his way in this respect, but on the other hand, he must not take it too much to heart if those things and people on which he has set his affections suddenly go back on him.

Uranus in the Sixth House

The principal indication of the sixth house, being the health of the native, it is to be expected that the presence of Uranus will cause strange subtle and sometimes sudden and violent diseases. In most cases these will be nervous or in some way affecting the will of the native, interfering with the connection between his sensory and motor apparatuses. The form which such a malady may take is not to be determined off-hand, but requires careful study of the sign on the cusp of

233. See note 172.

the house and its ruler. For example, the presence of Uranus in Aries on the cusp of this house presumably determined the deafness which has afflicted Edison, since Aries rules the head. The square of the moon to Uranus seems to indicate an affliction of the sensory rather than of the motor apparatus. Had Mars been afflicted thus, the trouble would probably have come through some form of paralysis.

The native should be extremely careful with regard to his health and keep himself in the best possible condition to resist disease when it actually arrives. Its onset is likely to be so sudden and unexpected, as a general rule, that precautions against it other than those indicated above, are likely to be useless. It is obviously no good to take an umbrella into the trenches. Pains should therefore be taken to live a life as free as possible from strain or worry, and the company of such people as jar upon the nerves is not to be endured with much patience as if no such threat to the stability of the system were in existence.

The sixth house also refers to servants, and, on the whole, the presence of Uranus is very unfavourable. Unless the native is a man of very strong character, his servants are likely to be better men than he is and to become his masters. The difficulties of Mary Queen of Scots with her subjects may have been due to this cause. Generally speaking there is liability to unexpected and unfortunate happenings in this connection. It is not that Uranus is malefic as such; we have seen that he is not; the point is that the idea of the servant normally precludes that of individuality, originality and independence. You do not want an inferior to do your thinking for you, you want him to do exactly what he is told and nothing else. Where, therefore, he insists on being himself, he becomes useless to you. The same remarks apply, to a certain extent, to every class of person with whom one may be thrown, from one's own father or wife, to a mere acquaintance. You want to know exactly what the other person is going to do and just so far as this is not the case, do you feel uneasy with regard to them.

The sixth house also indicates 'ambassadors', and this word may be taken, in extreme cases, to include inspiration. Messages are likely to come to the native from all sorts of important people and if he be in a position requiring the patronage of the great, he will probably obtain it. This is instanced by Wagner and Kant. The general liability of Uranus to upset things suddenly applies, however, also to all such affairs. The native cannot count upon the continued support of the great, as he could were Jupiter in this position. Exceptional aspects may, of course, modify the judgment. If for example, Jupiter were the lord of the sixth and true to Uranus, the combination would be ideal.

Uranus will indicate the character of the servants of the ambassador, and it will frequently occur that these persons are mentally or morally defective, or at the very least, eccentric. In the case of Mary Queen of Scots, the characters of Darnley and Bothwell,[234] to take only two of a host, were far from being all that could be desired, while with regard to Wagner, Ludwig II of Bavaria[235] is an extreme example of what the malice of Uranus can achieve. One may remark, moreover, upon the character of old King Leopold[236] in connection with the case of Cleo de Mérode,[237] who also had this position. It would perhaps be going too far, to comment upon the notorious proclivities of Frederick,[238] when considering the case of Kant.

The sixth house referring to speculative investment as distinguished from pure gambling for the love of the thing, we find Uranus exhibiting the same characteristics, *mutatis mutandis*, as in other matters. The native is likely to conceive great ideas, the carrying out of which will be liable to very great vicissitudes.

So far as the sixth house refers to small animals, the indication is that the native is not likely to be particularly successful in farming or breeding. Unfortunate accidents will constantly interfere with his success.

234. Darnley, husband of Mary Queen of Scots, was murdered by Bothwell, who married Mary soon after.

235. See note 111.

236. Leopold II (1835-1909), king of the Belgians and sovereign of the Congo Free State.

237. See note 157.

238. Frederick the Great of Prussia was alleged to be homosexual. Crowley, who was bi-sexual or pan-sexual, is writing with tongue-in-cheek.

So far as the house refers to apparel, the presence of Uranus will produce all kinds of eccentricity. The same peculiarities as are expressed by the presence of Uranus in the Ascendant, will be translated into terms of costume when he is in the sixth house.

Uranus in the Seventh House

So insensible is humanity at large to the facts of life that the most desperate of all adventures, marriage, is usually undertaken by them with the idea of settling down to quietude. Occasionally, success is obtained, exemplifying the fertility of nature in producing miracles to order. But this miracle is not likely to take place when Uranus is in the seventh house. It is only good for the adventurer, who may very likely obtain a partner very much above his or her social position. For there is always something big about Uranus. The person indicated by it is likely to be greatly superior to the native in one way or another. Such marriages are, of course, notoriously unhappy, because the suddenness of Uranus and the generally disturbing atmosphere which he creates wherever he goes, are unfavourable to peace and happiness in the conventional sense. There may, of course, be exceptions to this generalisation. Where the native has the lord of the seventh house well-dignified and Uranus is well-aspected, his presence there might merely indicate that the Uranus element in the partner, was, for example, science. A quiet little girl with no particular qualifications might marry a man famous in some department of knowledge or the President of a wealthy corporation or a government official and keep house very well for him. But such cases may be regarded as exceptional. As a general rule trouble is bound to ensue, of course, in many cases, he will prevent marriage altogether, causing the break-up of engagements, or the appearance of some other obstacle.

The obvious case, and one which needs no comment, is that of Queen Elizabeth; she was the last heir of the Tudors and marriage was more important to her than for almost any other person on the planet, yet the history of her reign is but the history of broken marriage negotiations.

An example of an unfortunate marriage is that of Louis

XVI to Marie Antoinette. Here the partner is indicated by Uranus, and as is stated elsewhere in this volume, it was the great eccentricity of her character which determined at least one set of causes of the French Revolution. Another example is the great Napoleon. His first marriage ended in divorce. In his second, the influence of Uranus is even more emphatically brought out, for Marie Louise was one of the greatest princesses in Europe and he was only a Corsican adventurer. The social again was consequently enormous, but there was, as the memoirs of time sufficiently prove, never even a glimpse of happiness in this ill-assorted union and the political gain expected from it did not materialise. Even as an alliance it rather hampered than helped. While the question of an heir was answered in none too friendly a sense, as is familiar to readers of history or of Rostand's *L'Aiglon*.

A further example of unsuitability is afforded by Madame Blavatsky. She again made an admirable match from the conventional point of view but there was no real marriage; and it soon broke up to free her for the career which we know.

Where the native is an artist and thus by nature ready to sympathise with the unusual, the effect of Uranus will not take this malignant form. In the case of Maurice Maeterlinck, who married a distinguished actress, the unusual nature of the profession does not come as a shock and consequently there was no reason for any upset. Only from the point of view of French Society could there be any scandal in such an affair, and this of course must operate to a certain extent. The reader will remember the trials of Marcel Schwob[239] caused by his marriage to one of the most charming and talented women in Paris, merely on account of her profession.

239. Even at the time this book was written (1917), the English reader was unlikely to know anything about the private life of Marcel Schwob, literary critic. In his youth, Crowley frequently visited Paris to meet his superior in the Golden Dawn, Macgregor Mathers, or to cool his ardour in one of the brothels there. In Paris at this time – about 1900 – he made the acquaintance of Marcel Schwob whom he persuaded a few years later to translate into French his 'chaplet of verse' which had been inspired by Auguste Rodin. See *Rodin in Rime*, 1907, by Aleister Crowley, and Crowley's *Confessions*, 1969.

It will be objected to all this that there is no sign of any trouble in connection with the marriage of T.H. Huxley,[240] who had Uranus right on the cusp of the house. But the lord of his seventh is admirably dignified by the conjunction of Venus and the sextile of Jupiter. And further, it may be said that in the case of a man so exclusively devoted to science, the effect of Uranus will not be so manifestly upon marriage as upon that other indication afforded by the house, i.e. public affairs.

With regard to this latter matter, the influence of Uranus will be tempestuous. He will cause the native to rise to great heights in all such matters, but the career will never be smooth. Huxley and Blavatsky spent most of their lives in controversies which literally shook the earth. The same remark applies to J.P. Morgan,[241] while Maurice Maeterlinck,[242] though not himself particularly controversial, has again and again been attacked from the days of Max Nordau[243] until now. The foreign policy of both Queen Elizabeth and Napoleon was war; there was never a period in the lives of either when they were not engaged in some desperate adventure. Queen Elizabeth, it must be remembered, was to all intents and purposes, a prisoner, during the reign of her sister.

It sometimes occurs that the presence of Uranus in the seventh house causes the sudden death of the marriage partner, or possibly the partner in business. With regard to the latter, all that has been said before with the necessary emendations will apply generally. He is likely to be the dominant figure in the partnership which is likely to break up after various vicissitudes. But an affliction of Uranus by the Moon in the case of a man or by the Sun in the case of a woman or any other trouble arising through aspects or

240. See note 3.

241. See note 4.

242. See note 135.

243. Author of *Degeneration*, an absurd attack on the Decadent movement in literature and art, based upon the views of the Italian alienist Lombroso, who ascribed certain artistic impulses and ideas to a degeneration of the brain cells. Poets Verlaine and Rossetti were classified by Nordau as 'imbeciles'.

transits of an unfortunate nature, of the partner's activities by sudden or violent death.

It is further to be remarked that Uranus often causes the native to marry in response to a sudden inexplicable impulse. Engagements to marry are also entered upon without sufficient thought. Such temptation should be watched and resisted. At the same time, it will be nugatory to seek for a mate of a conventional and inactive type; in fact to a person with Uranus in this position, there are no such people. In all men and women there is something extraordinary and incalculable, which would be brought out by the fact of marriage with any person having Uranus in the seventh house.

Uranus in the Eighth House

The presence of Uranus in the house of death does not always imply any strangeness in the manner of the death, as might at first sight be expected. Queen Victoria, for example, lived to a great old age and died in the most conventional manner possible, and this at first sight is more remarkable because Neptune is in conjunction with Uranus, with Saturn square to him. The trine of Venus is here sufficiently powerful to overcome those unfortunate indications and, besides this, Jupiter is the lord of the eighth house and is culminating in the mid-heaven in very close sextile with Mars.

There was nothing particularly strange, either, about the death of Anna Kingsford,[244] but there the moon is trine and Jupiter semi-sextile, while the lord of the eighth house Mars, is rising in conjunction with the Sun. Her death was unexpected and premature, but there was no essentially Uranian quality about it. These aspects explain why. Michael Angelo again, who passed peacefully away at an advanced age, though he too, like Queen Victoria, had Neptune also in the eighth house (it will be remembered that Neptune in this position often tends to prolong the life where it does not cut it off in infancy) has Mercury and Venus in trine to Uranus, and Venus is the lady of the eighth. Jupiter, moreover, is sextile and Saturn trine. It is a very remarkable complex and an entirely favourable one; Uranus consequently acts in his

244. See note 109.

best way. Queen Victoria had very little to do with death, but she had much to do with the goods of the dead. It was she who consolidated and enlarged and made prosperous her ancestral heritage. Here then we see Uranus acting in his governmental capacity. In the case of Michael Angelo, a very similar remark applies. It may be said that he, too, consolidated and enlarged the empire of his ancestors by the immense part that he played in the Renaissance. The glories of Greece lived again in him.

With regard to Sir Humphrey Davy,[245] one must recall the fact that death is only a secondary meaning of the eighth house; the essential significance is 'obscure and secret places'. It only comes to mean death because death is the chief of such. Davy has Uranus trine to Mars and Mars is the lord of the Ascendant, Scorpio, this sign being the natural cusp for the eighth house. He being a man of science, Uranus takes this colouring, and we therefore find that the discovery which made him famous is that lamp which insures safety in obscure and secret places. It is true that the lord of the eighth is squared by Mars, but Mars being himself so well-dignified by Uranus, the complex is not sufficiently bad to imply violent death. As we know, however, he constantly ran the greatest risks of such, and presumably it so happened that his directions on these occasions were good enough to enable him to escape catastrophe. This is to be taken as additional to what has been said above with regard to the peculiar quality in Uranus emphasised by the general scientific trend of the horoscope.

With regard to Dr L.L. Zamenhof, the inventor of Esperanto, the case is somewhat similar. Here we have a man investigating scientifically all sorts of dead languages, which are, as it were, a kind of ancestral possession, with the idea of forming from them, a new universal tongue. Here, again, there are no bad aspects which would suggest any strangeness, suddenness or violence about the death.

A last example of this class is Emanuel Swedenborg.[246] Here Jupiter is trine and Luna in conjunction. The latter

245. See note 90.
246. See note 113.

aspect suggests a certain obscurity and illusion with regard to the subject of death, and a great pre-occupation with the same is implied by the fact that Jupiter is lord of the Ascendant. This is undoubtedly the explanation of the tone of his being, as we see it expressed in his doctrine. It was investigations into what really happened at death that filled in his whole life.

We have now to change over to more conventional and obvious cases. The death of Vaillant[247] was certainly strange and violent, if ever death were. It is to be noted that Herschel in this case has no near aspects of any kind and his operation is consequently isolated and unchecked.

The death of Marie Bashkirtseff,[248] though premature, was not particularly strange, the cause being tuberculosis, but Saturn being square to Uranus seems to have given a sort of melancholy insight to her thought. Throughout her diary, full as it is of ambitious projects for a distant future, one can feel some subconscious certainty that these projects must be aborted. She senses her early death without knowing it in the ordinary way.

No comment is needed to explain the operation of Uranus in the case of Tolstoy, who feeling the hand of death upon his shoulder, fled instinctively from home and family to die in the waiting-room of a country railroad depot.

More remarkable cases still are at our disposal. First of all stands Shelley. Here the conjunction of Uranus with Venus and Sol operated no doubt to enlighten his mind in respect of antiquity. It conferred upon him that love for the ancient masters of literature and art, which formed the groundwork of his matchless style. But beyond this, there are no aspects to Uranus, who was therefore free to operate with characteristic violence, for while, when considering Uranus, we must regard him as helped by the conjunction of Sol, we must read this same aspect in an entirely opposite sense, with equal justice by saying that Sol being the lord of the eighth, the conjunction of Uranus threatened a violent termination to the life. With regard to the exact period of death, one may

247. See note 83.
248. See note 78.

note that Venus being in conjunction with both of these, it was open for him to die at one of the Venus ages.

Another case of suicide is Guy de Maupassant.[249] There are here no close or strong aspects to Uranus, only doubtful sextiles of Neptune and the Moon, which if they had any influence at all, would certainly not have had a good one. The lord of the eighth, Mars, is in conjunction with Venus and Jupiter, but there are no steady aspects. Conjunctions, even of the most favourable planets, are not to be trusted unless they have support from other parts of heaven.

From private sources we have also a case of death by drowning; curiously enough at just the same age as Shelley. Here Uranus is very close to the cusp of the ninth house, if not actually over it, but Luna, lord of the eighth, is upon the edge of the watery sign in exact opposition to Mars, while Uranus himself is in aspect to Neptune.

We have a case of drowning at the age of three, where, though Uranus is not in the eighth, Mercury the lord of the eighth is in a watery sign exactly squared by Uranus. Note that the presence of Mercury in the eighth house accounts for the early age at which the death took place.

There are one or two other examples of this second reaction of Uranus; Zola, for instance, who was suffocated by gas fumes, has the lord of his eighth, squared by Uranus and that lord is in a fiery sign.

Here is a case of a child strangled at birth, where the lord of the eighth is squared by Uranus, and another of exactly the same sort where the lord of the eighth, Jupiter, is in conjunction with Mars and squared by Uranus. Neptune is in opposition to Uranus. We have another case of a child strangled through falling off a chair, where the lord of the eighth, Mars, is in opposition to Uranus. The early age of the death is indicated by the presence of Luna in the eighth house. One may remark parenthetically that Neptune also can act in this secondary way, by afflicting the lord of the eighth. Thus, a child thrown at the age of 31 days by its mother into a mill stream, has the lady of the eighth squared by Neptune and by Saturn.

249. Henri René Albert Guy de Maupassant (1850-1893), novelist and writer of short stories, died of syphilis.

From these samples it will be clear that the action of Uranus when in a house and when afflicting its lord, may be very similar and this consideration should always be present in the mind of the astrologer, when attempting to estimate any condition.

With regard to the more general conditions indicated by this position of Uranus, one may observe that where he is in aspect to the lord of the first, third or ninth houses, the effect may be to cause the native to become preoccupied either with death itself or with the affairs of antiquity. He might become a collector of old coins, stamps, furniture, bric-à-brac, perhaps, or objects of art, or devote himself closely to such subjects as Egyptology, archaeology, palaeontology, and enjoy rummaging among old and musty folios. The exact pursuit might be chosen according to the indications afforded by aspects from other planets. For example a good aspect of Mercury might make him a classical scholar or cause him to employ his life in the deciphering of hieroglyphics or cuneiforms. A similar aspect from Jupiter might make him a historian or constitutional lawyer. But, of course, these determinations only come into force where Uranus is in some way connected with the personality or the mind. As in the case of the other houses, where we have to gauge the effect of Uranus on material affairs, the general result is bad. He may imply all sorts of trouble in connection with legacies or in the winding up of estates.

Where he is in aspect to the lord of the sixth, it is probable that any diseases to which the native may be liable will take one of those forms which we have learned to associate with Uranus. Death may come in consequence of nervous breakdown, or of some such disease as paralysis or epilepsy.

Uranus in the Ninth House

The ninth house, referring as it does to matters of science and religion in the first place, we may expect to find it one of the happiest of homes for Uranus, the best part of whose nature is concerned with the same subjects. As will be seen later there may be considerable danger when it approximates too closely to the cusp of the tenth. When fairly into the ninth, however, it may be described as altogether admirable, so far as it is a determinant of the quality of the subconscious mind.

Two of the greatest mystics of the religious type which this earth has ever produced are the Prophet of Nazareth and William Blake, both of whom had this position. The intensely religious quality of the subliminal outlook is indicated in the first case by a sextile of Luna and the presence of Saturn in the same house. While in the latter we find a sextile of Mars.

Pure literature has similar distinguished representatives in Emile Zola and Oscar Wilde. The extraordinary character of the point of view conferred by Uranus is well brought out in both these instances and the casual reader might think that one might have to go far and look deep to see the religious quality in either of these writers. Yet the religion of humanity informs both of them. As is evidenced in the case of Zola, less by his work itself than by the subtle quality underlying and inspiring it, while with the Irish writer, it expressed itself more clearly in such writings as 'The Soul of Man under Socialism' and *De Profundis*. It is to be observed, of course, in all these cases, that Uranus is not a religious planet in the same sense as Jupiter. He is always big, broad-minded and unconventional, more occupied with goodwill toward men than any problem of theology. Occasionally, he appears to devote himself exclusively to science as in the case of Copernicus, where the aspects are uniformly admirable. Uranus, however, being in Scorpio, one could not expect any but a scientific turn.

Two great poets, Swinburne and de Musset, have this same position and in these cases it will be noted that the religious instinct is expressed as is so often the case, in terms of absolute irreligion. As Fuller[250] remarks, 'the first Christians were called atheists, yet they believed in God; the last Christians are called theists, yet they do not believe in God; the first free-thinkers were called atheists, yet they believed

250. John Frederick Charles Fuller, born 1878. He was made a Major-General in 1930. Author of many works on warfare, his first publication, *The Star in the West*, 1907, was a panegyric on Crowley, his poetry and philosophy, a work which he excluded from the list of his publications in *Who's Who*.

in no-God; the last free-thinkers will be called theists, yet they will not believe in no-God.'

Swinburne's 'Hymn of Man', 'Before a Crucifix' and similar poems are far more truly religious than any number of those treatises which are usually considered pious, if only because their conception of the cosmos is so much greater and therefore so much more reverent. The conventional theological conception that this minute planet is the sole centre of the divine interest may be called the blasphemy of an egomaniac. Always assuming the justice of the courts which condemned George Edalji,[251] this position of Uranus is very instructive, with regard to the quality of his mind. For Uranus is in exact opposition to Mercury, a reference to the chapter on the aspects to Uranus will enlarge upon this point.

As to the more general indication of this position, it may be said that great activity of the subconscious nature is implied. The mind is usually very sensitive, very psychic, very intuitive and above all, has the faculty of that true kind of mysticism which understands all phenomena as necessarily correlated or to use the well-known phrase of the mystic's oath 'interprets every phenomenon as a direct dealing of God with the Soul'.[252] People born with this position nearly always continue mental activity through sleep and in many cases, especially if Uranus be afflicted, particularly by Luna or Neptune, they may be subject to disquieting dreams. During the childhood of such persons, they need the most careful guardianship. If they suffer from nightmare or are afraid of the dark, they must not be punished, but every precaution must be taken to relieve their troubles. If they find a lack of sympathy on the part of the parents, their whole lives may be ruined. Very often in the best cases, the activity of the sub-conscious mind during sleep will be extremely beneficial, leading to waking thoughts of an extremely valuable character. It will appear as if actual inspiration followed upon awakening, or sometimes may be carried on into the waking state and produce a kind of illumination. The problems that had worried one during the

251. See note 82.
252. The oath of a Master of the Temple $8^\circ = 3^\square$.

previous day will be solved in the morning. These tendencies are well worth encouraging; people with this position are often extremely well-suited for a life of meditation and prayer, or whatever they may choose to call it. We only imply the substitution of the consciousness of the world which lies behind and above phenomena, for that illusory and changing world itself.

Such people, however, should avoid externalising their views, as people of a more ordinary turn of mind are likely to be antagonised by their expression.

Besides the comparatively commonplace experiences spoken of above, it is quite probable that the native may be fitted in no ordinary degree for the obtaining of the very highest class of spiritual development. The names of the two great religious teachers cited above are sufficient evidence on this point.

As before, the quality of Uranus deteriorates, when we come to his influence upon material things. The brothers and sisters of the marriage partner are likely to be eccentric persons and to cause an infinity of trouble. In the matter of long journeys, Uranus again is unfortunate, especially if he be in a watery sign, when there is danger of drowning.

Care must be taken in deciding such points to look closely into the aspects of Uranus with regard to the lords of any other houses which may be concerned in such matters, and when the native wishes to start upon a journey, he should look closely into his direction and transits. There is, however, this to be said, that he will be liable to find himself compelled to undertake such journeys with the greatest suddenness, so that he will hardly have time to consider whether or no he be wise in doing so.

Uranus in the Tenth House

The primary indication of the tenth house being the mother, she will be indicated by Uranus in the same way as the father in the fourth house and the same remarks may be taken to apply to her, as were made in the case of him. It is however not quite so favourable because Uranus possesses qualities which may be forgiven in a man, but are quite inexcusable in a woman. It is also less antecedently probable that the best side of the planet will be brought out, while science and government remain principally in the hands of the sterner sex.

This incompatibility of Uranus with femininity is so pronounced that unless there is some strong reason to the contrary it will be wiser to look for the mother in the lord of the tenth rather than in Uranus.

Far more important is the reference of the tenth house to the professional career and reputation of the native. Here he finds ample scope for the development of all his peculiarities. He may exalt to the greatest heights, but this will nearly always be through vicissitudes and adventures of no mean order, and the chance of a crash is as great as, or perhaps even greater than when Saturn occupies this position, as is indicated in the proper place. Except, however, where it is death that closes the chapter, there is not the same reason for despair. Uranus knocks you down suddenly, but very often gives you a chance to get up again, whereas the calamities caused by Saturn are but the culminations of a process of attrition. Thus we find Gladstone defeated again and again by overwhelming majorities, only to come back to power with equal suddenness and vehemence within a few years or even months. A study of the meteoric career of Winston Churchill should also be instructive in this connection.

An even more splendid destiny was that of Paul Kruger.[253] Fate frequently seemed to desert him, but he always came back, until the final blow of the last Boer War.

The adventures of Jay Gould[254] on Wall Street form another chapter in the history of this position, and a very characteristic one. In the case of Rossetti, the reputation not only went through innumerable fluctuations, but owing to the conjunction of Mars and Neptune in the ninth, was hurt by his fall to madness. Ruskin's celebrity was of the same great and yet doubtful character, while with Chatterton[255] we see his fame based not really so much upon the work which he accomplished as upon the discovery of his forgeries,

253. See note 29.
254. See note 48.
255. See note 204.

his suicide and the scandal caused thereby. The square of Uranus to the Sun perhaps indicates that the loss of reputation caused by the exposure would threaten the life itself.

The extraordinary reputation of Ludwig II of Bavaria[256] and his deposition and death, whether that came about by his own hand or another's, is particularly characteristic of the actions of Uranus.

His influence is further shown in every one of these nativities as determining an extremely fantastic type of reputation, possibly quite undeserved. The publicity given by the planet combines with this cause to create the maximum of scandal, with the minimum of cause. Every one of the people we have mentioned was attacked persistently in the most shocking manner, in a manner quite out of proportion to any possible crimes that any human being could ever have committed. No one who was not living in England during the prime of Gladstone's power can possibly understand the ferocity of the hatred which pursued him. No lie was too absurd to circulate about him, no proposal for dealing with him too drastic. He was identified by quite orthodox clergymen with the Beast of the Apocalypse and quite responsible people who would not have hurt a fly, seriously counselled his assassination.

Winston Churchill has been attacked in a very similar manner. A most damaging story with regard to his escape from Pretoria was circulated again and again, until repeated prosecution for libel closed the mouths of his enemies in that particular respect, and that is only one of the hundreds of such attacks. One has only to read the English newspapers of 1915 to perceive the almost incredible bitterness of his enemies. A similar search through the files of the English newspapers of the nineties will disclose similarly insane fury towards Kruger. Rossetti was the victim of the most cruel persecution; witness Buchanan's *The Fleshly School of Poetry*.[257] Ruskin incurred the enmity of Whistler, and was

256. See note 111.

257. Robert William Buchanan, poet, author of several collections of verse and *The Fleshly School of Poetry, and other Phenomena of the day*, London, 1872.

as good as flayed alive by him in the 'The Gentle Art of Making Enemies'. Those familiar with American newspapers and magazines do not need to be reminded that Jay Gould was the victim of equally persistent and bitter attacks.

The native with this position must accordingly be prepared to take the rough with the smooth in the matter of reputation. Even in the narrow circles of ordinary private life, this is the case; and as Uranus with such people cannot expand in the same way as he does with public characters, the good side of him may be aborted. Women especially are certain to lose every shred of reputation; it is the most fatal indication possible.

So far as Uranus indicates the profession, the action is principally that of vicissitudes; it is very much better for anyone who has this to endeavour in every way to make his business as public as possible , to connect himself wherever he can with some great body. A doctor, for example, should try to secure a government appointment. If he sticks to private practice, there is almost certain to be trouble.

The tenth house also indicates the superior of the native and this is not so entirely bad. The employer will no doubt be a masterful person of great authority and strong will, but he will be broadminded and probably little inclined to petty tyranny. At the same time he may be apt to dismiss the native for some reason which the latter cannot understand.

With regard to the business of the native, he will be wise to enlarge it, as in the case of the professional man. He should look for government contracts and concern himself rather with wholesale than with retail business. He must always be on the look-out for bankruptcy, strikes, and other interferences with his trade. When all is said, this position of Herschel is not desirable; unless he is very well aspected, the career in whatever branch of life it may lie, is sure to be tempestuous.

A final point to consider is that where Uranus is in aspect to the lord of the Ascendant, he may cause the native to be extremely bold or even rash and over-confident. Let such a one remember, if he can, that 'at his initiation, he was taught to be cautious'.

Uranus in the Eleventh House

Although Aquarius is the natural sign for the cusp of the eleventh house, the influence of this planet is not especially excellent. For the idea of friendship connotes reliability above all things, and Uranus with all his virtues lacks this. The friends of the native may sometimes be of a very exalted kind, or distinguished for their attainments, in short, Uranus indicates the kind of friends, but where they are not so distinguished, they will show the worst side of the planet – the violent, eccentric side.

In the case of Nell Gwynn, for example, Charles II is clearly indicated by Uranus. In saying this, it is to be borne in mind that we do not mean that the king was altogether an Uranian, only that in his relations with her, he acted in the Uranian manner. These indications are, however, not universally true. In the case of Edward VI, for example, nothing could be more false than to say that his friends were Uranian in this particular sense and from the fact of his Kingship, they could not be more exalted than he was. The conjunction of Mars, the trine of Neptune, and the square of Mercury point rather to the determination of Uranus on its scientific side, as referring to the hopes and wishes of the native, which as we know, were quite in accordance with the best instincts of the planet.

In all ordinary cases, however, it may be said that the native is liable to make friends suddenly and impulsively, to adhere to them with great violence and then to drop them, as the saying is, 'like a redhot coal'. Some danger, too, is to be apprehended through friendships. Unreasonable quarrels are likely to be the rule; treachery is not impossible but the native is never likely to become cautious in this respect, however much experience may try to teach him. Great good, however, may result to the native from his association with persons of great position or influence, but the difficulty will always be to turn temporary success on these lines into a thing of permanence. It is also rather important to remember that the fascination of these curious friendships, which we have indicated above, may become a positive obsession, causing the native to waste his life in Bohemia. In some cases, even graver menaces may come from heaven. Though Ludwig

II of Bavaria has Uranus in the tenth house, where we have dealt with it, it must be remarked that it is only 2½ degrees from the cusp of the eleventh, and it is quite possible that some of his influence may have been carried over to that house. The reader will recall the fact that owing to his choice of companions which was hardly less eccentric than that exhibited by Heliogabulus,[258] he obtained a reputation for madness, which was perhaps not wholly undeserved. At the same time, it is evident that the influence of Uranus extends over both houses, so that his choice of friends and the loss of his good name were intimately connected. As explained in the chapter on the aspects of Uranus, the sextile of Luna is far more favourable, unless there be some strong impulse for sanity from another quarter. There is a kind of bewilderment of the brain caused by the closer aspects of these planets which often leads to disaster. Persons with this position should be careful to try to bring out the better side of Uranus in the choice of their associates.

Uranus in the Twelfth House

In the twelfth house, the effect of Uranus is very important. There is a certain secrecy about his method of action which agrees very well with the character of the house. So far, however, as secret enemies are connoted, the outlook is bad. For it gives to such the utmost freedom of activity. At all sorts of unexpected times they will spring upon you from behind and pull you down unless you are very careful. On the other hand if your Uranus is well dignified, it may make you a personage of the utmost importance in secret societies, or as a conductor of negotiations which depend upon any kind of trickiness or deception and also upon silence.

The house signifies confinement and detention and for this reason, Uranus giving the governmental qualities, it is likely that the native will hold an official position in such places as asylums, hospitals, prisons, work-houses, and even in out-of-the-way places. For example, he might be called upon to

258. Heliogabalus, or Elagabalus, the most epicene and apolaustic of the Roman emperors, assumed the purple in A.D. 218 at the age of 14 and was murdered four years later.

administer a remote district in the Sahara or some similar solitude. Even in minor matters, this might operate, causing mishaps, leading to delays and detention in inaccessible spots.

The native should be very careful as to whom he gives his confidence to. He is extremely apt to trust the wrong person. The hostile character of the house in most respects, is likely to cause the native serious trouble in many ways. In extreme cases he may be in danger of assassination. In others, of imprisonment or of exile. An example of the last Victor Hugo, who has Uranus on the cusp of the twelfth house and spent a great portion of his life in exile. The same remark is true of Dante, though in his case the planet is well within the house. As an example of assassination, we have the son of the late King of Portugal, Dom Carlos, who was shot while riding through the streets of Lisbon with his royal father.

The cases of Erasmus and Bernard Shaw are a little difficult to place. It must be remembered in these remarks upon the positions of the planets in the houses that very often the trine is not exact and that the difference of a very few minutes may bring a planet within the sphere of the next house. In both of these cases, it seems as if the position of Uranus was such that the more important parts of his influence at least belong to the Ascendant. But yet, we may say that Erasmus was constantly in danger of imprisonment and that Shaw has been all his life exceedingly unpopular with the more respectable classes of the community and that many attempts have doubtless been made to overthrow him. In particular, since the breaking out of the Great War, he has been in more or less continual danger of assassination.

In the case of Strauss, the conjunction of the Sun with Uranus does much to modify this particular part of the influence, since the nature of the Sun is wholly opposed in every point to that of the twelfth house.

A final remark is that danger is to be apprehended by the native in any dealings with large wild animals. It is probable that he will have great power over them, but at any moment a violent end is likely.

For example a man might become a splendid rider only in the end to be thrown from his horse and killed. Or he might acquire great reputation as a hunter of big game, and in the end fall a victim to his temerity. The atmosphere of Uranus is always one of adventure and of hair-breadth escapes. In whatever house he may be situated, this influence is pretty sure to manifest itself.

HOW HOROSCOPES ARE FAKED

How Horoscopes are Faked

I have always been opposed to the receiving of money for anything which has in any way to do with the occult sciences. Because they are so important and so sacred, one ought to be particularly on one's honour with regard to them. As the Scripture says: 'Avoid the appearance of Evil'. The more serious one is about the subject, the more careful one should be to do nothing which can make anyone justified in calling you a humbug.

The laws of the State of New York are supposed to prohibit fortune-telling, and they are, indeed, applied with great severity so far as the little fish are concerned. But the big fish, the most conscienceless swindlers of all, seem to dodge the police. A lot of bluff has been put up about 'scientific' astrology. I propose to show how the game is really worked.

Let us pay a visit to one of the best known of them. We find an expensive apartment in one of the best parts of the city. We are not very much impressed by the furniture. There is a good deal of muddle, a good deal of junk, a complete absence of taste. The spider of this web is a grey-haired old woman of exceedingly shrewd expression. She explains to us by pamphlets and by word that she is a really 'scientific' investigator. In setting up a horoscope, for example, she is very careful to calculate the places of the planets, not only to degrees, but to minutes and seconds. That sounds wonderfully accurate, doesn't it? However, when it comes to making the real calculations upon which astrology is based, an error of ten or twelve degrees is of no account at all. Which is rather like announcing that a man took 2 hours, 33 minutes and 14.25 seconds to run several miles. The alleged accuracy is quite meaningless. It is only a sham to impress the client. It is also to be observed that owing to the pressure of business she has these calculations made by her chauffeur. This, I suppose, is a point of war economy.

She is grotesquely ignorant of the first principles of astronomy. She has no conception, for example, of the Solar System as a Disk, but imagines that the planets are all over the place, like raisins in a plum-pudding. She calls her country house the Zodiac – and doesn't know what the Zodiac is.

One word more on the 'scientific accuracy' business. If astrology is to be done at all, if there is any sense in it whatever, which I do not for one moment deny, the calculations depend upon a fairly close approximation of the hour and minute of birth. For example, the seventh house, the place of the setting sun, refers to marriage, so that if a person is born with an unfortunate planet like Saturn setting, he may expect an unfortunate marriage. It is obviously of vital importance for the inquirer to know whether Saturn was setting or not. There is a certain amount of latitude, from about one to two hours, for Saturn would remain in that house for about that period. But where the birth hour is not known within about an hour the horoscope becomes worthless. If the time were six hours earlier, Saturn would be in the mid-heaven and bring misfortune in business or reputation rather than in marriage. However to the fashionable astrologer this must not matter. She has to get the dollars from the people who do not know in the least at what hour of the day or night they were born. She has the impudence to assure them that it doesn't matter, all the time insisting upon her wonderful scientific accuracy.

There is no need to cast any doubt upon the sincerity of the belief of the woman. She talks astrology day and night. She dreams of it. She sets a horoscope for her vast family of cats and dogs, and is scared out of her life when some planet threatens her horoscope.

But the people who deceive themselves most effectually are those who deceive others most effectually. Whether it is knavery or folly does not matter very much. What I want to do is to explain to the people who are paying five dollars that they are not getting genuine astrology at all. It may be said that a horoscope (granting for a moment the genuineness of the science) is a complete map of the life and character of the native. To read one properly would mean at least a week's continuous work. But the demand is for 5 dollar and 10 dollar horoscopes; and obviously no more than a few minutes can be given to each one if the lady is to clear her forty or fifty thousand a year. It is also necessary to give a good deal of apparent value for the money. There are only 12 signs and 9 planets to be considered. For the influence of the rising sign, therefore, one only needs twelve multigraphed pages. As each planet can be in any sign we shall need 9 times 12 multigraph pages to cover the action of the planets. Each planet can be roughly in fortunate or unfortunate aspect, and 162 more pages will be needed. These pages need not be prepared right away. A new one can be dictated as each aspect turns up in practice. These pages are all pigeon-holed, and by means of a chart the astrologer can tell her secretary which paper to pick out for any horoscope that comes along. The secretary can then pick them out and pin them together in a very few minutes, and there is your horoscope.

The objection to this proceeding is fairly obvious. In practically all horoscopes there are indications which clash with each other. To judge such a horoscope properly, the whole thing should be taken into individual consideration, and a reconcilement obtained. With the 'reach-me-down' method all this is necessarily ignored, and the client may be surprised to find on page two of the horoscope, that she is kind and considerate, and on page four, that she is selfish and inconsiderate. There is further a great theoretical objection; which is that a horoscope, to be a horoscope at all, must be a live thing. To get them out in this mechanical fashion is to offer a corpse instead.

It is true that the astrologer sometimes condescends to look upon a horoscope as a whole, and dictate one or two pages at the end, but this is not always done. There is no guarantee that it will be done.

It is probably difficult to take legal exception to this branch of the business, but it is only a very small branch. It is the thin end of the wedge. The fortune-telling, pure and simple, comes afterwards. The astrologer issues a series of so-called monthly forecasts which explain how the actual position of the planets in the heavens at the time should react upon any given horoscope. Another set of multigraphed pages is of course required for this. These pages are carefully examined by a lawyer, for we are now getting into the danger zone.

The phraseology is very carefully chosen, for nothing must be said which would be indictable as a prediction. Thus, instead of saying, 'You will be lucky in speculation during the first week of October', the phrase is 'financial conditions seem to be operating favourably during the first week in October'. These monthly forecasts are received at 24 dollars a year, and as they require a good deal of trouble in preparation, it is evident that the cheapness has something behind it. These forecasts are what you may call bait, and the fish to be caught is the 'personal consultation'.

Suppose I am told in my forecasts that financial conditions are favorable for a certain period, I am going to ask for more. I want to know exactly how to make the best use of the opportunity: so I ring up the lady and get an appointment. This appointment may ostensibly be a 5 dollar or a 10 dollar one; but in reality I may have to pay much more for it. I may have to let the lady in on a percentage of profits on the gamble in 'war babies'. Similarly, if I am an actress, or other easily exploitable person, I may have to pay a great deal extra. Once the fly is in the web, the spider can dictate its own terms.

Women are particularly foolish with astrologers. They tell all their love affairs. Again, even cautious Mrs A will tell one side of a story; prudent Miss B next day the other side. The astrologer becomes mistress of these women, body and soul. Perhaps she does not blackmail them; but she is in a position to do so if she wishes. At the very least, the victims realise their position, and are careful to do anything the astrologer may ask.

Then again there is the matrimonial agency graft; and the highly profitable business of *entremetteuse*. (We do not assert that in the particular case we are discussing these things are done, but they could be done. It is immoral to permit the existence of a secret of this kind.)

It is all done under the cloak of astrology. Mr G calls, and looks for a soul-mate; the astrologer soon finds some woman, 'whose Venus is on his Sun', and arranges a little dinner party. All in the sacred cause of astrology – scientific astrology; the old lady would be genuinely shocked if you called her by her real name. But she takes her commission just the same, and superstition is so extraordinarily strong that when faith is established, there is no limit to the amount of which the victim can be fleeced. This being the really dangerous part of the work, the astrologer is extraordinarily careful about making appointments. One has to have very good introductions. Word quickly goes round as to what the police are doing. For example a few months ago it was rumoured that a red-haired detective had been engaged, and all women with red hair, unless previously known, had to pass the 33rd degree before they reached the centre of the web. There is no doubt in the mind of the astrologer that she is breaking the law. She lives in continual terror of the police. She knows well enough that it was only a fluke that she was not convicted at her previous prosecutions. However, she boasts openly of her 'pull' with certain society leaders who can protect her from the police. Properly managed, evidence is easy to obtain. Will not Mrs Isabel Goodwin[259] look to it?

259. A popular American astrologer.

BATRACHOPHRENOBOOCOSMOMACHIA

Batrachophrenoboocosmomachia

sub figura

DXXXVI

Within His skull exist daily thirteen thousand myriads of Worlds, which draw their existence from Him, and by Him are upheld. – *I.R.Q.*[260] *iii.43.*

0. Let the Practicus study the textbooks of astronomy, travel, if need be, to a land where the sun and stars are visible, and observe the heavens with the best telescopes to which he may have access. Let him commit to memory the principal facts, and (at least roughly) the figures of the science.

1. Now, since these figures will leave no direct impression with any precision upon his mind, let him adopt this practice A:

A. Let the Practicus be seated before a bare square table, and let an unknown number of small similar objects be thrown by his chela from time to time upon the table, and by that chela be hastily gathered up.

Let the Practicus declare at the glance, and the chela confirm by his count, the number of such objects.

The practice should be for a quarter of an hour thrice daily. The maximum number of objects should at first be seven. This maximum should increase by one at each practice, provided that not a single mistake is made by the Practicus in appreciating the number thrown.

260. See Mather's *The Kabbalah Unveiled* for the translation of that section of *The Zohar* from which this quotation is taken. *Idra Rabba Qadesh*, The Greater Holy Assembly, pp. 109-257.

This practice should continue assiduously for at least one year.

The quickness of the chela in gathering up the objects is expected to increase with time. The practice need not be limited to a quarter of an hour thrice daily after a time, but increased with discretion. Care must be taken to detect the first symptom of fatigue, and to stop, if possible, even before it threatens. The practised psychologist learns to recognise even minute hesitations that mark the forcing of the attention.

2. Alternating with the above, let the Practicus begin this practice B:

B. It is assumed that he has thoroughly conquered the elementary difficulties of Dharana, and is able to prevent mental pictures from altering shape, size and colour against his will.

Seated in the open air, let him endeavour to form a complete mental picture of himself and his immediate surroundings. It is important that he should be in the centre of such picture, and able to look freely in all directions. The finished picture should be a complete consciousness of the whole, fixed, clear, and definite.

Let him gradually add to this picture by including objects more and more distant, until he have an image of the whole field of vision.

He will probably discover that it is very difficult to increase the apparent size of the picture as he proceeds, and it should be his most earnest endeavour to do so. He should seek in particular to appreciate distances, almost to the point of combating the laws of perspective.

3. These practices A and B accomplished, and his studies in astronomy completed, let him attempt this practice C:

C. Let the Practicus form a mental picture of the Earth, in particular striving to realise the size of the earth in comparison with himself, and let him not be content until by assiduity he has well succeeded. Let him add the Moon, keeping well in mind the relative sizes of, and the distance between, the planet and its satellite.

He will probably find the final trick of mind to be a constant disappearance of the image, and the appearance of the same upon a smaller scale. This trick he must outwit by constancy of endeavour.

He will then add in turn Venus, Mars, Mercury and the Sun. It is permissable at this stage to change the point of view to the centre of the Sun, and to do so may add stability to the conception.

The Practicus may then add the Asteroids, Jupiter, Saturn, Uranus and Neptune. The utmost attention to detail is now necessary, as the picture is highly complex, apart from the difficulty of appreciating relative size and distance.

Let this picture be practised month after month until it is absolutely perfect. The tendency which may manifest itself to pass into Dhyana and Samadhi must be resolutely combated with the whole strength of the mind.

Let the Practicus then re-commence the picture, starting from the Sun, and adding the planets one by one, each with its proper motion, until he have an image perfect in all respects of the Solar System as it actually exists. Let him particularly note that unless the apparent size approximate to the real, his practice is wasted. Let him then add a comet to the picture; he may find, perhaps, that the path of this comet may assist him to expand the sphere of his mental vision until it include a star.

And thus, gathering one star after another, let his contemplation become vast as the heaven, in space and time ever aspiring to the perception of the Body of Nuit; yea, of the Body of Nuit.

Index